Desktop Publishing with PagePlus 3

by

Andrew Marshman
and
Mike James

I/O PRESS

I/O Press

First Published 1994
©I/O Press
Cover Design: Mike James
ISBN 1 871962 38-2

British Library Cataloguing in Publication Data
A catalogue record for this book is available from the British Library

Although every effort has been made to ensure the correctness of the information
contained herein neither the publisher nor the author accept liability for any
omissions or errors that may remain.

Typeset by I/O Press

Printed and bound in Great Britain by Cromwell Press Limited,
Broughton Gifford, Wiltshire

Contents

Preface

Over recent years Desktop Publishing has been the boom area of personal computing and has brought the power of the press to both business and individual users. The rapid growth in this area has come about because the hardware required to even make a start on DTP has become affordable and so has the software. At the same time the software has improved to the point at which it is capable of impressive results.

This book is about the practice and theory of DTP using Serif's popular and prize winning software PagePlus. The latest version, PagePlus 3, has many additional features and we show how they can be put to good use in a series of hands-on examples.

To make the most of DTP you need to understand its many facets. In this book we cover ideas from traditional publishing technology such as fonts and leading, and areas that are specifically to do with the PC such as OLE, a topic that can and does baffle many users and so is discussed in detail.

Once you have created an effective design you need output, and this is the point at which many DTP users suddenly experience unexpected problems. This book has been written in the light of many years' experience of using DTP for real and we try to pass on the knowledge gained of how to make the transition from an interesting concept and a good design to physical paper output that lives up to your expectations.

Our aim has been to pass on some of our ideas for creating useful and interesting effects in PagePlus. We hope that this will encourage you to experiment.

Andrew Marshman
Mike James   July 1994

Publisher's Foreword

This book is one that we are especially pleased to publish since we find ourselves at the interface between the DTP environment and traditional publishing technology. This book has been originated and laid out in its entirety on PCs and its cover is not only the product of DTP but of PagePlus 3 in particular.

Acknowledgements

The authors would like to thank Serif Europe for their assistance and advice. Our especial thanks are extended to Darren Darvill, to John Marshman and to Marie Buck for their help in origination and checking the material included.

Companion Disk Information Sheet

The files created in many of the hands-on tours in this book have been collected together on a disk which also contains some shareware utilities that are likely to be useful in conjunction with PagePlus 3. As the contents of the disk may vary from time to time details are to be found on our Information Sheet which also lists useful contacts, details of other books of interest and further hints and tips. If you would like a copy of the latest Information Sheet send a stamped addressed envelope to:

I/O Press (DTP Information Sheet)
Oak Tree House,
Leyburn,
North Yorkshire
DL8 5SE

Chapter 1

PagePlus 3.0

Introduction to DTP

Desktop Publishing (DTP) is a relatively new term that has come to mean a variety of things to different people. It is therefore difficult to define exactly. To some, DTP is simply the production of attractive documents, perhaps including illustrations such as charts, logos and pictures. Looking at the term itself, publishing means creating and printing information, and desktop publishing means doing it all with a personal computer system, where previously a high cost set of traditional publishing equipment would have been required. In short, you could say that DTP is using your PC to produce documents that look as if they have been typeset and printed.

» PagePlus

This book is about PagePlus - arguably the best low cost DTP package available for the PC - but the principles and many of the practices of DTP hold true no matter what package you are using. As a result of their power to emulate, and even simplify, the traditional procedures of design and high quality printing, personal computers have enabled relative novices to undertake DTP work. Perhaps more importantly, they have made this process much easier and much less expensive. Even if the only experience you have of DTP is reading this book now, you could within mere hours of practice be producing exciting and attractive documents and all within a very reasonable budget. Before moving on to look at how PagePlus is used it is worth looking at some of the background of DTP.

» DTP means DIY

To use DTP successfully you may need to acquire skills in a number of different areas - computer operation, editorial and design. You should not be put off by any of these requirements. The computer is no longer a remote or impersonal piece of machinery. Instead it is an everyday and easy to use item of equipment which itself can help you to develop the other talents - as writer and artist - required. In these areas there are of course no hard and fast rules, especially when you are working with your own ideas. Editorial is primarily a matter of organising your material so that it conveys the message you want to put across, while design is about presenting it to satisfy your taste and preferences and to stimulate the interest and attention of your audience.

The advantage of DTP is that it allows people to do virtually everything involved in producing finished output by themselves. They are able to perform all the previously specialised tasks required in traditional publishing, at their desk, on a small personal computer. In other words, they are able to perform the functions of all the following:

>> Writer

>> Editor

>> Typographer

>> Paste-up artist

>> Compositor

>> Graphic artist

For people who require the production of attractive documents but do not make a living from such work, the possibilities offered by DTP are very welcome. It is cost effective and easy to do, allowing a small business to design advertising flyers and business stationery; a restaurant to create menus; a plumber to produce attractive quotes or invoices; a pressure group to compile a magazine or newsletter; a fan-club organiser to prepare the monthly fanzine; a student to produce a thesis complete with tables, illustrations and title pages; and so on. It has even been used to produce a CD cover for a professional pop group - a job that would normally be associated with a graphics program.

This is just one end of the DTP-user spectrum. It is certainly not confined to individuals working on a small scale and within tight budgets. Nowadays most national newspapers and magazines, and a host of other widely distributed literature, are also produced using computer publishing systems that are essentially larger scale and more costly examples of DTP packages. It is so versatile that it can readily accommodate these extremes and every other requirement in between.

PagePlus in particular will suit most applications ranging from advertising layout to newsletters. The new facilities included in version 3 also make it suitable for the production of manuals and books - something that PagePlus 2 could be used for but only with some extra effort.

» New technology

DTP is a remarkable application area because it is one of the few uses of a personal computer that has more or less wiped out a traditional industry. In most other cases the PC has simply altered working practices, made technology more accessible and made procedures more efficient. But DTP has removed a layer of highly skilled technicians who occupied a distinct world between the originator of the words and the printer of the words. With DTP it is entirely possible for a user to type directly into an on-screen representation of the printed page. It doesn't always happen this way because a single person will not necessarily possess the skill of writing and that of page layout but the technology makes it possible and a package like PagePlus encourages this approach.

The traditional publishing methods, however, have not been entirely replaced and superseded. There is an elusive and irreplaceable art to design and for high volume, low cost per page and high quality you still need to use a printing press.

DTP must allow for integration with the old traditional design and printing functions of the publishing industry and a variety of links have evolved between computer-based methods and the use of traditional publishing equipment and processes.

However, don't expect everyone in the printing industry to know all about the techniques and methods of DTP and PagePlus in particular. There is often a huge gap between the general printing world and the DTP user - and it is up to the DTP user to bridge this gap!

The DTP link with traditional publishing is illustrated by the use of PagePlus templates which allow you to take advantage of design work done by professional creative artists. In this way you can use your personal computer system to create your publication based on their design.

Similarly, some publications, such as high volume glossy colour brochures, usually require to have the final stages of the production (printing and finishing) done by a printshop. In this case, you use your DTP system to design and create your publication to the stage where camera ready artwork can be produced and sent to the printshop. Later in this book you will discover all you need to know about camera ready copy, film, bromide and how to get your finished layout into a form that a printer can use.

» What is page make-up software?

There is a very large range of software that could loosely be called DTP software. This includes drawing packages, paint packages, scanning packages, graphical word processors, font utilities, and so on. Such is the diversity of these packages that a variety of applications can be needed to produce exactly what you want. It is particularly easy to link packages together for this process with PagePlus. This means that you do not need to restrict yourself in the tools at your disposal but can instead use the most convenient for each aspect of the production process.

One definition that identifies DTP software more specifically is to consider it as 'page make-up software'. This would encompass packages such as Corel Ventura Publisher and Aldus PageMaker and of course PagePlus, which includes almost all the features of these well established and well known packages and can even claim to outperform them in some areas.

Since the introduction of the Windows environment, a number of word processors have developed the capability of basic page make-up DTP work. Such packages allow graphics to be imported, text to be set in columns, drawings and charts to be produced, and so on, and may provide some people with all their document production requirements. These word processors, however, are not as versatile as dedicated DTP packages nor do they offer the range of features that distinguishes specialist page make-up software - typographic control; screen and colour control; and document management. These are advanced features and are covered in later chapters of this book.

Page make-up software lets you design exactly how pages look. Text and graphics can then be added, precisely positioned and manipulated to match that look. Pages can then be printed to the desired quality. This is the DTP equivalent of the traditional pasteboard. In the days before DTP a paste up artist would gather together all of the material - text, photos and illustrations - and would assemble the pages by cutting and gluing the elements together on a page grid.

Different software focuses on different aspects of page make-up. PagePlus has features that are especially good for short, design-intensive publications. It can handle long documents such as books or manuals and, as already mentioned, new features introduced in version 3 make this easier. PagePlus has now evolved into a package that is capable of performing well in any DTP environment.

One of the features that makes PagePlus easy to use is the incorporation of the idea of an electronic pasteboard. You can gather together the elements required for your layout in the area around the document itself. This of course models the real-world use of a working surface on which you assemble the items to be pasted onto the page being designed. Layout grids are used to help with the positioning of objects in your design. Unlike the ruled layout grids on the traditional pasteboard these are invisible on the final printout and you don't have to remember to erase them!

» Equipment needed for DTP

Although a detailed discussion of the merits and disadvantages of specific equipment is beyond the scope of this book, a few general pointers may be helpful if you are setting up a new system or upgrading existing equipment specifically for the purpose of doing DTP with PagePlus.

» Personal Computer

Clearly the first and most essential constituent of any DTP set-up is the computer itself which must be capable of running PagePlus and storing your work. To run PagePlus 3 you must have an IBM compatible running Windows 3.1 which means at the very least a 386SX. If you are purchasing from new or can upgrade your existing hardware you would be well advised to aim higher. The reason for requiring a more powerful machine is simply that DTP is a time consuming activity. PagePlus would be irritatingly sluggish on a 16 MHz 386SX and, even on a full 386 moving around a complex design would be slow. So, if you intend to make intensive use of DTP you would appreciate the speed of a 486 or even a Pentium.

Although the minimum memory requirement for PagePlus 3 is 3MBytes of RAM, 4MBytes is recommended, and of course, a hard disk is a necessity. PagePlus itself requires 5MBytes of disk space for installation but if you want to use its add-in options the demand for space grows to over 20MBytes of disk space. Given that you are likely to want a word processor and perhaps a drawing package and that you that will quickly fill disk space with layouts you are working on, a 100MByte disk drive should be thought of as a working minimum.

» Colour Monitor

PagePlus will run with an EGA display but Serif recommend at least VGA graphics. Our advice would be for a colour monitor and graphics adapter with an even higher resolution - preferably SVGA (Super VGA) 1024x768 in 256 colours. This resolution allows you to see two thirds of an A4 sheet in reasonable detail and lets you make best use of PagePlus's WYSIWYG display. WYSIWYG - What You See Is What You Get - means that what is shown on the screen is exactly what gets printed on paper. If you can, choose a non-interlaced monitor and matching adapter - this produces much less screen flicker than an interlaced system.

Users sometimes wonder why they need the extra expense of a colour monitor if they are going to print on a black and white printer. The reason is that the software supports colour. Even when you print to a monochrome device it will be reproducing colour - using grey shades to correspond to colours - and not just solid black and white. You need not be restricted by your own printing device and when you use the program's colour separation facilities you need a colour monitor to check that each separation shows the correct items.

》 Mouse

All but a few of PagePlus's features are controlled with the aid of a mouse, or similar pointing device, which is used to move both cursors and objects around your screen and to select most PagePlus functions. It is essential that you have a pointing device, and the appropriate driver software for it, installed as otherwise the PagePlus installation program will not allow it to be installed. The exact type of pointing device - usually a mouse - is unimportant and it needs only one mouse button for all PagePlus actions. If your mouse has multiple buttons, the only active mouse button is the leftmost one. Information will also need to be typed in using the keyboard and you can perform many operations using the keyboard if you prefer.

》 Scanners and OCR Devices

Until recently, virtually all graphic images had to be designed using art/graphics software. Now, however, there are scanning devices on the market for under £100. These devices enable pictures (or even photographs) to be scanned in, storing the image as a graphics file in a variety of formats. For most DTP use a hand-held scanner that can read in grey level images (256 shades of grey) at 300 dpi (dots per inch) is good enough. Colour hand scanners are available but choose one that can work at 300 dpi or better. If you are going to be scanning a lot of artwork then a flat bed scanner makes the task easier and quicker. Flat bed scanners are of course more expensive than hand held units but this is their only disadvantage!

As an alternative to a scanner you might like to consider an electronic digital camera. The Logitech Fotoman works in black and white and can download already digitised photos to your machine. The Canon Ion camera works in colour and records its images on a small floppy disk which can be downloaded into a PC using a special interface board. Both the Fotoman and the Ion camera do away with the need to use standard photographic processes and provide a fast way of getting pictures into DTP documents.

As well as capturing images, scanners can also be used to convert printed documents into text files using OCR (optical character recognition). This can save a lot of time typing in printed material. You can add OCR software to most scanners but at the moment this generally isn't cheap.

» CD-ROM Drive

A CD-ROM drive is rapidly becoming an important accessory for the DTP user. The reason is the growing popularity of the Photo CD process. This was invented by Kodak and is a process whereby a standard 35mm film is transferred to CD-ROM which can be read in almost any CD-ROM drive. What this means is that you can use it to read high quality photos into your machine without the need to use a scanner. There are also a wide range of photo libraries available on CD-ROM. For example, Serif's own PhotoPack CD is very useful, as is the library of CDs from Corel and the Hulton Deutsch photo-library containing contemporary photos of famous people, landmarks and events. The trend towards using CD as the standard method of supplying stock photos and graphics is set to continue, making CD-ROM an essential for DTP work. You can also buy font libraries on CD-ROM but at the moment these are either very expensive or very low quality.

You don't need a very expensive drive for reading in still images. Any drive that conforms to the MPC level II standard will do and there are a number of suitable models for just over £100 that can be easily added to an existing machine.

» Printer

To print your designs you obviously need a printer. The type of printer you choose depends on your requirements. PagePlus can print directly to any printer supported by Windows 3.1 or later. This includes anything from a 9-pin dot matrix printer through to a high quality laser printer.

If you intend having the end results of your work printed by a printshop, you may decide to have just a basic printer for proofing your work or even no printer at all. To produce the final copy you simply print to disk and send this to a bureau to be transferred to a high quality laser printer or image setter. The use of a bureau for output is discussed in Chapter 7.

You can, however, print final output with your own equipment. The more graphics you intend to use, and the better the definition you want, the more you will need to pay. Colour adds to the cost and high definition colour printer quickly goes beyond a personal or small business budget. Depending on its quality, a dot matrix printer can be suitable for proofing and for finished output. A 9-pin printer can be used to produce results good enough to proof-read but to produce the finished page, complete with graphics, you need a 24-pin printer. You also need to keep in mind that a dot matrix printer is slow when printing in graphics mode - typically less than one page in five minutes!

Bubble or inkjet printers can represent excellent value for money if you wish to produce acceptable quality output. The quality is high, almost as good a laser printer output but, as with dot matrix printers, they can be very slow. A colour ink jet is currently the only reasonably priced form of colour output which has the necessary quality- but it is very slow and so only suitable for proofing and for one-off, or very short, runs.

There is now a wide choice of laser printers for less than £1,000 that are suitable for satisfying most requirements that do not involve colour. In many cases a Hewlett Packard (HP) LaserJet compatible printer will be sufficient but it is important to realise that to produce a full A4 page of graphics it will need at least 1MByte of memory. Printer memory can be added at a later date in the form of upgrade modules.

Although you can use any printer that Windows supports with PagePlus, there are advantages in using a PostScript laser printer. PostScript is almost the universal language of DTP. If you want to send your output to an imagesetting bureau then the high resolution output device that they use will be a PostScript machine. As PostScript printers only differ in the resolutions they offer, testing the output using a PostScript printer can save a lot of money and time. In addition there are some output features such as colour separations and the ability to print certain types of graphics which are only supported if you are using a PostScript printer.

What all this means is that if you are serious about DTP then it is worth investing in a PostScript printer or a PostScript upgrade to your existing printer.

The newest generation of laser printers - for example the HP LaserJet 4 family - works at 600 dpi (dots per inch) and this is sufficient resolution to be able print text and grey level images to a quality that will be good enough to be used as camera ready copy. However, the majority of laser printers still work at 300 dpi and although is appears good at first glance a closer inspection reveals the dots! A 300 dpi printer is usually good enough for camera ready copy containing nothing but text and black and white line images but not for grey scale photographic images.

Even working at 600 dpi there are still times when you need to use an image setter which writes directly to photographic film. A typical image setter works at anything from 1200 dpi to more than 4800 dpi - and at this resolution you definitely cannot see the dots! You will find more information on using imagesetters in Chapter 8.

» Software requirements

Windows 3.1 (or a subsequent version) is required to run PagePlus 3. In addition, to follow the tutorials in this book you will be required to use the application Paintbrush that comes with Windows and some of the sample images that are installed along with it. You can of course add any or all of the Serif Publishing Suite to PagePlus to extend its range of abilities.

» The PC versus the Mac

The Apple Macintosh (Mac) began the DTP boom and established itself as the industry standard for DTP. In 1987 the Mac held over 70% of the DTP market which was then characterised by relatively expensive hardware and software However, the Mac's market share has now shrunk dramatically and is still decreasing.

The reason for the initial dominance of the Mac in the DTP market is the simple reason that from its outset the Mac was well suited to such work. The Mac has a distinctive WYSIWYG user friendly interface. Its methods of operation using windows, icons, menus and pointers (WIMPs) facilitated the rate at which software could be learnt and used. This was ideal for DTP software where the cursor needs to be moved around the screen with ease and selections to be made at the click of a button. Compare this to a PC of the same era which still lacked good graphics hardware and was mostly used with text based applications.

While the initial lack of suitable alternatives allowed the Mac's domination to occur, this situation has now changed. The development of the graphical desktop interfaces on the PC has allowed it to become equally user-friendly in its method of operation. The best known and most powerful of these graphical interfaces is, of course Windows.

At the moment the PC offers the best price/performance ratio and there is very little that the Mac can do that the PC cannot. However, the Mac still has one advantage by virtue of being the first machine used for DTP. Many professional DTP users have been trained using a Mac, and continue to use them in their day-to-day work. This means that when you need to speak to a DTP bureau or a traditional printer then they are likely to know something of the Mac and very little about the PC. Indeed many will assume that if you are doing DTP you will also be using a Mac. In practice this isn't a real problem but it helps to recognise that there may not be much common ground.

» What's new in PagePlus 3

PagePlus was originally launched in January 1991 and was the first inexpensive Windows DTP package to appear. The greatly upgraded version PagePlus 2 was released in March 1993 and PagePlus 3, the subject of this book, was launched in June 1994. If you have used an earlier version of PagePlus then it is worth outlining some of the differences you will encounter.

» **Improved user interface**
PagePlus 2 was easy to use and well organised and version 3 has built upon this start. Now the user interface can be switched into one of three levels - Intro, Publisher and Professional. The level that you select determines what features you are able to gain access to and the default settings that are used. For example, the Intro level has an expanded help box by default. Although other levels can use the same help facility it is considered unnecessary as a default. You will also find more on-screen information available. The hints and tips feature aims to extend your knowledge of PagePlus as you use it and tool hints tell you what each tool does as you move the cursor over it.

A more advanced improvement is that now the pasteboard area is "global". What this means is that any object you place on the pasteboard is accessible even if you move to a different page. This allows you to use the pasteboard as a way of moving objects to new pages.

» **Automatic page layout**
In the past PagePlus has been open to the criticism of being capable only of producing small, design-intensive, publications. This is no longer true, now that PagePlus has the use of master pages and automatic page numbering. Page numbering is self-explanatory. You can add a page number to any page or allow PagePlus to assign the page number relative to the entire document. Inserting or deleting pages will cause the numbers to be updated appropriately.

You can now design a Master Page, a non-printing page on which you can add graphics, text or other layout features which then occur on all the other pages within your document. This is particularly useful in conjunction with page numbering, and for creating headers and footers etc.. You can also define right and left master pages to make the production of booklets easier.

» Easier text handling

PagePlus now has its own text editor, WritePlus, which can be used to enter and edit text. This includes a spelling checker and thesaurus and, as it works with PagePlus styles, it is more convenient than a separate word processor.

PagePlus also now supports auto-kerning and hyphenation. Typographical control has been implemented to allow you to set word and letter spacing to achieve custom tracking.

» Sophisticated graphics facilities

Several new features are available for the manipulation of pictures and graphics within PagePlus. Firstly, objects can now be flipped vertically or horizontally. So if you want a piece of clipart to face the other way you can now flip it over. Pictures also now have an automatic wrap 'avoid me' area that follows the outline of the image. This saves you having to manipulate the wrap outline manually. Another new option enables you to convert a single letter or any text object into a picture and then manipulate as a graphic, making it possible to flip it and use the automatic wrap perimeter.

An entirely new feature, the Color Mapper enables you to take a picture (usually imported) and redefine all the colours used by it so as to re-colour the picture. This isn't just useful for creating artistic effects, it is vital to the production of spot colour separations.

PagePlus now has the capability to deal with a whole new range of graphic filters. It can now import clipart from Corel Draw, WordPerfect and numerous other packages, and can import CD ROM pictures.

>> **Pre-press, printing and production**
PagePlus's output capabilities have been improved. You can now print a booklet automatically, placing two layout pages to each sheet of paper. There is support for trapping, a technique where spot colours are overlapped to avoid white gaps or smudging. For really high quality colour work OPI (Open Prepress Interface) comments will be automatically inserted into an output file so that high quality scanned images can be inserted at a later stage in production.

There are many other improvements that will be discussed as and when they become relevant in the remainder of this book.

» Learning DTP

The only way that you can really learn how DTP works is to do it. To help you come to grips with PagePlus in particular this book includes a number of examples that you are encouraged to try out. As well as the practical side of things you also need to know something about how things work. Throughout this book you will find explanations of what is happening. This should give you a deeper understanding of the process of DTP and ensure that you are able to make the right choices when things go wrong. As the book progresses and you become more comfortable with PagePlus you will find that the emphasis shifts from the fine detail of how to achieve something to the more general considerations. These are still practical but you may find that rather than being told which tool to use or button to press the instructions are in terms of what you are trying to do rather than exactly how to do it.

» Levels

To make PagePlus appropriate for users with varying experience there are three different levels that you can select between - Intro, Publisher and Professional. The only difference between these three levels is the number of features they offer you and the default level of help. The idea is that when you first start using PagePlus you begin with the simplest level and work your way up as your familiarity with the program grows.

The Intro level allows you to use all the basic features without being confused by the inclusion of more advanced options.. You can create and manipulate your objects, and setup your page almost without restriction. However, most of the selections have to be made using the Menu Bar as the shortcut keys are limited.

The Publisher level gives you all the features of the Intro level plus a few extras. The most significant difference is that you can use the ChangeBar and Properties Palette fully, and additional shortcut buttons. This makes most tasks much quicker for experienced users, who then need not make selections from as many menus and dialogs.

The top level, Professional, has access to all of PagePlus 3's current features, some of which are not available to the lower levels. Most of the extra help is turned off so that you can get on with using PagePlus without having to read unnecessary instructions.

For the first few chapters of this book the examples will use Intro level but we will quickly graduate to Professional.

» A first look

Before taking a first look at PagePlus it is worth examining what sort of tools you would expect to find in a DTP package. Having some idea of what you are looking for is a help whenever you approach a new applications package - no matter what the application!

Any DTP package has to give you some way of placing the standard components - text and graphics of various kinds - in a layout. As well as positioning we need some way of altering the objects. A text tool to edit text is an obvious example. We need to be able to alter the size of objects, assign colours and type styles to text, to rotate objects etc.. All of these positioning and editing abilities have to be provided in an easy to use way.

When you first start PagePlus you will see the welcome screen. You can get rid of this screen by registering your product. Just phone Serif and they will give you a registration number which you can type in by clicking on Register Now. Until you register you will see this screen each time you start.

If you have registered, or have clicked on the Register Later button, you will see the StartUp Assistant. There is an option to stop this screen from appearing but many users find it helpful. To start a new layout simply click on Blank Page.

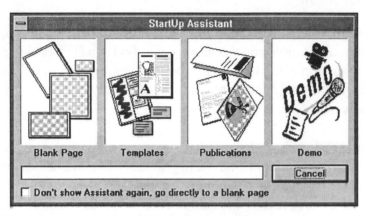

This takes you to PagePlus in Intro mode.

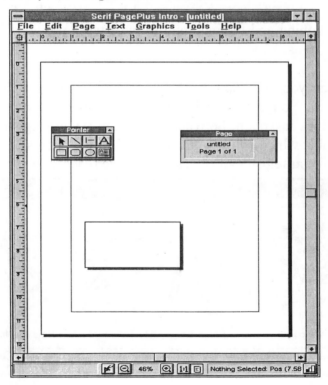

All layouts consist of objects - both text and graphics - positioned and sized on the page. In the middle of the screen is an image of the page on which you are going to place the objects. The area around the image of the page is an area representing the traditional layout pasteboard where you can place objects while you are trying to decide where they should go. Think of the pasteboard as a work area.

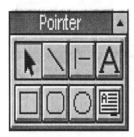

The small rectangular block of icons is your ToolBox. To use a tool you simply click on its icon. Don't worry for now what all the tools are - you will find out soon enough in the following chapters.

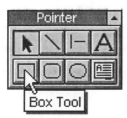

Box tool. Use this tool to draw a box.

You should be able to guess roughly what each tool is used for from its icon - but as icons are subject to interpretation a short text description of each appears in the QuickHelp box - the large text panel below the ToolBox. In fact as you move the cursor around the screen the QuickHelp panel does its best to describe everything it passes over. It's up to you how much notice you take of its information! A second level of explanation appears if you leave the cursor positioned over a tool. This is ToolHint and a small bubble of text will appear whenever you hover over any tool or menu.

It is possible disable these help facilities and so if you find
they do not appear then you will need to restore them. This
can be done in the Ease of Use Preferences dialog box which
is reached using the command Tool,Preferences,Ease of Use.
We return to the subject of customising PagePlus 3's
Preferences in Chapter 10.

The only tool it is worth telling you something
about at this early stage is the Pointer tool - the
arrow in the top left-hand corner. Using this you
can select objects, move them, resize them and rotate them.
The pointer is the equivalent of your hand picking up objects,
moving them, stretching them and rotating them. It will be
the tool you use the most.

» Remember: the ToolBox is used to add new objects to the
   layout or to move, size or rotate existing objects.

As well as the ToolBox there is the Menu bar at the top of the
screen.

This is used to give commands that are usually not directly
related to objects on the page. For example, you use the Menu
bar to set the page size, to save and load documents and of
course to print your finished work.

Many of the commands in the Menu bar are duplicated in the ChangeBar for ease of use.

The ChangeBar only appears on the screen when you have an object in the layout selected. Exactly how it looks depends on what is selected and what level you are working in. In Intro level it  only allows you to change the single most important property of the object. For example, if you select a text object then the ChangeBar only allows you to change its size. Later, when we work in higher levels, you will discover that you can change almost any aspect of an object using the ChangeBar.

» Remember: the ChangeBar changes a property of the object that you have selected. Later we will find out how to select which property of the object is changed.

This concludes our introduction to the most general features of the PagePlus interface. You will find out exactly how they work and how they all work together in the following chapters. For the moment it is enough that you can identify the ToolBox, Menu bar, and the ChangeBar.

Key points

» Desktop Publishing is using a personal computer to produce documents that look like traditional printed, typeset material.

» DTP has largely replaced a traditional industry that looked after the stages between the origination of material and its printing with a process that can be undertaken by any individual with their own PC and a suitable DTP package like PagePlus.

» Although the Apple Mac used to dominate the DTP scene, the development of the Windows interface has enabled the PC to capture an increasing share of the market. The problem is that the PC user has still to contend with a largely Mac-oriented printing industry.

» To embark on DTP you need a moderately powerful PC - a 386 or 486 based machine is recommended - with a sizeable hard disk and preferably an SVGA display. To use PagePlus 3 you need Windows 3.1.

» It is page make-up software that lets you design the precise layout of any document and PagePlus comes into this category.

» PagePlus 3 has a number of notable enhancements over earlier versions in its user interface and in its functionality - notably in text and colour handling.

» The basic PagePlus interface is centred on the use of a ToolBox to add, move, size and rotate objects on the page; a Menu bar for more general commands such as printing and saving files; and a ChangeBar which is used in conjunction with it to change the attributes of an object.

Chapter 2

PagePlus
Fundamentals

A good way to learn about any software is to go ahead and use it for the type of task it has been designed for. It is even better to be guided step-by-step through a small example before you start to use it 'for real'. This chapter runs through the fundamentals of using PagePlus 3, introducing its terminology, and then gives you a hands-on practical tour. The tour itself uses some technical terms that might well be unfamiliar - don't worry as they will all be explained in due course. It is assumed that you know how to use Windows. Specifically that you know how to click, double click and drag using a mouse. You also need to know how to select commands from the menu, fill in dialog boxes, use drop down lists and scroll bars. If you are in any doubt then run the on-line tutorial that is part of the standard Windows Help. To do this go to use the Program Manager and give the command Help,Windows Tutorial.

» Object manipulation

Essentially PagePlus deals with every object in the same manner, whether it be a piece of text, a graphic or a picture. Note that a *picture* is a piece of artwork imported into PagePlus whereas a *graphic* is a piece of artwork created using PagePlus's own drawing tools.

Objects are initially created using PagePlus's tools or they are imported from other applications. Once placed on the page you can position them and change their size or other properties. As the methods for manipulating objects don't really depend very much on what the object is, it is worth outlining the most common operations. Selecting, moving and resizing objects are all achieved using the *pointer tool* - the arrow in the top left-hand corner of the ToolBox. When you have this tool selected the mouse cursor also changes to an arrow.

» Selecting objects

An object is selected by clicking on it with the pointer tool, although a newly created object is initially selected automatically. A selected object is surrounded by small black squares, called *handles*, to indicate this. The rectangle formed by the handles is the object's *bounding box*. It is the bounding

box that you see when you drag the object and it acts as a guide to the space on the page that the object occupies. You can actually select an object by clicking anywhere within its bounding box but most users prefer to aim at something more tangible!

If two or more objects overlap each other, repetitive clicking *toggles* the selection between those objects. For example, if there are a group of objects together, including one that you want to select, just keep clicking on that object until it becomes selected. Notice that two objects overlap if their bounding boxes overlap at the point that you click. You can sometimes select a particular object by choosing exactly where you click so that you hit only one object's bounding box.

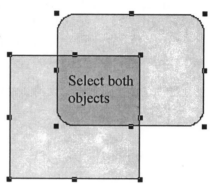

Select both objects

You can select multiple objects by either clicking on additional objects while holding down the shift key or by 'lassoing' the group by dragging with the mouse. If you drag with the mouse when the pointer tool is selected an outline box appears and any objects that are included in the box are selected. The shift key can be used to add or remove selected objects from the group. If you click on a selected object when the shift key is pressed it is de-selected.

》 Holding down shift when you click adds to the selection.

» Selecting tools

The tool that you will be using most of the time is the Pointer, or selection, tool. If you select another tool to create an object on the page you will find that after you have used the tool you are automatically given back the selection tool. The reasoning is that after you have drawn a line, a box or placed some text on the page the next thing you will need to do is adjust it. In other words you will need the selection tool!

Most of the time this swapping back to the selection tool is exactly what you want to do. Sometimes, however, it is a nuisance. For example, if you are trying to draw a set of lines or boxes then to be swapped to the selection tool each after each line you draw means that you have to reselect the line drawing tool. The solution is to hold down the Shift key while selecting any tool that you want to keep in operation until you change to using a different tool.

» Holding down the Shift key when you select a tool makes the selection permanent.

» Moving objects

An object is moved or positioned by dragging it with the pointer tool cursor. You can drag an object using any point within its bounding box and sometimes it is worth considering exactly where to pick an object up so that the pointer doesn't obscure the feature of interest. To save time only an outline box is drawn while you are dragging, but if you pause for a moment the compete object is redrawn, allowing you to see it at its new position.

In many cases rough positioning by eye is sufficient but, for more accurate positioning, you can use rulers, guides and snapping, all of which are described later. If you want to make sure that you move an object only horizontally or vertically then hold down the Shift key after you start to move the object.

» Holding down the Shift key after you start to move an object restricts the move to either a horizontal or vertical move.

» Resizing objects

Resizing an object is simply done by first selecting it, so that handles appear, and then dragging any one of the handles. Dragging the handle of your choice causes the bounding box to change its shape accordingly and, when you have finished dragging, the object is resized to fit the new bounding box.

Thus, dragging on one of the handles at the side of the object causes its width to be altered; dragging inwards makes it thinner and outwards makes it thicker. Dragging on one of the handles on the top or on the bottom of the object causes it to get taller or shorter. By dragging on the corner handles you can change both dimensions at the same time.

It is worth saying that the effect of resizing a text object might not be what you expect. Instead of altering the size of the letters making up the text it alters the spacing of the words so that the text fills the bounding box. The reason is that the size of the letters in a text object is governed by a property - the font size. In the case of artwork the shape is compressed or stretched to fit the bounding box.

If you hold down the Shift key while sizing an object, the object will be constrained to some predefined aspect ratio (i.e. width to height ratio). For example if you try to resize a rectangle while holding down the Shift key it will change to a square, similarly an ellipse will change to a circle. It is important that you do not press the Shift key before you start to drag the handle as this will only deselect the object!

» Holding down the Shift key after you have started to resize an object restricts its aspect ratio - i.e. makes a rectangle a square and an oval into a circle.

» Copying objects

Although you can copy an object using the familiar Windows operations Edit,Copy (or its keypress shortcut Ctrl-C) and Edit,Paste (Ctrl-V) it is worth knowing another simple shortcut. If you want to copy any object on the page simply select it and then drag it as if you were trying to move it - but hold the Ctrl key down before you start to drag. This allows you to drag a new copy of the object to another position. It's easy to remember as **C**trl for **C**opy.

» Holding down the Ctrl key when moving an object creates a new copy of the object.

» Deleting objects

You can delete any object or group of objects by selecting them and then either pressing the Delete key or selecting Edit,Cut from the menu (the shortcut keypress for which is Ctrl-X). However, although these two actions appear to be similar they are not.

The Cut operation removes the object to the Clipboard from where it can be pasted back onto the page any number of times using the command Edit,Paste (or Ctrl-V). Using the Delete key on the other hand removes the object without transferring it to the Clipboard. Pressing the Delete key is the same as using the command Edit,Clear. To get a deleted object back you can use the command Edit,Undo (or its shortcut Ctrl-Z) which will also undo any command.

» Edit,Cut or Ctrl-X removes an object to the Clipboard.

» Delete erases an object and doesn't use the Clipboard. You can "undelete" an object using the Edit,Undo command or Ctrl-Z.

» Tour One: a cover design

Tour One is a hands-on tutorial that you can follow to produce a relatively simple design - a front cover to a football game manual. It is designed to illustrate the basics of DTP, and the use of PagePlus in particular. The tour is uses the Intro level of PagePlus. For this reason, the Properties Palette is not used nor are the other features that are only available at the higher levels. The Menu Bar will be used to apply most of the property changes to objects. Bear in mind that once you move to the higher levels you will be able to do the same things in a variety of ways, often using the more direct shortcuts.

You will only be able to follow the steps of this tutorial exactly if you have Intro mode in force. Arrange for this by selecting Tools,Level,Intro or by toggling (i.e. clicking on) the level icon on the right of the Status Bar to the first level.

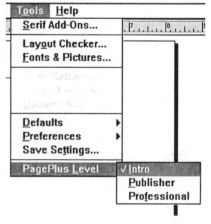

One of the pictures used in the tour is taken from Serif's ArtPack1. However, if you do not have this it is still possible to follow the steps by substituting a suitable alternative.

Whatever your level, the principles of simple page design are the same. So if you are new to DTP or new to PagePlus this is an ideal starting point. Tour Two in the next chapter covers many of the same fundamentals but using the Publisher level.

If you are not running PagePlus 3, you should now start it up from Windows. It is assumed that you have not altered any default settings. If you have and you wish to reset all the defaults, just reinstall PagePlus 3. When PagePlus starts, select a blank page from the initial StartUp Assistant dialog and cancel any subsequent tips that you might be offered.

You should now have a blank page and be ready to begin. Notice that your page has a magenta box to represent your margins. You will also see the ToolBox, from which the Pointer is currently selected, and the ChangeBar which at present contains a number of general options (print, save, etc.). The area surrounding your page is your pasteboard which you can use as a convenient place for storing objects while you are working on them, or even for creating objects, before finalising their position. Objects on the pasteboard will not be printed and are accessible no matter which page in your document you are using. That is, you don't get a new pasteboard for each page in your publication.

● Double-click anywhere on your blank page to open the Page Setup dialog. The first thing you must do in any publication is to set your page up. The Page Setup dialog allows you to change the size of your page, the margins and set up any columns.

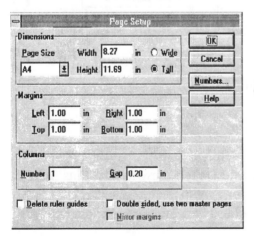

● From the Page Setup dialog select the Page Size box and then select A4 from the drop-down menu. Click on the OK push button to apply your changes and return to your page.

- Click with the Pointer tool on the vertical ruler near the 5-inch mark. A magenta line will appear across your page. This is a guide to help you with the positioning of objects. Drag with your cursor (currently the Pointer tool) on the guide line so as to position it at exactly 5 inches from the top of your page.

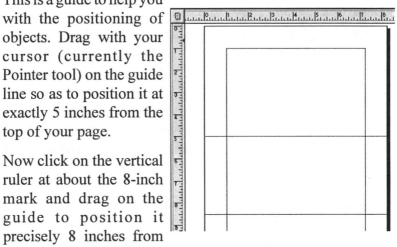

- Now click on the vertical ruler at about the 8-inch mark and drag on the guide to position it precisely 8 inches from the top of your page.

- Next, click on the Box icon in the ToolBox to select the Box tool.

- With the cursor (which is now a cross-hair) drag from the top left corner of your page, where the top margin and the left margin meet, down to first guide and across to the right margin.

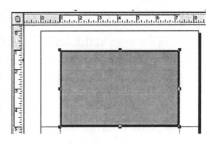

Notice how when you drag to create the box, the object is not dragged smoothly but in small increments making it easy to align it with the guides and margins. This is caused by the snapping feature, which is set on by default. Snapping causes objects to be pulled, almost magnetically, towards margins or guides and to the snap grid which is an invisible grid based on the ruler increments. Snapping is discussed in Chapter 4.

You have now created a box in the top section (down to the first guide) of your margined page, with default properties. After you finished dragging the Box tool, you will have noticed the ChangeBar open. This is used to manipulate your object's properties, though at the Intro level its use is restricted. The ChangeBar applies to the object that is currently selected - your box in this case.

A selected object is indicated by the handles surrounding it and can be selected by clicking on the object with the Pointer tool. An object can be deselected by clicking with the Pointer tool anywhere else.

- If for some reason your box is not already selected, click on it to select it.

- Select the Show/Hide third row icon on the ChangeBar to open the set of shortcut buttons.

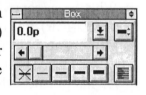

- Select the No line thickness button (the one at the left of the ChangeBar) in order to give your box no border line. It automatically sets the line width to 0.0p.

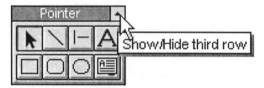

- Now change the colour of your box to cyan by selecting the Graphics menu from the Menu Bar.

- From this menu, select Color, and then choose Cyan from the side menu that appears. You can leave the shading of the box at the default 20%.

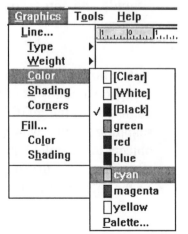

Changing properties such as the colour and shading can be done more directly from the ChangeBar and Properties Palette when you are working at the Publisher or Professional level.

● Select the Box tool again from the Tool Box by clicking on the Box icon.

● Now create a box in the central section of your page by dragging from the left margin at the 5-inch guide across to the right margin and down to the 8-inch guide.

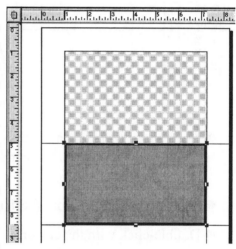

● Once again, select the No line thickness button from the ChangeBar to remove the box's border.

● To change the colour and the tint of your box, first make sure that your object is selected. Then select Graphics,Fill... by choosing the Graphics menu from the Menu Bar and the Fill... entry in that menu. This opens the Fill dialog box allowing you to manipulate both colour and tint from one dialog.

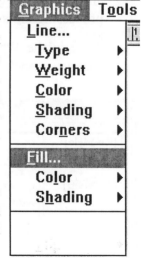

Note that you can alter the colour and the tint individually by using the menu commands Graphics,Color and Graphics,Shading respectively.

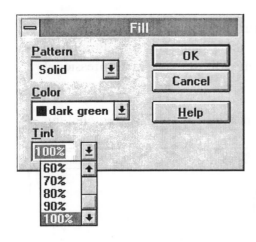

● From the Fill dialog, click on the down arrow beside the Color window. From the drop-down menu, scroll down, using the down arrow, to select dark green.

● Similarly select the Tint box and, using the drop-down or by typing in, set the tint to 100%.

● Now apply these changes by selecting the dialog's OK button. You now have a second box which is dark green and tinted fully (100%).

● Select the Text tool from the Tool Box.

● Double-click with the cursor, which is now an I-beam, on your page's top box (the cyan one). This opens WritePlus Serif's own word processor which you can use to create and edit text. You will notice that various standard word processing tools are available.

● Type in the WritePlus word processor the text: Soccer Manager - each word on its own line.

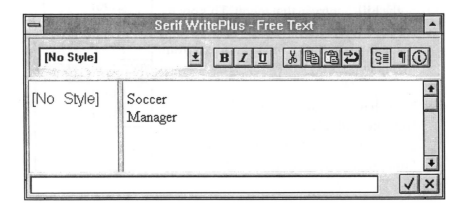

● Click on the tick icon that is in the bottom right-hand corner of the WritePlus window to return to your page with the text object applied. Note that the cross icon would cancel the text object and return you to your page.

● Select the Pointer tool from the ToolBox and click on your text to select it if it is not already selected.

● Now drag on the centre right handle of your text object and pull it across to the right margin and drag the centre left handle across to the left margin.

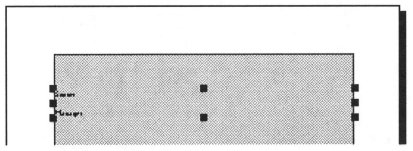

This makes the bounding box for that text object the same width as the page. Therefore, when you align centre your text it will be positioned exactly in the middle of the page.

● Now select Text,Align,Center to centre your text.

● With the object still selected, select the Bold and Outline shortcut buttons on the object's ChangeBar.

● The primary property available from the ChangeBar at the Intro level is Size. So click on the down arrow and scroll down to select 72.0p as the size of your text.

Note that you can change this property using the data-entry window or the scroll-bar if you prefer.

- Now, with the text still selected, select Text,Character to open the Character dialog.

- Select the Font box and select Arial from the drop-down menu as the chosen font type.

- Then select All Caps from the Case drop-down menu to make all the characters in your text appear as upper case on the page.

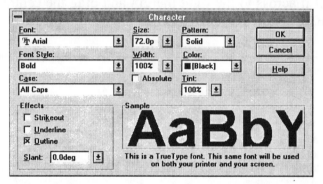

- Select OK from the Character dialog to apply these properties.

- With the text still selected, finally select Text,Leading and 90% from the side menu.

Leading, which is discussed in Chapter 5, is a measure of the distance between the lines of text so decreasing this to 90% tightens up the lines.

- Select the Pointer and drag the text to the top of the page. If you drag quickly on the text, the object will be represented by its bounding box only, so you can accurately position the top of this box on the top margin, helped by the snapping.

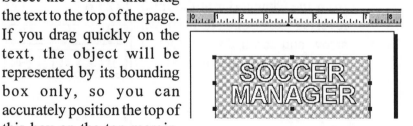

● Select the 45° Line tool from the Tool Box which is the one used to draw horizontal, vertical and diagonal lines.

● Drag, just beneath your text, 0.25 inches in from the left margin to 0.25 inches from the right margin. A horizontal line then appears between these points with default properties of 6.0p thickness and black colour.

● Adjust the precise position with the Pointer tool if you need to.

● Select the Text tool again and double-click near the bottom right of your page to open WritePlus.

● Type in:
> Manual in English
> Manual en francais
> Handbuch auf deutsch
> Manuale in italiano

● Click on the Tick button to apply the text to your document.

● Drag the left and right centre handles to the left and right margins respectively, like you did before.

● Then use the command Text,Align,Right to right align your text with the right margin.

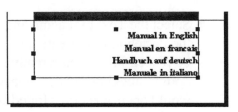

- With the text selected, select the Bold button and set the text to 24.0p in size.

- Select the Pointer tool and accurately position the text if you need to do so.

- Select the Text tool again and double-click near the bottom right of the green box.

- Using WritePlus, type in:
  ## Player's Handbook

- As you did before, drag the handles to the left and right margins and select Text,Align,Right.

- Using the ChangeBar increase the size of the text to 30.0p.

- Select Text,Character to open the Character dialog again and, from the Font box, select Arial.

- From the Color box, select White.

- Select OK to apply your changes.

- Select the Pointer tool and make any positional adjustments to the text if you need to do so.

- With the Pointer tool, ensure the right handles of the text object's bounding box are dragged across to the right margin.

- Select the Text tool again and double-click somewhere on the pasteboard to create another text object. It is going to be placed in an area already occupied by a text object so double-clicking on the area where you actually want it would open WritePlus for editing which you don't want to do. So use the pasteboard as a convenient "scratchpad" instead. Type in:

    S

and click on the tick icon to apply the text object.

- Use the ChangeBar to select Bold and then increase the size to 72.0p. Select Text,Character and then select Arial from the Font dialog.

- Select the Pointer tool and then manually position the S just above the bottom margin and 0.5 inches in from the left margin.

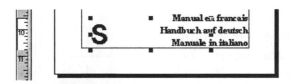

- Select the Text tool again and double-click on the pasteboard to enter another new text object. Type in:

    CORE
    OFT

and click on the Tick icon.

- Use the ChangeBar to increase the size of the text to 24.0p.

- Select Text,Character and set the font to Arial.

Before manually positioning this object you need to prevent the object snapping to the ruler grid. This will allow you to move this object smoothly and more precisely.

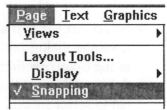

- Select Page,Snapping to toggle snapping off.

- Select the Pointer tool
  and drag your text
  object to position it
  next to the 'S'.

Your text objects are now complete, so all there is to do now
is to add the two picture objects.

- Select the Show third row icon on the ToolBox to make
  the third row of tools available. The third row of tools
  includes the Import Picture tool which you now need to
  use.

- Select the Import Picture
  tool from the ToolBox to
  open the Import Picture
  flyout.

- From the flyout, click on the
  Art & Borders icon to open
  the Art & Borders dialog.

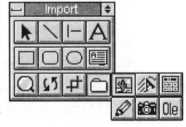

Note that single clicking on the Art & Borders icon opens the
Art & Borders dialog which is what we currently require.
Double-clicking the Import
Picture dialog to allow you
to import any supported
artwork by specifying its
name and location.

- Select Art (or ArtPack1)
  from the dialog box. Go
  to the Sports section and
  then scroll down the file
  list to select soccer1.

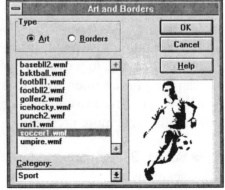

- Select OK from the dialog, which currently shows a preview of the picture, to import the object.

- Click with the cursor, now shaped as a paste icon, somewhere on your page or pasteboard to apply the object.

- Drag on one of the corner handles of your picture object to increase the size of your object. Keep the shift key held down to maintain the aspect ratio (the ratio of width to height) whilst you drag the picture to a size of approximately 4 inches by 7 inches.

When you size the object use the rulers which change colour to indicate the size of your object allowing you to measure it accurately.

- Drag on the picture itself (not the handles) to position the picture, by eye, so that the head overlaps the text slightly, and the feet are on the far left of the page, an inch below the green box.

- Now import the second picture, soccer2, by selecting the Import Picture tool again, followed by the Art & Borders icon.

The picture soccer2 is included in ArtPack1 but not in the sample images supplied with PagePlus 3 itself so you may have to improvise. You could use soccer1 again at a smaller size, or you could import the file c2_ball.wmf from the

I/O Press companion disk. To access a file not already included in the Art & Borders dialog, double-click on the Art & Borders icon to open the Import Picture dialog where you can specify the filename and location of the picture you want to import. So if you wanted to import c2_ball.wmf from a disk in your a: drive you would first select a: from the list of drives and then select it from the list of files that would appear.

- Click on the page with the paste cursor to apply the object.

- Again, resize the object by dragging inwards on the picture, with the Shift key held down, until the picture is approximately 1.75 inches wide by 1 inch high.

- Use the ChangeBar's horizontal flip icon to turn the picture around to face the other way.

- Now drag the picture to position it, again by eye, so that the tail of the ball's flight just touches the top of the 'S' text object. You should be able to position the picture precisely as the snapping should still be set to off.

Your design is now complete and all that

remains to be done is to save your work and print it if you want to.

● To save your design, select the Save icon from the Page ChangeBar to open the Save As dialog.

● Use this dialog to supply a filename (e.g. **tour_one.ppp**) for your work and to select the drive (e.g. **C:**) and the directory (e.g. **pp30\document**) where you want to keep it. Leave the file type as Publication. You can save a thumbnail sketch of your design to help identify it in the future if you wish, by checking the Save preview checkbox.

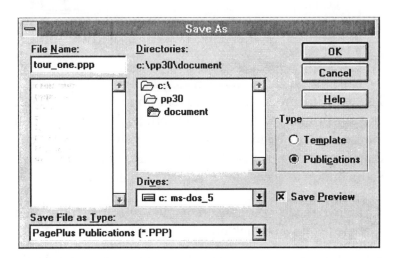

● When your selections are complete, select OK to save your file.

You only need to go through this procedure the first time you save a publication. Subsequently, you can select the Save icon and the file will be saved using the same name and location, replacing the previous version.

● The first step in printing your document is to select the Print icon from the Page ChangeBar to open the Print dialog.

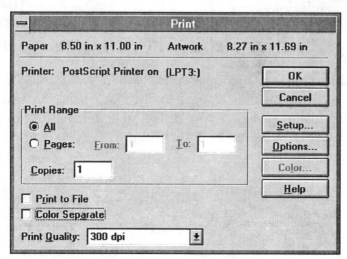

The exact nature of the subsequent option dialogs depends on your printer set-up but if your printer is normally set up for use through Windows applications, you shouldn't need to change anything. If you do want to make alterations use the Setup button to access the Print Setup dialog.

● Having made your selections and specified how many copies you want click on OK to start printing.

● Finally, you can exit PagePlus, if you wish, by selecting File,Exit which returns you to the Windows desktop.

You can re-open your document, if you ever want to alter it or print it again. To do this just open PagePlus and then select the Documents icon on the StartUp Assistant dialog that pops up when you start PagePlus. This opens the Open dialog from which you can specify which document to open.

You can also open the document from within PagePlus by selecting the Open icon from the Page ChangeBar or select File,Open. The Open dialog can then be used to specify the filename and its location.

If you saved a preview of your document it can be viewed in the Open dialog before being opened for editing by selecting the file with one click only - select OK to fully open it. A double-click will open the file, without first previewing it.

The File menu also offers a quick route to opening a recently used file in that it lists the last four documents you worked on at the bottom, below the other choices on its menu.

» What next?

Your first PagePlus 3 document is now complete and you will now be aware of the fundamentals involved in using PagePlus. Most of the functions and tools are intuitive and therefore you will already be armed with the knowledge to use them. Tour Two in the next chapter builds on this first lesson in order to illustrate how to produce more complex designs.

Key points

» The selection tool can be used to select a single object by clicking within its bounding box, and to select multiple objects by 'lassoing' them, that is dragging with the selection tool. To add or remove objects from a selection use Shift and click.

» Moving an object is just a matter of dragging it and resizing is performed by dragging its handles.

» If you drag an object while holding down the Ctrl key then a new copy is made.

» The first step in any layout is to set the page size and margins.

» You enter text using the text tool. Double clicking with it displays the text editor WritePlus.

» You can change the properties of text objects both by commands in the menu and by using the ChangeBar.

» The rulers can be used to position text and other objects.

» The Box tool can be used to draw rectangles.

» Pictures can be easily added to a publication and can be used for decorative effects as well as illustration.

Chapter 3

Moving up to
Publisher

Now that you have seen the basic methods of working with PagePlus - selection, moving and resizing objects - it is time to find out about properties. Intro mode tries to shield you from the full range of facilities that PagePlus offers you but the idea of controlling properties is logical and so simple and should by now cause you no difficulty. So it's time to change to Publisher mode.

» Change to Publisher mode

If you use the command Tools,PagePlus Level, Publisher you are immediately switched into Publisher mode. The most obvious difference is that the third row of the ToolBox is automatically on display and the ChangeBar gets bigger.

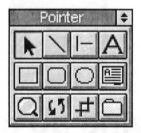 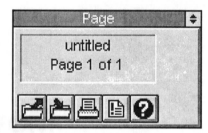

You can hide the bottom line of the ToolBox if you want to by clicking on the arrow in the top right-hand corner. The enlarged ChangeBar may be something of a puzzle to you at first because it simply seems to display a few additional tool icons. However, as you will see, its new purpose isn't as an extension to the ToolBox. The ChangeBar now allows you to set not just one but any of a range of properties. It also gives you quick access to the most common property changes that you are likely to make. But before all this makes sense we need to look at the third member of the team, the Properties Palette.

» Changing the properties of objects

In addition to position and size, every PagePlus object has a set of properties that controls the way it looks. In any DTP package how to give the user an easy to use and yet comprehensive way of changing an object's properties is a major problem. PagePlus's solution to the problem is to provide the ChangeBar working in conjunction with the Properties Palette.

In Publisher (and Professional) level the ChangeBar has a row of icons which allows you to select from a range of commonly used settings for the property that you are changing. For example, if you select a box then by default the ChangeBar allows you to alter its line width property. You can do this in one of four ways.

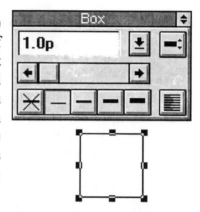

» You can type the line width directly into the text box where the current width is displayed.

» If you click on the arrow at the right-hand side of the text box then a list of standard sizes drops down and you can select the size that you want to use.

» Moving the slider to the right increases the property value and moving it to the left decreases it.

» Clicking on one of the line width icons below the slider sets the line width to 0, 1, 4,6 or 12 points. Notice that the range of standard property values available varies according to the type of object.

Use whichever method of setting a property suits the occasion. If you know the value you are trying to set then typing it in is usually faster. If you are trying to judge an effect then the slider is often a good way to make rough changes before using the drop down list to pick the closest round value. Notice that the tool button to the far right of the ChangeBar is different from the others. It sets a 'Wrap' setting which controls the way objects and text interact and is discussed in Chapter 7.

» The Properties Palette

The ChangeBar may now have an extended function but it still only controls a single property. If you look closely at the ChangeBar you will notice that the tool button in the top right hand corner indicates the property that you are currently changing. If you click on this button the Properties Palette appears next to the ChangeBar.

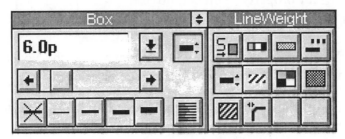

The Properties Palette contains a large number of buttons and their use is not always immediately obvious. However, in principle all you have to do is select the property that you want to change by clicking on its button in the Properties Palette and then change it using the ChangeBar. Once you have selected the property that you want to change the Properties Palette vanishes so that you can concentrate on the changes. To make the Properties Palette appear again you click on the button in the top right of the ChangeBar that indicates the current property.

That's all there is to it! As you work you will find that you quickly get used to making the Properties Palette appear, selecting the property you want to change and making the change. This is a very easy and efficient way of working and it represents a level of logical organisation that other DTP packages do not have. Your only problem is in discovering what all the properties are and how they interact together to produce the visual effect you are interested in.

This isn't as difficult as it first appears because the properties fall into a number of simple groups each of which apply to a range of object types.

For example, a line has a small and fairly obvious set of properties. The first property button controls styles which are described in Chapter 4. The other buttons can set the colour of the line, its tint or shade, its type, width and pattern.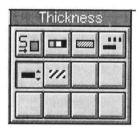

This seems simple but what's the difference between line colour and shade? The answer is that the shade sets the intensity of the colour that you have selected. For example, if you set a line colour to black then setting its shade to 50% means that the line will be drawn using 50% black ink - in other words it will look grey. Similarly, if you select red and a shade of 20% it will look light pink. The reason for using colour and tint settings is explained in detail in Chapter 8.

You may also be puzzled as to the difference between line type and line pattern? The line type controls how the outline is drawn - dotted, dashed, thick double, thick-thin double and so on. The line pattern controls how any parts of the line that are drawn are inked in. For example, if you select a dashed line type and then a hatched line pattern the result is a dashed line with each dash hatched in!

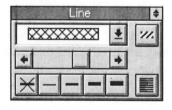

Once you are familiar with the basic line properties you will immediately recognise them as part of the set of properties that you can set for a graphics object such as a box or a circle. The line properties control the way the outline of the object appears in just the same way that they work for a simple line.

The only extra line property needed in this case is something to control the curvature of the corners of the box object - something a circle object doesn't need!

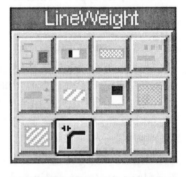

There are of course a number of properties that are needed to control the way the interior of shapes are displayed. The three new properties are fill colour, fill shade and fill pattern. Colour and shade interact in the same way as the line colour and shade. That is, you can select a black fill with a 50% shade to produce a grey. The fill pattern allows you to fill a shape with hatching.

You can see that line and fill properties are basic to many types of shape. Once you are familiar with these two groups of properties only the text group and one or two extras wait in store for you!

» Tour Two: an advertising flyer

Tour Two covers similar ground to Tour One except that it is assumed that you are working at the Publisher level.

The design is a flyer or a magazine advertisement for a classical concert. Just one picture is used in this design. It is included in the music category of the Serif ArtPack1 and is also supplied as one of the art samples.

If you are not running PagePlus 3, you should now start it up from Windows. It is assumed that you have not altered any default settings. If you have and you wish to reset all the defaults, just reinstall PagePlus 3. When PagePlus starts, select a blank page from the initial StartUp Assistant dialog and cancel any subsequent tip dialogs.

You should now have a blank page and be ready to begin. As usual, the first thing you must do in any publication is to set your page up. The Page Setup dialog allows you to change the size of your page, the margins and set up any columns.

- Open the Page Setup dialog by double-clicking anywhere on your blank page.

- Click on the Page Size box and select A5 from the drop-down menu.

- Then select the Wide radio button on the same dialog.

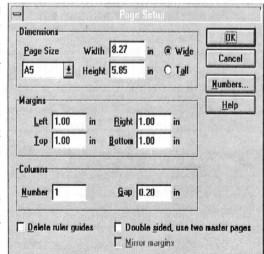

- Click on the OK push button to apply your changes and return to your page.

Your page size is now set to A5 and by setting it to wide it is effectively the same as having an A4 sheet folded in half. It would be possible therefore for two of these designs to be printed on a single A4 sheet.

Note that setting the page to wide turns it to lie on its side. This is referred to as *landscape* as opposed to the standard *portrait* orientation.

The next step is to create some guides on the page to help with the positioning and alignment of objects. Although you could create each of them individually as they are needed it's easier to do it in a single operation.

It is well worth knowing that you can move the rulers from their default positions at the edge of the page. For this Tour it is a good idea to move them to the page margins. To do this click on the button at the intersection of the two rulers, the *ruler origin*, and drag - to the right or left to move the vertical ruler and up or down to move the horizontal one.

- Click on the top ruler, 1.5 inches in from the left margin. This creates a red line, a guide, down your page which you can drag to position it precisely where you want, using the ruler mark if necessary. Note that you can remove a guide by dragging it off the page.

- Now create another guide by clicking on the top ruler, and position it 1.5 inches in from the right margin, i.e. at 4.75 inches from the left margin.

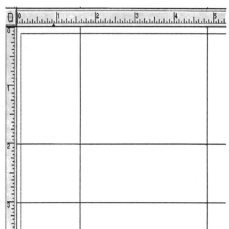

- To create the first horizontal guide click on the vertical ruler at the left side of your page, and position it on the 2-inch mark if 0 is aligned with the top margin.

- Create a second horizontal guide and position it at the 4-inch mark.

All your guides are now in place so you can begin to add the objects in your design.

- Select the Box tool from the ToolBox by clicking on the Box tool icon.

Notice how the cursor then becomes a cross-hair indicating that you have a drawing tool selected, and the title of the ToolBox changes to Box.

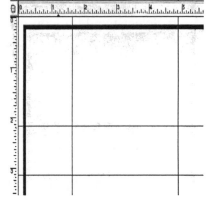

- Drag the cursor from the top left corner of your margined page (where the top margin and left margin meet) to the bottom right corner of your margined page (where the bottom margin and right margin meet).

The point at which you started dragging from creates one corner of your box and the point at which you stop dragging marks the opposite corner. Consequently, you now have a box covering the whole of your margined page. The precise positioning of your cursor for the creation of this box should have been easy as a result of snapping.

When dragging to create the box, notice how the object is not dragged smoothly but in small increments making it easy to align it with the guides and margins. This is caused by the snapping feature which is set on by default. Snapping causes objects to be pulled, almost magnetically, towards margins or guides and the snap grid, an invisible grid based on the ruler increments.

As soon as you finish dragging the Box tool you will notice the ChangeBar open. The ChangeBar becomes available when any object is selected and applies to that object. You use it to control all the properties of the object. Once you finish creating the box it remains automatically selected, as indicated by the eight black squares (*handles*) surrounding it. If an object is not selected, you can select it by clicking on it with the Pointer tool. Deselecting objects can be done by clicking on a blank area of the page or pasteboard.

● Select the 4.0p icon on the ChangeBar to set the thickness of the rectangle's border to 4 points in the default colour of black.

You could have altered this property using the drop-down menu, the slider or the data entry box, but in this instance the icon is the quickest way.

● Click on the Properties Palette icon on the ChangeBar to open the Properties Palette. (Notice that the Properties Palette is a feature not available to Intro users.) This is a collection of icons, each representing a property that when

selected can be manipulated and applied to the current
object, using the ChangeBar.

- Select the
  F i l l C o l o r
  property from
  the Properties
  Palette.

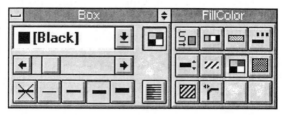

Notice how the Properties Palette title changes to FillColor
and the ChangeBar's icon for selecting the Properties Palette
changes to the icon of the selected property. Now that the
FillColor is selected, the ChangeBar can be used to
manipulate your box's interior colour.

- Select Clear from the drop-down
  options menu.

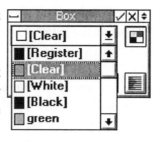

Your box then becomes transparent
except for the border and is now
complete. A second box within the
current one is now required.

- Select the Box tool
  again and drag
  with the cursor to
  create a box that is
  0.375 inches
  inside the page
  margins. Again
  moving the rulers
  temporarily will
  help.

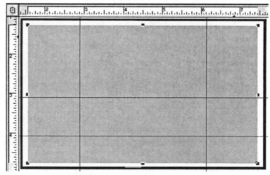

Snapping will help you with the positioning of the box. If you have trouble, though, remember that you can drag on the box's handles to change its size and position.

● With the box selected, use the ChangeBar's Properties Palette icon to open the Properties Palette again.

● Select the FillTint property from the Properties Palette.

● Slide the ChangeBar's slider all the way across to the right, by using the scroll-bar, to change the tint level from the default, to 100%. As you move the slider, you can see the incremental effect of the changing tint level on the object in WYSIWYG mode.

You needn't worry about the border thickness as it is the same colour as the interior, so it doesn't show. That leaves just one last box to create.

● Select the Box tool again and drag from the point where your first vertical guide crosses your top horizontal guide to the point where the second vertical guide crosses the lower of your horizontal guides. This creates a smaller box within your black box.

● Select the No thickness icon from the ChangeBar so that the box has no border.

● Use the ChangeBar, as you did before, to open the Properties Palette and again select the FillColor property. Then select the colour White from the drop-down menu.

The background to your design is now complete. All you need to do now is to add the pictures and text.

● Select the Import Picture tool from the ToolBox. The Import Picture flyout then opens giving you several options. Click on the Art & Borders icon to open the Art & Borders dialog and select Violinist as the picture you want to use (this is included in the Entertainment section of the sample images as well as in ArtPack1). You will be shown a miniature of your chosen picture and simply click on OK to import the object.

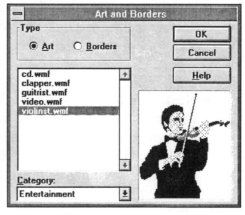

● Click with the cursor, now shaped as a paste icon, somewhere on your page or pasteboard to apply the object. Then drag the object so that the top left corner of the picture area is positioned where the top margin and the left margin meet.

Note that pausing for a moment before dragging the object allows you to see it in WYSIWYG mode as you drag it. Alternatively, if you drag without a pause the object appears simply as a bounding box - which is useful for accurate positioning as it allows you to align the boundary of the picture with the top and left margins. The snapping facility also helps with this positioning.

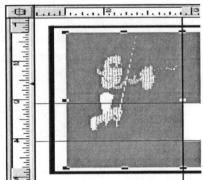

● Now drag the picture's bottom right corner handle down to the point where the bottom margin meets the first of your vertical guides.

This has the effect of altering the dimensions of the picture. Not only has the picture become larger but it has also been stretched as the height has increased proportionally more than the width. Although this effect is deliberate in this case, note that you can preserve the original aspect ratio of the picture by holding down the Shift key as you drag.

● Next, with the Ctrl key held down, drag the picture to a free area on your page or pasteboard. By dragging with the Ctrl key, you have created and moved a copy of the picture, whilst leaving the original in place. Note that you can also do this by selecting an object and then using Edit,Copy followed by Paste.

● Make sure that your copied object is selected, and then select the Flip Horizontally icon on the object's ChangeBar.

This creates a horizontal reflection of the original, so that the picture faces the other way.

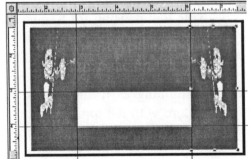

● Now drag the picture to fit it in the area on the right of your design between the right margin and the second of the vertical guides.

The picture should be exactly the right size for the area and the snapping should make it easy to fit. Your design should now look symmetrical with the pictures in corresponding positions on opposite sides of the page.

● Now select the Text tool from the ToolBox and double-click somewhere central near the top of your page.

This opens Serif's WritePlus which is PagePlus's own word processor. Note that if you single click on the page with the Text tool instead, you can type the text in WYSIWYG mode.

● Within WritePlus type in:
   ## In Association with

and click on the Tick icon to apply the text object to the page.

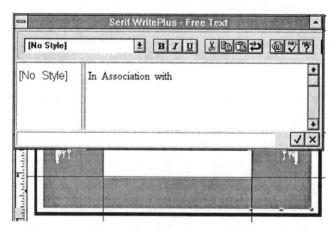

Note that the Cross icon allows you to cancel any text object, returning you to your page.

At this point it is a good idea to re-position the horizontal ruler so that it is aligned with the top of the page. This will make it easier to follow the next few steps.

- Select the Pointer tool from the ToolBox and drag on the text object to position it 1.75 inches from the top of the page.

- Drag the centre left handle of the text object across to the first vertical guide and drag the centre right handle across to the right vertical guide.

This sets the object's bounding box, and therefore its overall size, to the width of the central area of your design. The reason for doing this is that when you align text it is positioned within its bounding box. So to centre text on the page its bounding box has itself to be centred.

- Use the ChangeBar's option list or the data entry box to increase the size of the text to 14.0p. You shouldn't need to select the Size property from the Properties Palette first as, being the default property for text, it should already be selected.

- Open the Properties Palette, select the Align property and choose Align center from the drop-down menu. Your text object should now be precisely aligned in the centre of your page.

- Select the Text tool again and double-click just below the text object you just created. Using WritePlus, type in:
  The Wessex Philharmonic Orchestra

and then click on the tick icon to apply the object.

● Select the Pointer and drag the text to a position approximately 2.5 inches from the top of the page. As before, drag the left and right handles to the left and right guides, respectively.

As it was the last property that you used, Align should be the current ChangeBar property, so it makes sense to alter that property first rather than having to select it again afterwards.

● So, with the object still selected, use the ChangeBar to centre align your text, as before.

● Next, from the ChangeBar select the Bold and Italics icons.

● Open the Properties Palette and select the Color property to change the colour to white.

● The select the Size property and increase the size to 18.0p.

Notice that with this size there is not enough room for the text to fit on one line within the confines of the text object's bounding box, so the text wraps onto a new line, but still remains centre aligned. You may find that, instead of the whole word 'Orchestra' going onto the second line it is, split up and hyphenated. In this case use the command Text,Spacing and uncheck Auto hyphenation to turn this feature off. This is discussed in Chapter 5.

● Select the Text tool from the ToolBox, double-click just below the other text objects and, using WritePlus, type in:
we proudly present

and select the Tick icon to apply the object and return to your page.

● Select the Pointer tool and position the text approximately 1/8 inch above the white box (2.875 inches from the top of the page). Then drag the new text object's left and right handles across to the left and right guides, respectively, as you did before. Increase the text size to 14.0p, set its colour to white and centre align it.

● Select the Text tool again and double-click on the white box that you created earlier in the centre of your page. In WritePlus, type in:
    VIVALDI
    The Four Seasons

● When you've finished typing the text, drag the cursor right across all the text to highlight it. Then select the Bold and Italics icons.

Previously, you've changed these properties from the ChangeBar but this illustrates how you can apply certain properties from within WritePlus. These properties will be applied to the text when you return to your page and the

ChangeBar will indicate that these properties are selected. These properties can still be changed using the ChangeBar.

● Select the Tick icon to return to your page.

● Select the Pointer tool to position the text centrally in the white box. Drag the left and right handles to the left and right vertical guides respectively, and use the ChangeBar to increase the text size to 24.0p.

● Open the Properties Palette, select the Align property again and centre align the text.

● Select the Pointer tool and drag the text object to position it vertically in the middle of the white box.

● Select the Text tool from the ToolBox. Double-click near the bottom of your page and, using WritePlus, type in:
Great Griffin Entertainment Ltd

● As usual apply the object to your page using the Tick icon.

● Select the Pointer tool and drag this item to position it approximately 4.5 inches from the top of the page and drag the left and right handles to the left and right margins, respectively. (Make sure you drag to the margins and not the guides.)

● Use the ChangeBar to centre align your text and the Properties Palette to set the text size to 14.0p and to colour it white.

● Select the Letterspace property from the Properties Palette.

● Use the ChangeBar's slider to increase the letter spacing to 40%. Notice how using the slider allows you to see the incremental effect on the object as the spacing is increased. This property allows you to move the letters closer together or further apart as in this case. This activity is often referred to as *kerning* and is discussed in Chapter 5.

● Select the Width property from the Properties Palette.

● Use the ChangeBar's slider again to increase the letter width to 110%. Increasing the letter width has the effect of stretching the text, so it shouldn't be overused here.

● Finally, select the Bold and Underline icons from the ChangeBar.

The publication is now virtually complete, but just when you were considering attending, you find out that it's all sold out!

- Select the Text tool from the ToolBox and double-click on a free area of your page or pasteboard to open WritePlus. Then type in:
  ## SOLD OUT

- As usual, click on the Tick icon to apply the text to your page. Then set the text to Bold and to a size of 36.0p.

- Select the Font property from the Properties Palette and choose Arial by scrolling up the list of options.

- Select Color from the Properties Palette and choose the option red.

- Now select the Pointer tool and drag the text to position it approximately in the centre of your page.

- Select the Rotate tool from the ToolBox.

- Drag on the bottom left handle of the SOLD OUT text object in an anti-clockwise circular motion. As you drag, the text will rotate in proportion to the length of your drag movement. Watch the HintLine as you rotate the object and notice how it tells you the position and the rotation angle of the selected object. If you double-click with the Rotate tool on a rotated object it returns it to the horizontal (0°).

- Set the rotation angle of the object to approximately 30°.

- Click on the Snapping icon on the Status Bar at the bottom of the page to deselect snapping.

By disabling snapping you can move objects without them being pulled towards guides or margins and they do not follow the snap grid. This means you are able to move them more smoothly and precisely for positioning them by eye.

● Drag on the text to reposition it centrally on your page. Note that the Rotate tool acts in the same manner as the Pointer tool when you drag on the object itself for positioning purposes.

So your design is now complete and all that is left to do is to save your work (as TOUR_TWO.PPP) and print it out if you wish to do so. How to do this was described at the end of Tour One.

» Coming soon...

The key ideas introduced in this tour are the use of objects and the control of object properties. Many of the other ideas introduced in a practical way are developed in later chapters. For example, we have seen how useful guidelines and snapping to the page grid are. The whole subject of page layout is discussed in detail in the next chapter.

In this example a range of special effects was created by changing the properties of text objects. Text and typography are discussed in much more detail in Chapters 5 and 6. Printing out the final product out and planning how to use colour and tone so that it can be reproduced are topics we will return to in Chapters 8 and 9.

Key points

» In Publisher mode the ToolBox and the ChangeBar have an extended range of facilities and you can now access the Properties Palette to select which property the ChangeBar controls.

» The ChangeBar allows you to change a property in a number of different ways. The slider bar can be used for experimental effects and typing in the value can be used to set the property exactly.

» The Properties Palette contains a large number of buttons each of which selects a particular property that the ChangeBar controls.

» Line and fill properties are two groups which apply to a range of objects.

» Text has its own particular range of properties. You can use the ChangeBar and the Properties Palette to change the size of text, align it, change its font and colour, control letter spacing, and select effects such as bold and italics.

» You can position objects accurately using guidelines and snapping to the page grid. The movable rulers are another useful facility.

Chapter 4

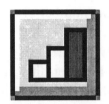

Professional Page Design

By following the tours in the previous chapters you will now be confident about PagePlus 3's fundamental methods and techniques. You are now ready to work with more complex layouts that require you to make design decisions before you even make a start. You are also ready to make the change to Professional level. This chapter presents a further hands-on tour which builds on the experience of using PagePlus 3 developed in the previous ones. To follow this chapter, therefore, now select the highest level, Professional.

» Page size, margins and columns

Before you can begin creating and manipulating objects in a DTP environment you must have the first basic elements of design. You can experiment on screen or on paper. Either way, you must decide on the page size, the margin sizes and the number of columns on which your design will be based.

It is fairly easy to change all these factors at a later date. However, this may entail a lot of realignment of objects as the relative position of margins and columns will have moved and so it is worth paying attention to these details at the outset.

The page size, the margin sizes and the number of columns are consistent throughout most well designed publications. Consistency is important for neatness and makes a document easier to follow.

The page size you use depends largely on the type of design you are creating. PagePlus allows you to choose from a variety of predefined sizes, like A4, A5, Letter, etc., or you can create your own custom size by specifying its dimensions. You can also define the *orientation*. The default, in which the long side is the vertical, is referred to as *portrait*, but you can, if you wish, turn the page on its side so that the long side is horizontal, which is referred to as *landscape.*

The choice of page size is complicated because there are in fact always two page sizes involved in any design. There is the logical page size of the design and the physical page size available to print it - and these two are not always identical. Sometimes you will want to work with a page size that is larger than the design so that you can produce multiple copies of it on a single physical sheet of paper. Other times you will want to work with a page size that is exactly the same size as the space available to the design. Questions of page size are closely related to production details and in particular *imposition*, i.e. how the logical pages are to be arranged on physical sheets of paper. This is discussed in Chapter 6.

You can define the exact size of each margin: left, right, top and bottom. These sizes again depend on your objective and the style of your design. Any objects positioned off your page, as defined by your margins, will still print. The margins are only guidelines to make object positioning easier or even in some cases automatic. Although objects in the margins defined within PagePlus will print, you need to realise that there are physical margins around the edges of the paper which cannot be printed on. The size of the printable area of a sheet of paper depends on the printer or the printing process. It is usually best to assume that you cannot print closer than 1cm to the edge of the physical page.

The number of columns you decide to use is an important factor in the design. All the text flows through these columns and they, along with any guides that you set, form the grid which is the basis for your design. If it is more appropriate for your design, you need not have any columns as such, and instead just let the text flow across the entire page from margin to margin. Once you have defined the columns you need not use every one for text; some columns can act as guides for graphics, adverts or even as an indented margin. Equally, it is often pleasing to the eye to have the boundaries of these columns occasionally broken by illustrations, tables, adverts etc..

» Controlling the page

The simplest way of setting the details of the page you want to work with is to double click on an empty area of the page. This causes the Page Setup dialog box to appear. Alternatively you can use the command Page,Page Setup which also displays this dialog box.

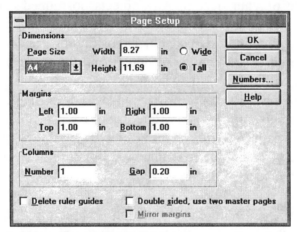

Using the Page Setup dialog box you can select the page size from a range of standard paper dimensions. If you want to create a layout to a non-standard size, which is more common a requirement than you might think - see Chapter 9 - then you can select Custom paper size and type its dimensions into the Width and Height boxes. You can also select the paper orientation - Wide or Tall - which corresponds to the more traditional terminology of "landscape" or "portrait".

Notice that if you only want to change the paper size and its orientation then a quicker method is to use the Page menu command and select the Size and Orientation options.

The four page margin specifications are easy enough to set, as are the columns and gap width. The only complication is how these should differ on right and left pages - see Master pages later in this chapter. You can change the units that page sizes, margins and gap width are measured in using the command Preferences, General.

» Guides, rulers and grids

Once your basic page has been defined and set up, you may need to add *guides* to help with the design and the positioning of objects. The columns that you have selected act as vertical grid lines, though more may be needed, and guides should be used to form any horizontal grid lines that are necessary.

Guides appear as red lines running across your page. You can position them exactly where you want, move them and remove them whenever you want. They act merely as guides, like construction lines in drawing programs, and they do not print. Each page in a multi-page document can have its own set of guidelines - but see the section on Master Pages.

You can use guides to align objects by eye but this is difficult. What really makes guides useful is the ability to turn on a 'snap to guides' mode of operation. When *snapping* is turned on the guides appear to attract objects that you move near them. As soon as an object is moved near enough to a guide it seems as if it jumps or snaps into the exact position of the guide. You can turn snapping on or off as you require. Objects do not automatically move to the nearest guide when you turn snap on - you have to re-position each one yourself.

You can select whether or not the guides are displayed using the command Page,Display,Guides. When the guides are not displayed objects do not snap to them, even if snap is turned on. If you want to delete all of the guides you have set you can do so by checking the Delete ruler guides box in the Page Setup dialog. But be warned, unchecking this box does not restore them.

PagePlus also provides *rulers* to help with the positioning and sizing of objects and to define guides. By default the rulers are positioned at the top and the side of your design with the zero point of the calibration corresponding to the top left of your page. You can, however, move the rulers by dragging on the point where they intersect. This is called the *ruler origin* and appears as a raised box with a miniature page icon on it.

To move either the vertical or the horizontal ruler click on the ruler origin and then drag across or up/down respectively. The zero point will move so that it remains at the point the rulers intersect. If you want the zero point to stay in its default position of the top left of the page hold down the Shift key while you drag. Double clicking on the ruler origin when you have an object selected moves the rulers to surround it and sets the zero point to its top left-hand corner. Double clicking on the ruler origin when you do not have an object selected restores the rulers to their default positions.

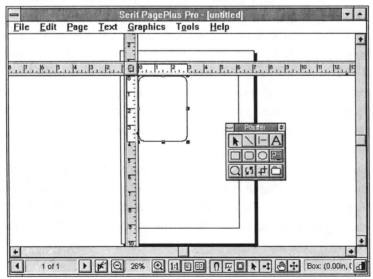

A new feature in PagePlus 3 is the use of shading on the rulers to show the height and width of an object as you move or resize it. This makes it much easier to size an object accurately.

You can lock the rulers to guard against them being moved unintentionally once you have placed them in a particular position by using the Page,Layout Tools command and checking the Lock rulers box.

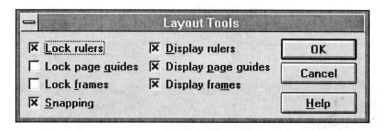

The rulers also define a positioning grid. When snap is on you can only move an object in steps given by the increments shown on the rule. In other words the rulers define a snap grid across the whole page. If you choose not to display the rulers then the snap grid isn't used, as objects will only snap to visible guides or rulers. Notice also that when you move guides they too snap to the current grid if snap is on.

You can select the scale used for the rulers using the Options,Preferences,General command. You can select a different scale for horizontal and vertical measurement if you want to. It is very important that you select the ruler scales that you are going to use for the entire layout. Changing scales can mean that every object already placed on the page is misaligned with respect to the new rulers and grid. Notice also that there are two inch scales that you can select. The Inch scale is divided into 1/2 inch, 1/4 inch, 1/8 inch and so

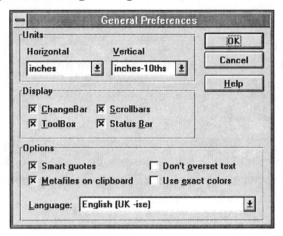

on. The "inch-10ths" scale is divided into tenths and swapping between the two can cause layout problems!

» Multi-page documents

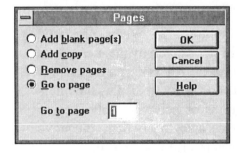

You can add pages to a document by double clicking on the page number box at the far left of the HintLine. This displays the Pages dialog box which can be used to move to an existing page, add blank pages, add copies of the current page or remove pages. Notice that you can add or remove multiple pages in one operation.

Navigating through a multi-page document is mostly a matter of using the arrows next to the page number box but you can jump to any page using the Pages dialog box. If you double click on either arrow you are taken straight to the start or end of the document. If you try to move beyond either point you will be offered a chance to insert a new page via the Pages dialog box.

◀   1 of 2   ▶

» Master Pages

Each page in a multi-page document can have its own page setup which can be completely different from any other page in the document. This is a powerful feature that allows you to mix page sizes and margins within a single document. However, more often the problem is trying to keep the page setup identical within a multi-page document. The Master Page, a new feature in PagePlus 3, makes this very easy.

Every document has at least one master page. The master page acts as a sort of page template for every page in the document. Any object or guideline placed on a master page appears on all of the pages that it controls. This means that if you want to create a document consisting of pages that use the same basic layout then it is sensible to create a master page that contains all of the guides and objects that you want to appear on each page. So for example, if you want a heading to appear on each page then create the heading on the master page.

Any changes that you make to the layout of a master page will affect any page that it controls. So if you change the text of a header on the master page, the change will be made to all of the pages in the document controlled by the master page. Any object that appears on a page that belongs to the master page cannot be selected. In other words, the relationship is one way - the master page affects the content of every page it controls but they do not affect the master page. Notice, however, that this is not true of changes made to individual page setup - page size, margins etc. - see later.

To work with a master page all you have to do is click once on the page number box at the bottom left-hand side of the HintLine or use the command Page,Goto Master Page.

(Notice that this option is only available at Professional level and if you access the Page menu from either of the lower levels it will not appear at all.) You can then work with the master page as it it was a normal page. When you have finished click on the page number box again or use the command Page,Leave Master Page and you will be returned to a normal page.

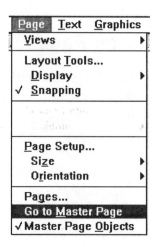

Multi-page layouts can either be single-sided or double-sided. A double-sided layout has left and right pages and these generally need different margin arrangements to take account of the position of the fold in the paper. That is the "outside" edge on a right-hand page is on the right but it is on the left for a left-hand page. To make double-sided layouts easy you can opt to use two master pages - a right page and a left page. Simply select Double sided, use two master pages in the Page Setup dialog box. After this when you go to the master pages you can select the left or right master page using the arrows next to the page

number box. If you want the left and right margins that you set to be automatically reversed on right and left pages then also check the Mirror margins box.

Once you have set up a single master page or a right and left master page you can add pages to your layout confident that each one will be modelled from the appropriate master. However, there is one complication. Each page keeps its own page size and margin settings. If you want to change a page's size to B5, say, in the middle of a set of A4 pages then you can. You can also set any margins you want on any page. If you subsequently change the master page's margins this only affects the page you selected immediately before going to the master page.

In other words, the master page does not actually set the page size or margins for all of the pages in the document. So how is the page setup of a new page determined? What happens is that when you insert a new page in a single-sided layout the page size and margins are copied from the previous page. For example, the page setup for a new page 5 is copied from page 4. In a double-sided layout the same principle works but now the page size and margins are copied from the previous page of the same handedness. For example, a new page 5 takes its page setup from the existing page 3.

What this means is that if you change the page size or margin of an individual page then this change will affect every page of the same handedness you insert after that page. If this sounds complicated then stick to the rule that you will not alter the page setup of any page once it is inserted into the document. As long as you do not change the page sizes or margins on a page by page basis it looks as if the master pages do determine the page setup. The reason is that when you set the right master page it determines the page setup of page 1. The left master page determines the page setup of page 2. When you insert new pages the page setup of these initial pages propagates through the document. See Chapter 6 for an example of how this works in practice.

The final question is what if you don't want the objects on the master page to appear on a particular page? The answer is that you use the command Page,Master Page Objects. When a tick is shown beside this menu item the master page objects show. When the

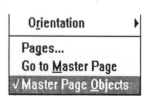

tick is absent they don't. You can go through a multi-page document turning off or on the display of master page objects on a page by page basis.

» Page numbers

One of the most common requirement of page design is to include a page number somewhere on each page. Of course there is nothing stopping you from placing text that announces the page number but if you insert or remove a page you will have no choice but to manually edit all of the page numbers to take account of the change. A much simpler and less error prone solution is to use the Text,Insert Page Number command. This inserts a special symbol, #, into any text that is guaranteed to display as the page number of the page that the text finds itself on, even if you insert or remove pages. The only confusing aspect of the page number symbol is that it looks different on the page to the way it looks when you are editing it - on the page or using WritePlus.

The page number symbol works well together with the master page facility. To number a complete document it is simpler to place a page number symbol on the master pages. As the master page objects are placed onto each page the page number symbol is replaced by the actual page number - so numbering the entire document correctly. Although page number symbols and master pages seem to be made for each other it is important not to miss the fact that you can place a page number symbol manually on any page.

You can control the way pages are numbered using the Numbers button in the Page Setup dialog box. This displays the Page Numbering dialog box which you can use to set the style of numbering and the number of the first page. Notice that you can only select one numbering style and one first

```
┌─────────────────────────────────────────────────────────┐
│ ▬             Page Numbering                             │
├─────────────────────────────────────────────────────────┤
│ ┌─Style──────────────────────────────┐   ┌─────────┐     │
│ │                                    │   │   OK    │     │
│ │ ◉ Arabic numerals 1, 2, 3, ...     │   └─────────┘     │
│ │ ○ Upper Roman   I, II, III, ...    │   ┌─────────┐     │
│ │ ○ Lower Roman   i, ii, iii, ...    │   │ Cancel  │     │
│ │ ○ Upper alphabetic  A, B, C, ... AA, BB, CC, ... │ ┌───────┐ │
│ │ ○ Lower alphabetic  a, b, c, ... aa, bb, cc, ... │ │ Help  │ │
│ └────────────────────────────────────┘   └─────────┘     │
│                                                          │
│  First Page Number      │1                    │          │
└─────────────────────────────────────────────────────────┘
```

page number for each document. So if you need different numbering systems you have to split the layout up into separate PagePlus documents.

» Tour Three: a complex design

Tour Three incorporates some features available only at Professional level. It is a more complex design than the previous tours and the steps are explained in a more descriptive manner and less formal instruction is given as you will already be aware of how to select and use the features we have already covered in the previous tours. See the end of this chapter for a sneak preview!

» Page setup with Master Pages

From the previous tours you will be aware of the concept of setting up your page. However, as this is a multi-page publication it is worth using the master page feature which allows you to set a few objects, such as page numbers, headers and footers, which repeat on all your other pages.

● Click once on the page number box on the StatusBar or use the command Page,Go to Master Page to select the master page feature. (Note that you don't double click on the page number box because that would display the Pages dialog box.) You

```
┌─────────────┐
│   1 of 1    │
└─────────────┘
```

can tell that you are viewing a master page because the pasteboard area is grey rather than white.

● Define the master page setup by double-clicking on a blank area of page to open the Page Setup dialog. The setup you define applies to all the pages within the document unless you specifically redefine a page.

● Use the Page Setup dialog to set the Double-sided, use two master pages checkbox on, allowing you to define a left and right master page. Set the margins to 0.5 inches for all the margins except the left margin, which you should leave at the default setting of 1 inch. These margins are applied to your right master page.

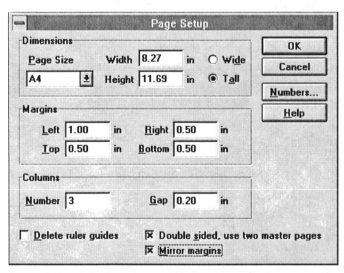

As the publication is a bound document, facing pages need to be defined slightly differently from each other to account for the differences between left and right pages, in particular, the effect of the centre binding. Effectively, the facing pages should have margins that are the opposite of each other. You can easily do this by setting the Mirror margins checkbox on. This means that you need not redefine the margins for the facing page (the left page) as it will automatically be the opposite of the right page. The result of these settings is that there is a larger gap down the centre bind of the publication than on the outside edge of the pages.

● Set the number of columns to three using the data-entry box in the Page Setup dialog, and leave the gutter (the gap between the columns) at the default value of 0.2 inches. Once you have made all your selections, click on OK to apply them to your publication.

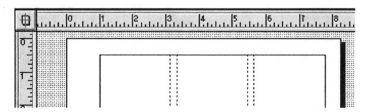

At this stage it is worth defining any headers or footers to be used in the document, so that they do not have to be repeated on all the pages manually.

● With the right master page still selected use the 45° Line from the ToolBox (which is used for horizontal vertical and diagonal lines) to drag a line from the left margin across to the right margin, 10.5 inches down your page.

Doing this precisely should be easy with the snapping feature on, resulting in the start and end of the line being "pulled" towards the margins. Use the ChangeBar to set the thickness of the line to 1.0p, but leave the other properties at the default.

● Select the Text tool from the ToolBox and double-click near the bottom of the page. This opens WritePlus, where you can then type in:
    Keely Travel Ltd Summer Breaks Brochure

You need to use a small trick to achieve the desired effect which is to align the text to both the left and the right. When you type in the text object above, instead of using the spacebar to create the spaces, use the en-space, (type Ctrl-Alt-n) except for the space between 'Ltd' and 'Summer', where you should use a normal space using the spacebar.

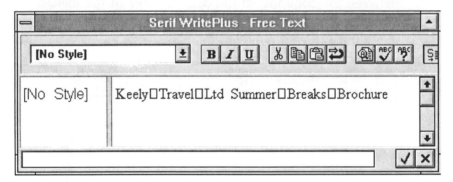

The en-space is a special character of a space which has a fixed width equal to the width of an 'n' character. You can create them by holding down the Control and Alt keys whilst performing a single press of the 'n' key. In WritePlus these characters are represented by small boxes but in WYSIWYG mode on your page they give the desired effect.

● When you have finished typing in your text, complete with en-spaces, click on the Tick icon to apply the object to your page where you will see that the en-space special character appears as a genuine space.

● To complete the effect, you must drag the left and right handles of the text object across to the left and right margins respectively (as illustrated in Tours One and Two), using the Pointer tool. Then use the ChangeBar's Properties Palette icon to open the Properties Palette. Select the Align icon and then use the ChangeBar to set the alignment to Force justify.

The alignment option Force justify makes a text object take up the full width of its object area, which in this case is the width of the page. The text is stretched by increasing any spaces. In this object, the only genuine space lies between 'Ltd' and 'Summer', because of the use of en-spaces, causing the two sets of text to left and right align about this point.

● Finish this text object by using the ChangeBar to set the text to italics and set the font to Arial with size 14.0p.

● The footer also needs the page number added, so select the Text tool again and click just once in the bottom right corner of your page - one click allows you to type in WYSIWYG mode which makes adding the page number easier. Type in:

    page

and without deselecting the text object, select Text,Insert Page Number. This adds a page number marker where your text cursor is currently positioned (after 'page'). The marker initially appears as a special character on any master pages, but is replaced by the correct number on the actual publication pages. PagePlus also supplies a space between the word 'page' and the page number.

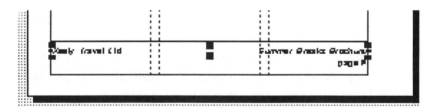

● Once you have created this object, use the ChangeBar and Properties Palette to set the text to italics and set the font to Arial of size 14.0p. Also right align the text and then use the Pointer tool to position it right in the bottom right corner of the page.

Make any necessary positional adjustments to your footer objects using the Pointer tool. If you want to move the objects more smoothly, without the positional aid of snapping, you can deselect it by depressing the snapping button on the StatusBar at the bottom of the screen.

● When you are satisfied with the footer, you need to transfer it to the right master page as well. This is easily done by copying it across. Do this by dragging the Pointer tool around (lassoing) all the footer objects, or selecting Edit,Select All to select all the objects. Then use Edit,Copy (Ctrl-C) to copy the objects onto the Windows clipboard.

● Move to the right master page by selecting the page right arrow key on the Status Bar. When you are on the right master page you will notice that the margins are the reverse of the left master page as you selected. Select Edit,Paste (Ctrl-V) to apply the copied objects onto the page. These objects are all automatically selected, so using the Pointer tool, drag them all in one go to the equivalent position on the right master page (10.5 inches down). To position the objects precisely make sure that snapping is on, using the icon in the StatusBar.

Your master pages are now complete. The setup you have applied to your left master page, and all the objects on it, will appear on the left pages in your document and the setup you have applied to your right master pages and all the objects on it will appear on the right pages in your document.

● Click on the Page number box on the Status Bar or select Page,Leave Master Page to return to your first document page, where you will notice the effect of the right master page on page one of your document.

This page is effectively the front cover of your publication, and, being the first page, is a right-sided page. This tour is only concerned with the next two pages, the centrefold spread. We will return to the design of the front cover in Chapter 10.

- Select the page right arrow button on the Status Bar to move to the second page. Notice that the page number you inserted in the footer now shows as a '2'.

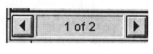

We are now going to work on pages 2 and 3 of the publication.

» Creating a shadow text box

The shadow text box we are going to create is made up of a clear text frame with text in it. A text frame is a container that is used to hold large quantities of text. If you are working with a single line of text or a small block then there is no need to use a text frame - but for longer blocks or groups of paragraphs it is essential. Text frames and free text, that is text not in frames, are discussed in detail in Chapter 6.

In the design we are going to implement here there are going to be two coloured rectangles (or tint panels) which will show through the clear frame to create the background for the main box and the header banner. Beneath the rectangles there will be another coloured box, the same size as the text frame, which will be offset to create the shadow.

As the illustrations in this chapter indicate how the document should look as we proceed, it will help if you position your rulers to correspond to those shown and use inches as the units.

● First, take the rulers back to their default position by double clicking on the ruler origin without having any object selected. The vertical ruler now measures from the top of the page - which is what we require for this particular step. However, the zero point on the horizontal ruler in this and later screen dumps is lined up on the left margin. To do this, position the cursor over the ruler origin and drag the vertical ruler right until it reaches the purple line that indicates the left margin. Then, holding down the Shift key, drag the ruler to the left until it is in a convenient position outside the page area. Although the ruler moves, the zero point remains fixed at the left margin.

● Now select the Frame tool from the ToolBox and drag, with snapping on, from a position 2 inches from the top of the page and 0.25 inches in from the left margin, to a position 0.25 inches above the footer line and the right boundary of the first column.

● Notice that with the new frame selected the shading on the ruler shows its exact position.

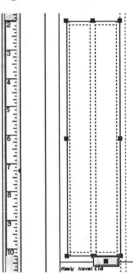

● Remember that you can always select the frame and drag on its handles or on the object itself to resize or reposition it, respectively. When you've created the frame, the Frame Assistant dialog opens. Just cancel the dialog this time.

● The frame you have created will automatically have two columns. Set the number of columns to one by using the one column button at the left of the Frame's ChangeBar.

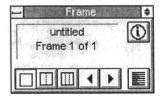

- By default the frame is clear with no colour which is just what we want.

- Making sure that snapping is still on, select the Box tool. Drag to define a box with exactly the same size and position as your text frame. Start in one corner of your frame and drag to the opposite diagonal corner. Use the ChangeBar to set the box colour to cyan and leave the tint at the default 50%. Set the box border thickness to 1.0p and select the LineColor property from the Properties Palette before using the ChangeBar to set the line colour to blue.

- Select the Box tool again and drag to create another box on top of the one just defined to provide the background for its heading. Drag from the top left corner of the previous box across to its right edge and drag down to make the depth of your new box 1 inch. Make its colour blue and again leave the tint at 50%. Use the ChangeBar and Properties Palette to give it a 1.0p border thickness coloured blue.

The two rectangles you have just created obscure the text frame which you now need to bring back to the front.

- With the Pointer tool click on the text frame to select it. As three objects overlap in this area you may need to click repeatedly as each object becomes selected in turn. Watch the ChangeBar and the HintLine on the StatusBar to see what object is `Frame: (0.75in, 2.00in) 1.87in x 8` currently selected.

- When your text frame is selected use the Wrap icon on the ChangeBar to open the Wrap flyout from which you can select the Bring to front icon. This brings your text frame to the top but does not obscure your coloured rectangles as the frame is clear (transparent).

● Before proceeding, reposition the rulers so that the zero point on the vertical ruler corresponds to the top margin.

● You now need to add the shadow. Use the Box tool again and beginning at the left margin 2.25 inches down the page drag to the bottom of the page 0.25 inches to the left of the text frame's right edge. This creates a box that is the same size as the first but is offset by 0.25 inches down and to the left of the text frame. You may need to make adjustments with the Pointer tool to create the shadow effect.

● Once the box is properly positioned and sized, use the ChangeBar to set the colour to blue and select the Shade or Tint icon from the Properties Palette before using the ChangeBar to set the tint to 100%. Give the box no border thickness. Complete this box by selecting the Wrap icon from the ChangeBar and then selecting the Send to Back icon.

● To complete the shadow box, you now need to add the text. Select the Text tool from the ToolBox and double-click within the frame. This opens WritePlus where you can type in:
What Your Tour Includes

Return overnight flights
Scheduled flights
Departures from Heathrow or Gatwick
Top 5* hotels
All rooms - private bathroom, TV and telephone
Reserved coach tour places
Meals provided on all scheduled tours
Additional nights at cheap prices
Business class upgrade at cheap prices

When you click on the tick icon in WritePlus to apply this text object to the page it automatically pours into the frame.

● With the text blocks (each paragraph) still selected, use the ChangeBar to set the text to size 14.0p and centre align it. If you need to reselect the paragraphs, just select each one in turn with the Shift key held down.

● Now select Text,Spacing to open the Spacing dialog. Use the auto-hyphenation checkbox to set hyphenation off and set the paragraph spacing to 120%. This means that the text will not be hyphenated but will wrap as whole words and there will be a space equivalent to a blank line between paragraphs.

● With the Text tool drag across the shadow box heading 'What Your Tour Includes'. This highlights that area of text which means that any properties you now apply will affect that text and not the rest of the text object. Then use the ChangeBar to increase the text size to 20.0p, set the font to Arial and set bold on.

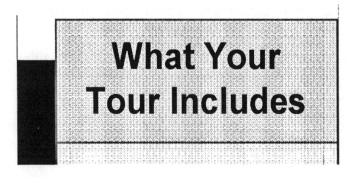

» The page heading

● Select the Text tool from the ToolBox and double-click near the top of your page. In WritePlus, type in:
   OURING AMERICA'S WEST COAST

Note that the 'T' from 'TOURING' has been omitted. It is easier to create this as a separate object since it is radically different in style and position to the rest of the text.

● When you've created the text object and returned to your page, use the ChangeBar to make the text bold, apply Arial as the font, make it a size 24.0p and colour it red. Make sure the size of the text's bounding box is big enough for the text to fit on one line, increasing the size by dragging on the right or left handles if you need to. Don't worry too much about the precise position for now. In fact, it's probably best if you move the text out of the way for the moment.

● Now with the Text tool, click once on the page to type in WYSIWYG mode:
   T

● Set this text object to bold and choose an appropriate font for it. (The one used here is ZurichCalligraphy but any fancy font that you have installed will do.) Increase its size to 120.0p and set its colour to red. With snapping off move this 'T' using the Pointer to the top left corner of the page. You may find that the text object's bounding box overlaps the margins but this doesn't really matter.

● With snapping still off, move the rest of the heading text with the Pointer to a position next to the 'T' so that it is beneath the overhang of the T-bar.

● You also need to enlarge the letters that start each word of the heading. Do this by selecting the Text tool and drag across the 'A' at the start of 'AMERICA'. This letter will become highlighted and any properties you now apply will affect only that letter and not the rest of the text object. Using the ChangeBar increase the size to 30.0p. Do the same with the 'W' in 'WEST' and the 'C' in 'COAST'.

● Now select the 45° Line tool from the ToolBox and complete the heading by dragging a line beneath the heading text (except the 'T'). You may need to use the Pointer to adjust it to get it right but the line should be the same width as the text. Using the ChangeBar set the thickness to 4.0p and the colour to red.

» Graphics for the left page

There are five items of clipart that you need to import for this design - two of which are on this page - and they all come from the Travel category of the Serif ArtPack1. All but one of the images are included in the standard samples and it is easy to find a substitute for the one that is not.

You should be familiar with how to import graphics from the previous tours. The general method is to select the Import Picture tool from the ToolBox and then select the Art & Borders icon from the flyout - clicking once for pictures that are available as clipart in one of the PagePlus directories or twice if you need to get them from elsewhere.

● Import the picture bridge.wmf and then paste it onto a free area of your page. To help position the picture, create a guide by clicking on the vertical ruler at the side of your page at the 3.5-inch mark and set snapping on. Drag the picture so that the bottom right-hand corner is at the junction of the guide and the right margin. Drag the top left-hand corner handle of the picture, with the Shift key held down, across to the left edge of the second column. The picture should thus span the width of the final two columns on your page. The Shift key preserves the height to width ratio (the aspect ratio) of the picture.

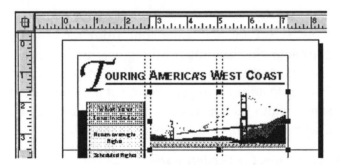

● Import the second picture, flag.wmf, and paste it on your page. Drag the graphic with snapping on to position it so that its top left-hand corner is at the same point as the bottom left-hand corner of the first picture (that is, where the guide meets the margin of the second column). When you've positioned it correctly, drag the bottom right-hand corner of the picture down to the footer line and across to the right margin. Don't use the Shift key when you drag the picture as the original dimensions don't correspond very well to the area you want it to occupy. Although this distorts the picture this doesn't matter as it is only going to be used as a background and therefore won't be very prominent.

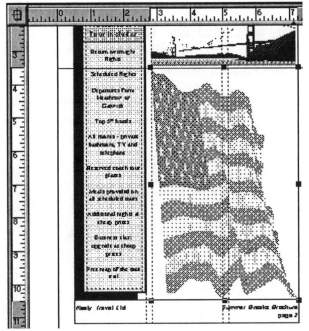

- When you've positioned the flag picture correctly, and with it still selected, select the PictureTint tool (the right-hand icon) from the Properties Palette and use the ChangeBar  to tint it to just 10% - so that when you position text over the top it remains readable on top of the faint backdrop.

» Graphics for the right page

- Now move onto the right page of the centrefold by clicking on the page forward button on the Status Bar. As you do not already have such a page you will be prompted to create one by the Add Pages dialog. Click on OK to add a new

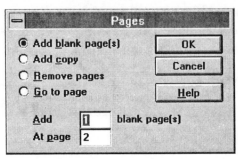

page after your current page. This new page will, of course, be created complete with its margins and footer as defined by your right master page.

- Select the Import Picture tool from the ToolBox and then the Arts & Borders icon and specify the map picture (map.wmf) to import. (You can use globe.wmf as an alternative). Paste the picture onto your page. Like the flag, this picture is to act merely as a background to your text story. So, with snapping on, position the object so that the top left-hand corner of the picture's bounding box is at the position where the top margin meets the second column's margin.

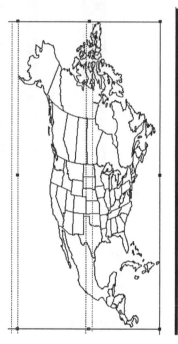

- Then drag the bottom right handle of the object down to the footer line and across to the right margin, stretching the picture to fill the whole of the last two columns on your page. Use the ChangeBar and Properties Palette to set the picture to a tint of 20%.

- In the same way, now import the picture of the Statue of Liberty (liberty.wmf). Paste the picture anywhere on your page. With the picture still selected, use the ChangeBar to flip the picture horizontally so that it faces the other way. Drag on one of the picture's corner handles, with the Shift key held down, to resize it and preserve its aspect ratio, until it is about 2 inches in height.

- Next select the Wrap icon from the ChangeBar and then select the Wrap outside icon from the flyout.

● You will notice that the picture then becomes surrounded by a dotted line which closely follows the bounding of the picture itself rather than the picture's bounding box. This is effectively the picture's *avoid-me area*, so that any text that meets this perimeter will wrap around it and not overlap the picture itself. You can manually adjust the avoid me area by dragging on the perimeter lines themselves and by creating new joints, or *nodes*, by double-clicking on the lines.

In the case of this picture you will notice that the perimeter runs into the statue's arm area because that part of the graphic is transparent.

● You do not want text flowing into that area, so drag the perimeter out to the bottom of the picture. Then position the picture, with snapping on, right in the top left-hand corner of your page.

● Now import the last picture needed, rushmore.wmf which depicts Mount Rushmore, and paste it onto the page. Use the Pointer tool with the Shift key held down to reduce the size of the picture by dragging inwards on one of the corner handles until the picture has a height of approximately 1.75 inches.

- With the picture still selected, set its wrap to make text flow around it by selecting the Wrap icon and then Wrap outside from the flyout. In this case the avoid me area is a simple box which is what we want.

- With the snapping off, drag the picture to a position at the bottom of the page 1/8-inches above the footer line and the right of the picture 1/8-inches in from the right margin. This leaves room for a shadow box beneath the picture.

- Select the Box tool from the ToolBox and drag from a position 1/8-inches in from the left and 1/8-inches down from the top of the picture to the point where the footer line and the right margin meet. Use the ChangeBar to set the box to black with 100% tint.

- Reselect the rushmore picture and then select the Wrap icon from the ChangeBar and select the Bring to Front icon from the flyout. The picture then reappears above the shadow box.

» Including the rotated text

- The rotated text required for this design is easily created. First select the Text tool, double-click and type in WritePlus:

    Mount Rushmore

● Return to your page and use the ChangeBar to increase the size of the text to 30.0p and make the text blue and appear in outline. Resize the bounding box of your text by dragging on the handles so that the words are on separate lines - so make the bounding box just a little wider than the word 'Rushmore'.

You can if you wish rotate the text by using the Rotate tool and dragging on one of the text object's handles in a circular motion. This causes the object to be rotated about the top left handle in proportion to the rotational drag you make and allows you to rotate the text to about 20° but it is imprecise.

● A way of specifying the rotation angle precisely is to use the Status Editor dialog by selecting the object and then choosing the Position icon from the Status Bar. Then use the dialog to type in the X (horizontal) and Y (vertical) co-ordinates of the top left-hand corner of your object. You can also specify the object's size in terms of height and width. More importantly in this case you can specify the rotation angle with 0° being the horizontal. If you decide to use this method for your rotated text, you need not worry about the size and position, just specify a Rotation angle of 20° and then click on OK.

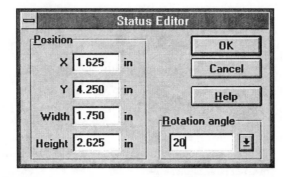

● With snapping off, use the Pointer, to position the text object in the first column below the picture of the Statue of Liberty.

● Follow the same procedure to create three more rotated text objects, 'Golden Gate Bridge', 'Grand Canyon', and 'Zion National Park' but give each alternate one the colour red instead of blue. Position each of them in turn in the first column, with about a 0.5-inch gap between each object.

» Creating the frame text and importing the story

Before importing your story text you need to create a chain of frames for the text to flow through. Start by going to the first page of your design, where your story starts.

● Select the Frame tool from the ToolBox and, with snapping on, drag from the point where the start of the second column meets the 3.5-inch horizontal guide, to the point where the footer line meets the right margin. (This is the area the flag picture occupies.)

● When the Frame Assistant dialog opens, select Add more frames.

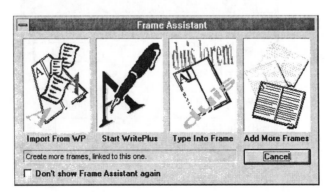

- Then select the page forwards button from the Status Bar to move to your second page design. With the Frame tool selected drag from the top left margin of the second column down to the footer line and across to the right margin.

The Frame Assistant has automatically linked these frames for you. Note, however, that you can link frames together manually by creating the frames and then selecting the frame push button, which then displays a linked chain icon, followed by the frame you want to link to. You can unlink and frames by selecting the link button and then clicking on a "frame-free" area of page. Double-clicking on the frame button allows you to import text into the text sequence.

- Now it's time to import the text story into your frame sequence. Select the frame on the first of your two pages and double-click on the frame push button to open the Import Text dialog. Use this standard Windows dialog to specify the location of a text file to import. The text used here, **travel.sam** originated in Ami Pro, is included on the companion disk to this book but you could, of course, use any available text file created using any word processor.

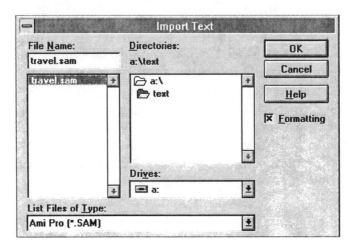

● Make sure that the Formatting box is checked, so that any properties such as indents and bold are kept by the text story.

The text then pours into your first text frame, column by column, before moving onto the next frame. The text takes on the properties of the default style which can be applied in WritePlus. Styles are groupings of property settings that can be used to format text consistently, see Chapter 6. The default style is appropriate for this design except that it is not justified.

● An easy way to make this style justified is to click on the first paragraph of the text to select it. Then use the ChangeBar and Properties Palette to set the text alignment to justify. Once you've made this change the ChangeBar itself changes to include tick and cross icons in its top right-hand corner. The tick accesses the AutoApply dialog and the cross cancels the change. Select the tick icon to open the AutoApply dialog.

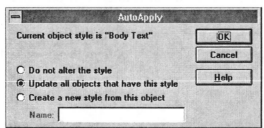

This dialog can be used to save the current text object's properties as a new style which can then be applied from the ChangeBar (with the Style property selected from the Properties Palette) to other text objects, or you can update the existing style. This is explained further in Chapter 6.

● For now, just select the Update all objects that have this style button before clicking on OK. The effect of this is that all the paragraphs in the story automatically become justified.

In this particular instance it's probably easier to change one paragraph and update all the rest of the text using the Tools,Update story option. However, if the text consists of several styles, as will often be the case, this is not practical.

● Having imported the text, it is worth doing a quick spell check. So double-click on the story with the Text tool, or use the WritePlus shortcut button on the Status Bar, and then select which of your publication stories to use.

WritePlus has most of the standard word processor tools such as cut, copy and paste, bold, italics, underline and strikethrough, a spelling checker and a thesaurus.

● Click on the spell check icon to check your story for any spelling errors. When the Check Spelling dialog opens, leave the default options and click on Start to begin the spell check. When a word that the spell checker does not recognise is actually what you require use the Ignore button to skip it but correct any mistakes it finds by accepting one of the alternative suggestions or typing directly into the Change To box.

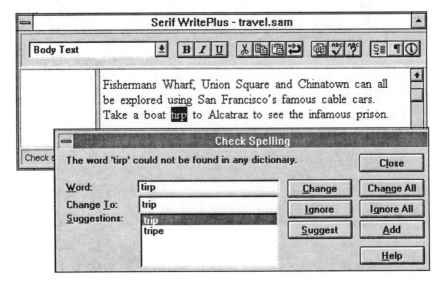

● Reading through the story also reveals another common problem - namely a sentence with two occurrences of the same word, in this case 'stroll'. PagePlus 3 offers help for this situation. Position the cursor on the word you want to replace and select the Thesaurus icon. The window on the left of the dialog allows you to identify the meaning of the word in this context and then the right window gives you suitable alternatives to that meaning. Select an appropriate alternative, such as 'promenade', to replace 'stroll'.

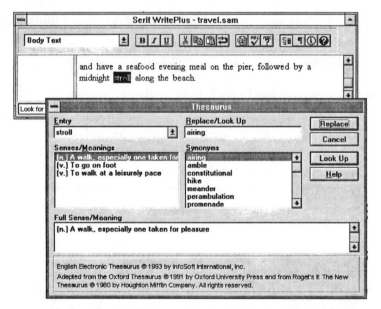

● When you are satisfied with your story you can click on the Tick icon to return to your page with the story updated. But before you do that, delete the first letter of the story by simply positioning the cursor before the letter and pressing the delete key.

This first letter needs to be removed because you are about to replace it with a more attractive first letter - a dropped capital.

» Creating the dropped capital

Dropped capitals are an easy effect to create and are commonly used because they are a way of adding visual interest to a long story. It is done by replacing the first letter of the story by a bigger, bolder, more attractive first letter that takes up more than one line and has the text that it displaces wrapped around it.

- Make sure you are on the first of the two pages of your publication and then select the Text tool and click once a free area of page or pasteboard. Type in 'T' and use the ChangeBar to set the text to bold, italic and make it Arial of size 55.0p. Use the Pointer to drag the right handles in towards the 'T' so that the text's bounding box is only slightly bigger that the object itself.

- The real trick comes from manipulating the 'T's wrap avoid-me area. Set the text to wrap by clicking on the ChangeBar's Wrap icon and selecting the Wrap on icon from the flyout. The object now has a perimeter line surrounding it, representing the text's avoid-me area. Drag the lines on the bottom and to the right of the 'T' close in to the object but do not overlap the 'T'. Then click just below the T-bar to create a new node so that the perimeter can bend at this point. Create another node just to the right of the stem of the 'T' by clicking on the perimeter line. Then drag the bottom right-hand corner node of the broken line in towards the 'T' right up into the junction. This creates an area that text can flow into.

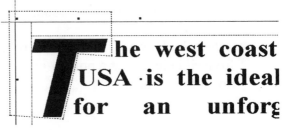

The west coast USA ·is the ideal for an unforg

Another way of doing this is to create the 'T' and then select the Tools, Convert to Picture command. Then with the 'T' acting as a picture you can set it to wrap and have an automatic avoid-me area. It still needs a bit of manipulation, however, to get it just right.

A useful tip here is to select Tools,Preferences,General and then the option Don't overset text in from the Preferences dialog. This should stop any letters that might otherwise be forced into small gaps from overlapping. This might also be useful where the Statue of Liberty graphic overlaps your story.

● Position your 'T' at the start of your story. In order to achieve the precise positioning you require magnify this area by selecting the Zoom or Magnify tool from the ToolBox then drag the cursor to lasso around the area you want to magnify. Wait a few moments for the display to update with the magnified view. Make sure snapping is off and then position your object.

● When you are satisfied with the position of the 'T' return to your normal view by selecting the Fit page in window icon.

» The quotation and the acknowledgement text

The quote used in this design is a simple free text object but to ensure that the story text does not overlap the quote an invisible box, with wrapping on, is placed in the text frame for the free text to be placed upon.

● Select the Box tool and drag across the second column, from right to left, at a point 4 inches down the page. Drag down to 5.5 inches.

● With the box still selected, set its colour to clear, so that you can still see the map background, and use the Wrap flyout on the ChangeBar to set the box to wrap outside. Also, give it no border thickness.

The text now avoids the box allowing you to work easily upon it. The two sets of lines at the top and bottom of the quote, known as 'thick and thin' are used to emphasise quotes or headings etc..

● To create these, first make sure that snapping is on but turn the rulers off with the icon in the ChangeBar. This means that snapping will now only affect guides and margins with the snap grid being disabled. Then select the 45° Line tool and drag across the column at the top of the clear box. Set the thickness to 2.0p and draw another line just beneath it and set its thickness to 1.0p. You may need to reposition the lines a few times to get them just right. Magnify the area if you need to.

● Create the bottom "thick and thin" in the same way but make sure that the thin line is the upper of the two.

● Create the text by selecting the Text tool and double-clicking on a free area of pasteboard. Type in:
    The trip of a lifetime - Wish You Were Here

● Add a single open quotation mark in front of the text using Ctrl-Alt-(. That is, hold down the Ctrl and Alt keys and then pressing the left bracket once before releasing the keys. Add a single closing quote after the word 'lifetime' using a similar key combination with the right bracket, Ctrl-Alt-).

An alternative to this standard method of producing single quotes, which works in cases like this where the quotes marks are paired, is PagePlus 3's *smart quotes* option. Smart quotes are created using the key combination Ctrl-Alt-" which automatically creates an open quotation mark the first time you use it and the corresponding closing quote the second time you use it.

- Once the quotes marks have been entered, return to your page and set the text to bold and italics with size 24.0p, and centre align it.

You may need to drag on the handles of the text to resize the bounding box in order to spread the text across the three lines. Then position it using the Pointer in the middle of the clear box, whilst holding the F4 key to keep the text as free text.

- There is also some acknowledgement text at the bottom of the first column which is easily created. Double-click in a free area of your page and type in WritePlus:

    Pictures courtesy of Jan Rees
    Text courtesy of Steve Power

● When you return to your page set the text to italic with size 14.0p and right align it before repositioning it, with snapping on, in the first column, up against the first gutter. You may need to resize the bounding box to get each sentence of the text spread over two lines.

» Using the Layout Checker and CleanUp

To be entirely satisfied with your work you should check complex publications with lots of objects, like this one, for any design errors. PagePlus 3's Layout Checker can look for various inconsistencies, such as widows and orphans, over-spaced text, objects that overlap the margins, etc..

● Select the Check Layout icon from the Page ChangeBar. Then choose which pages you want to check, and whether to include master pages or not. You can also use the Options button and then the Layout Options dialog to specify what you want the Layout Checker to look for.

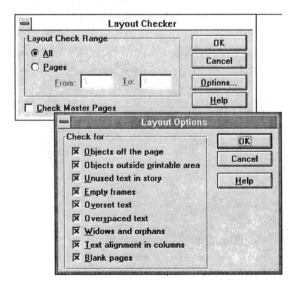

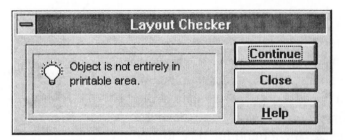

When the Layout Checker reports a problem you can decide whether it is something that needs altering or if in fact it is a deliberate feature of your design.

It is also worth using the CleanUp feature to remove all frames, margins, guides etc. from your design so that you can get a better look at your publication before you print it. You can also use this feature during the creation of a publication if you don't want its 'construction lines' and the screen furniture to show and it is a safe option to use because you can restore the display to its former state simply by clicking the CleanUp button a second time.

● Double-click on the CleanUp button on the Status Bar to select your clean-up 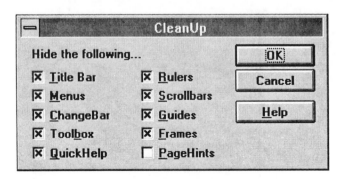 preferences. Use the CleanUp dialog and choose the features you want to hide. Then select OK to return to your page. Click the CleanUp button again to hide the items you have selected. Next time you click on the button the display will switch back to its former state.

Your design is now complete and you can save it and print it as explained in the previous tours.

» From practice to theory

This has been a very long tour but, having completed it, you have seen most of the facilities in PagePlus. You have also encountered the sort of techniques used to create a complex layout. Some of the terms - leading, letter spacing, text flow, etc.- have been introduced here without exact definitions or further discussion. This doesn't matter while you are doing the tour because you can see the effect each one has on the layout and appreciate why they are being adjusted. In the following chapters these terms are explained in more detail so that your understanding can grow and you will know for yourself when to use these fundamental printing techniques.

Key points

» Before starting any layout you should choose the page size, margins, number of columns and units to be used for the rulers.

» Column guides will be automatically added and you can create additional guides by clicking on the rulers. If snap is turned on objects are attracted to the rulers and guides making it easier to align and position objects accurately. If you hide the guides and rulers then objects no longer snap to them, even if snap is on.

» As well as providing a default snap grid, rulers can be moved to aid precise positioning of objects on the page.

» Master pages can be used to create layout features which are repeated on every page in a document. You can create single-sided documents which have a single master page or double-sided documents which have right and left master pages.

» Objects and guides placed on master pages appear on every page that the master is appropriate for unless you disable this on a page by page basis.

» Unless you deliberately change the page setup for a new page, it takes its page size and margins from the appropriate (right or left) master page.

» The page number symbol can be included on any page and is always replaced by the page's actual number. Placing a page number on a master page is the easiest way of numbering an entire document.

Chapter 5

Fonts and Typography

In nearly all layouts text objects form the most important, or at least the most numerous, elements. We have already seen how to create both free and frame text and how to manipulate it to alter the way that it looks by assigning properties to it. However, complete mastery of the text component of a layout is vital to making good use of PagePlus so in this and the following chapter the focus falls on text objects.

In this chapter we look at matters of typography - letter shapes and how they are placed on the page. In the next chapter we look more closely at frame text and the way it interacts with free text and layout at the paragraph and chapter level.

» Fonts

A *typeface* is a set of characters, usually an entire alphabet in upper and lower case, all conforming to the same style. A *fount* or, as it is pronounced, *font* is a specific typeface at a specific size. (The word fount is from the French fonte meaning a casting and harks back to the days when printing involved metal type.) Due to the American English influence on computer and printing terminology, the spelling 'fount' has disappeared and 'font' has been adopted in its place. Furthermore, though not strictly correct, font has come to mean typeface or 'text style'. PagePlus 3 uses this generalisation and this is the meaning we shall continue to use in this book.

A font can therefore be considered to be a typeface that can be manipulated in size, and to a lesser extent in appearance. Fonts can be italicised, emboldened, underlined, etc., and generally come in families containing these subsets and often also with lighter (thinner) or heavier (darker/thicker) styles.

» Units

The printing industry has a number of archaic units of measurement still in use. These are so entrenched that it is inconceivable that they will be changed to something more modern so it is up to us to fit in with them! The size or height of a font is generally quoted as its *point size*.

This measurement is quoted in terms of *points* and *picas*. It is important therefore that you know exactly what these terms imply and exactly what point size measures.

A point is approximately 1/72 of an inch, and there are 12 points to a pica. A pica is therefore approximately 1/6 of an inch.

If you insist on being 100% accurate then 1 point is exactly 0.01387 inches and there are 72.27 points to the inch - so a point is actually just a little smaller than 1/72 of an inch. In practice this tiny difference isn't of practical importance. Other units of measurement in use include the didot point - a sort of metric point in use in Europe but very little used in the UK or the US. One didot point is 0.3759 mm (0.01479 inch) which is larger than a point. If the didot is the European equivalent of the point then it is also worth knowing that the cicero is the European equivalent of the pica. You can set PagePlus's rulers to measure in inches, centimetres, points, picas, didots or ciceros. However, you can only select font sizes and line widths in points.

» Point size

It is easy to see how point size can measure the width of a line or the distance between objects. However, what is not quite so obvious is how text can be measured in points and picas: what does a text size of 12 points mean? Originally point size referred to the height of the lead blocks used to carry the typeface. Today the measurement is used in the same way but now there is no need to use lead blocks. You can think of the point size as specifying the amount of vertical space available for the letters in a font. Any given letter in the font does not have to use the whole of the space specified by the point size and indeed there is no need for any letter of the font to use the whole of the space allocated to it.

The way that the available vertical space is used by the letters in a font varies according to the letter. All of the letters are aligned so that the body of the letter sits on a *baseline.* It is usual for the body of each letter to be the same height - the so called *x-height.* Some letters, such as 'h', have a line which extends above the x-height - this is called an *ascender.* Some letters, such as 'y', have a line which drops below the baseline - this is called a *descender.* Thus, in any font the maximum amount of vertical space used is from the bottom of a descender to the top of an ascender and this distance is usually the point size. Notice that the point size is not the size of a capital letter in the font - this is called the *cap height.*

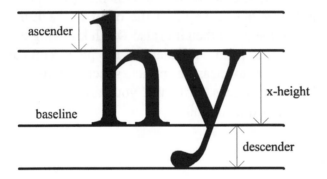

Beginners are often confused by the fact that different fonts in the same point size actually look bigger or smaller. In other words, not all 10 point fonts actually look the same size. The reason for this is that different fonts do not have to use all of the vertical space allotted to them. What this means in practice is that some fonts come with some built in vertical spacing, see the section about Leading later in this chapter. For example,

this is Times Roman 12 point but

this is Arial Super 12 point which appears to be smaller.

» Point size only specifies the maximum height of a font. Individual fonts will use more or less of this space and so you may need to change point size when you change font.

Also notice that the text baseline should not be confused with the outline box that appears around a string of text when you move it. The outline box surrounds the entire text object including ascenders and descenders. This box cannot therefore be used to position a baseline accurately.

» Serif, sans-serif and script fonts

There are three broad categories of fonts - serif fonts, sans-serif fonts and script fonts.

A *serif* is a curl, or additional stroke, on the end of a line forming part of a letter. A serif font is, therefore, a font where the letters contain these embellishments. Popular examples of serif fonts are Times, Baskerville, Century Schoolbook and Garamond.

A *sans-serif* font is a font where the characters do not have these additional strokes. The letters are made up of more rigid and singular strokes. Popular examples of these are Helvetica, Futura and Arial.

Script or *cursive* is a style of font which attempts to emulate handwriting by providing curls, loops and extensions to letters so that when a word is typed the letters have a joined up, handwritten style. This does not always work, however, as certain letters do not join together well and extra loops often occur where they would not if the handwriting were genuine. Examples include Script and BriemScript.

There are also symbol fonts in which the characters are not ordinary letters, numbers and punctuation. The font named Symbol comprises the Greek alphabet and mathematical symbols while other symbol fonts, such as Wingdings, include generally decorative motifs plus items like a smiling

A serif font - Times New Roman

A sans-serif font - Arial

A script font - ChurchScript

A σψμβολ φοντ – Σψμβολ (Symbol)

A monospaced font - Courier New

face and a skull and crossbones and they are useful in the context of artwork rather than text.

The obvious problem in using Wingdings and similar fonts is in knowing which key produces which character. The Character Map solves this problem by letting you select symbols and copy them to the Clipboard and then paste them into your work. This utility is supplied with Windows and by default is in the Accessories group. You can also run it from within PagePlus by selecting the command Edit,Character Map.

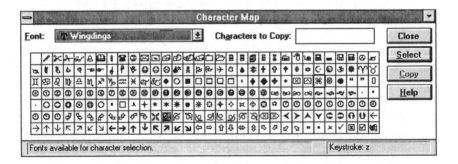

With the character map displayed you can select any character or group of characters that you are interested in and copy them to the Clipboard. Once on the Clipboard they can be pasted into the text as usual. If you look at the box in the bottom right-hand corner you also will see the keystroke that you have to press to enter the character.

Another important difference between fonts is whether they are proportional or monospaced. Most fonts are proportionally spaced - that is the space between characters varies to take account of wide or narrow letter shapes. A monospaced font uses the same amount of space for each letter irrespective of its width. Monospaced fonts generally look as if they had been produced using a typewriter and they are not at all attractive. However, they can be useful in tables or where you want to make a text insert look as if it had been typed.

» Using TrueType fonts

With releases of Windows before 3.1, fonts came in the form of bitmaps and vectors. These fonts, while adequate for some applications, cannot be accurately scaled to desired point sizes and the printed font often looks different to its equivalent display on the screen.

Bitmap fonts consist of a collection of redefined pixels making up the appropriate shape. You can think of each letter in a font as being represented by a small picture. The disadvantage of bitmap fonts is that you need a picture of each letter for each point size you want to use. This is workable but it takes a great deal of disk storage. If you try to use a point size for which there isn't a font file definition on disk then scaling is used to create it. Unfortunately this scaling is very crude and results in jagged edges and curves. For DTP you have to have a bitmap font file for the point size you are trying to use or the result is unacceptable. In fact the result is so unacceptable that PagePlus 3 doesn't allow you to use any bitmapped fonts that are installed on your system.

Vector fonts, like vector graphics, consist of a collection of predefined lines which merge together to produce the desired overall shape. Vector graphics are more easily and accurately scaled but due to their nature are often stick-like and rather oddly shaped. Both bitmap and vector fonts have the added disadvantage that they are often incapable of being rotated or having their letter-width condensed or stretched. PagePlus does allow you to use vector fonts.

The only alternative to bitmapped or vector fonts used to be to install type managers such as Adobe Type Manager (ATM) or Bitstream FaceLift. These products are able to provide fully scalable fonts which can be accurately scaled to any size for printing purposes and screen display. A scalable font makes use of a mathematical description of each letter shape which can be scaled to any point size with no loss of quality. As well as scaling, it is also possible to rotate or distort the letter shapes in other ways - however, the real advantage is that a single font definition serves for all point sizes and for all display devices. The mathematical description of the letter shape can be converted to a pattern of dots which can be reproduced on any Windows display or printer. As the fonts on all output devices are generated in the same way this is as close as you can get to true WYSIWYG.

You can still use ATM or other font managers but in most cases there is no need. Windows 3.1 provides its own scalable fonts - TrueType - and these are the fonts that PagePlus prefers to use. A basic set of TrueType fonts is installed along with Windows but you can add to it either by way of the PagePlus FontPack or by using any of the many TrueType font libraries that are available. Any fonts, TrueType or otherwise, that you install will automatically be available for selection in PagePlus for any item of text. This can be done from the ChangeBar, when Font is selected from the Properties Palette.

» Printer fonts

There is one complication with respect to using fonts in PagePlus. As well as the Windows supplied fonts, some printers come with their own set of fonts. These are fonts that are stored within the printer's own electronics and while Windows will allow you to use them it has very little to do with them. When you select a printer font Windows attempts to find one of its fonts that it can use to show you what the printed document will look like. In most cases this is reasonably effective and in any case you can always be sure that each letter on the screen is positioned in exactly the same way it will be on the printer and broad details of layout, such as page breaks and line endings, are accurate. What might not be accurate are the shapes of the individual letters because what is happening is that one font - the Windows font - is being spaced according to the rules for another font - the printer font.

You might be wondering why you would bother to use a printer font when TrueType fonts are so effective. The answer is that in some cases printer fonts are much faster to use. Also in some cases the match between TrueType and printer fonts is so good there is nothing to gain by not using them. For example, all PostScript printers come with a standard set of 35 fonts and each one has a TrueType match - Times is New Times Roman, Helvetica is Arial and so on. However, if you stray from the basic set and want to use a wider range of PostScript fonts then you will almost certainly need to add Adobe Type Manager (ATM) to your system. The reason is that ATM fonts are PostScript (Adobe type I) fonts. Adding ATM means that you can see printer fonts on the screen.

This said it is important to know of another disadvantage of using printer fonts. If you lay out a document using a printer font and then change the selected printer, using the command

File,Printer Setup, then the range of printer fonts will change. PagePlus tries to cope with this change by altering the printer font to another font that matches. However, this remapping of fonts isn't particularly successful and you will almost certainly have to re-lay the document.

» If you use a printer font the document layout is dependent on the existence of that font. If you change the printer so that the font is no longer available the layout will change.

If you want to avoid creating documents tied to particular printers then you should clearly avoid printer fonts and only use TrueType fonts. You can  identify a printer font in the font list because it has a small printer icon next to it whereas a TrueType font has a TT icon. You can also opt to show only TrueType fonts in the font list - see TrueType Font Options later in this chapter.

There is one situation where selecting and using a printer font can be advisable. If you are planning to send output to an imagesetter bureau then using PostScript printer fonts is a sensible option. The reason is that all current imagesetters use PostScript fonts and you have to take special steps to allow them to use TrueType fonts. This is a complicated issue and one that has to be considered in the wider context of pre-press, see Chapter 8.

» Installing fonts

Windows initially comes with a small selection of fonts which are installed automatically along with the rest of the software. If you install any other packages which come with additional fonts, they will normally be installed automatically too. However, if this is not the case or you acquire additional fonts separately, you can install them manually via the

Windows Control Panel (found by default in the Main group of the Windows desktop).

Control Panel

To install a font for use with Windows applications, including PagePlus, first select the Fonts icon from the Windows Control Panel. The Fonts dialog then opens, displaying a list of all of the currently available fonts.

Fonts

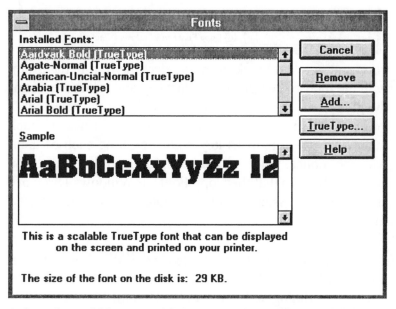

Select the Add button which causes the Add Fonts dialog to open, listing all the fonts in the current directory.

If the default location is not correct, select the drive and directory that contains the fonts you wish to install. The fonts you wish to install should now be contained in the List of Fonts box. Select the ones you require from this list. Notice that the Select All button lets you select all the fonts in the list and there are shortcuts to selecting more than one font. If

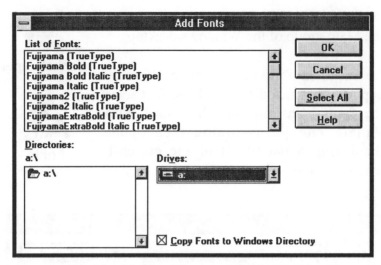

you want to add a block of fonts select the first in the group
with the mouse then press the Shift key and select the last of
the group. All the fonts in between will also be selected. If
you want to install multiple fonts that are not next to each
other hold down the Ctrl key while selecting each of them
with the mouse. Once you have highlighted the fonts to be
added make sure that the Copy Fonts to Windows Directory
check box is crossed then click on OK to install the selected
fonts.

The selected fonts are then installed in the **\Windows\System**
directory. Click on the Cancel button in the Fonts dialog box
to close the dialog and return to the Control Panel.

» Removing fonts

You may decide to remove some fonts from your system.
This is a good idea in the case of any fonts you are unlikely
ever to use and even with those you might want very rarely
as they take up a relatively large amount of disk space. You
can of course reinstall them at a later date if you decide you
need them.

The procedure to remove a font from your Windows system is the converse of that just described for installing fonts. First select the Fonts icon from the Windows Control Panel which opens the Fonts dialog, displaying a list of all your available fonts. Select the fonts you wish to remove from this list. Once you have identified the fonts to be deleted click on the Remove button which displays the Remove Font dialog box.

You have to confirm each removal by clicking on Yes. Click on Yes to All if you wish to proceed with the deletion of multiple selected fonts.

Notice that unless you check the box Delete Font File From Disk the font will not appear on the list of fonts but its associated files will still take up disk space.

If you have a lot of fonts installed then you might want to reduce the number displayed in the font list without having to remove the files from disk. This would of course make reinstallation much simpler as the font files would still exist in the directory \Windows\System. In this case leave the Delete Font File From Disk option unchecked when performing the Remove Font operation.

Important Note: Do not remove the Arial or New Times Roman TrueType fonts as these are used by applications programs to display their own text and menus.

» TrueType font options

There are two main options regarding the use of TrueType Fonts which you can set to on or off from the Windows Control Panel. These are Enable TrueType Fonts and Show Only TrueType Fonts in Applications. By default, TrueType fonts are enabled (set to on) and the Show Only TrueType Fonts in Applications is disabled (set to off).

If you want to change these options select Fonts from the Control Panel, by double-clicking on the Fonts icon, then click the TrueType button in the Fonts dialog. The TrueType dialog box then appears.

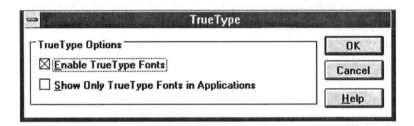

Disable TrueType fonts only if you are committed to using some other type of scalable font - for example Adobe fonts as provided by ATM.

The Show Only TrueType Fonts in Applications option restricts font lists to include only TrueType fonts. This is mainly of use in eliminating printer fonts from font lists. However, it is worth noticing that if a printer supports a TrueType font then this will appear in the list. If this option is enabled, work already containing non-TrueType fonts will still appear with the appropriate fonts; the fonts have not been removed, they merely do not appear in selection lists.

» How to select the right font

The objective of the written word is to communicate something to the reader. It must therefore be easy to read and attract the attention of potential readers. Selecting the correct font is very important in this context. There are many generalised rules that relate to font selection but, as with all rules relating to matters of taste and design, they can all be broken to good effect!

Generally, serif fonts are used for the body text of a publication - the main articles or stories. Research has shown that such a style is easier to read for large areas of text due to the letters flowing into each other. This is visually more attractive and apparently causes less eye strain. The Times newspaper uses the appropriately named Times serifed font for its main body text, as does our Tour Three.

Conversely, sans-serif fonts tend to be used for headlines as they stand out more, gaining attention. Tour Three used the sans-serif font Arial for the main story headline. Arial is the TrueType equivalent of the much better known Helvetica sans-serif font. These fonts are commonly used in advertising, where an immediate or dramatic message needs to be communicated.

The size of text is also important. The larger the text in relation to the page, the greater its perceived importance. Clearly the main title should be the largest text on the page and the main body should be amongst the smallest with all other headings in between. For a full page design a point size of one pica (72 points) or more is often used for the main headline. Sizes in the region of 10 to 14 points are normally used for body text, and smaller text such as footnotes are 8 to 10 points.

In this book the chapter titles - the largest text - are 26 points; the subheadings - the largest frequently occurring text - are 16 points and the body text is 12 points.

Emboldening and italicising text can be done to provide variety where there is a need to keep the same font. Headings look more prominent in bold and it can be is useful for emphasising a single word or short passage. However, too much use of bold within body text can make a layout look dark and 'over-emphatic'. Italics are a useful method of discriminating a separate string of text from the main body, for example to pick out a caption for an illustration, or to differentiate a quote within the story itself, or to draw attention to words you want to make sure the reader notices. Italics are generally a cleaner lighter way of differentiating text but you need to make sure that they blend with the rest of the text spacing. For example, it is often a difficult decision whether or not to include punctuation within italics.

Different fonts and font sizes are used for different elements of publications. Each font has a different mood and personality. Some are chosen because of their readability qualities and others because they are decorative or symbolic of a relevant era. For example: Times is informative, serious and scholarly; Bodoni is dramatic and sophisticated; Garamond is graceful, refined and successful; Invitation is informal and frivolous.

You should, however, avoid using too many different font types and font sizes. This can quickly make a design appear cluttered. It is better to stick to one style and size for each heading level and one for the main body. Use italics, bold, letter spacing and leading for variety. However, even these features should be used sparingly as they too can make a design look untidy. Furthermore, make sure that a publication has consistent fonts; do not change the main body font style for each different heading or story. Whenever you select a new font ask yourself if it is really necessary and always take a final overview of the fonts that you have used in a layout when it is nearing completion.

Bear in mind the following guidelines:

» Restrict yourself to one or two font types.

» Use fonts in contrasting pairs - serifed and sans-serif.

» Vary the properties of text - using bold, italics, colour, tint, etc. - to give emphasis and variety rather than using additional fonts.

» If you make use of decorative fonts check to make sure that your message is still readily comprehensible to people who don't know it beforehand!

» Typography

Choosing a font defines the letter shapes and some of the basic rules for spacing the letters on the page. This, however, is only the start. You are free to define the word spacing and vary the letter spacing from the default. You can also set the inter-line and inter-paragraph spacing. All of these adjustments alter the look of the text on the page and are collectively referred to as *typography*. PagePlus is set up so that the default typography will be acceptable in many applications but to really take control of your layout you must understand each of the typographic features. The most basic elements of typography are the horizontal spacing of text - letter and word - and the vertical spacing of text - line and paragraph. We start by examining horizontal spacing.

» Tracking

Every font supplies a specification for the way individual letters in the font should be spaced. You can think of this as defining how much space each letter takes up. Normally this default letter spacing is acceptable but there are times when a more compressed or expanded spacing is desirable. Changing the inter-letter spacing in this way is called *tracking*.

PagePlus allows you to set the inter-letter spacing in a number of different ways. You can select the Letter-space icon in the Properties Palette and then set the spacing using the ChangeBar. Letter spacing is specified as a percentage - 0% means no additional letter spacing, positive percentages increase the spacing and negative percentages decrease it. The best way to discover the effect of any given letter spacing percentage is to try it out. By using the scroll bar slider on the ChangeBar you can see the effect of letter spacing on the selected text interactively.

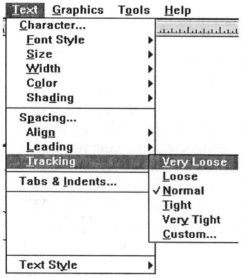

As an alternative you can select one of the options in the Text,Tracking menu. Each of these descriptive options sets the percentage letter spacing to a predetermined value. For example, Loose sets the letter spacing to 3% and Tight sets it to -3%. If you select Custom then the Spacing dialog box appears.

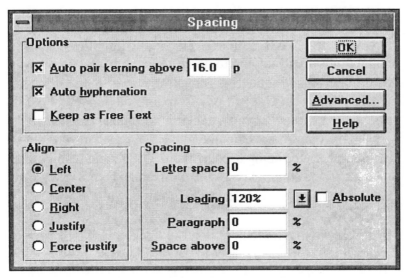

The Spacing dialog controls all of the typographic features of the text as well as letter spacing. You can go straight to it by selecting the menu command Text,Spacing. Use whichever method of setting the inter-letter spacing you find most convenient. What matters is that you realise that these three methods all set the same single quantity.

This only leaves unanswered the question of why you might want to alter the letter spacing. Occasionally, you may want to space letters wider than usual as part of a special design effect. You might also want to alter letter spacing to make a block of text exactly fit the space available to it - although this is a dangerous way to work because it often results in too much or too little tracking being used.

The most legitimate reason for tracking text it to alter its overall density. By altering the letter spacing you can make a block of text look darker or lighter. You may also find that the default spacing of a font appears to be too wide at the large point sizes used in headings. Some DTP packages apply a *tracking curve* which automatically increases the tracking as the size of the font is increased. Tracking curves have to be designed to suit each font and this is a difficult job. If you have the time and patience then adjusting the tracking manually is always going to do as good a job, and possibly a better one, than a predefined tracking curve. As in all cases where there is an element of discretion, the tendency is for the beginner to over-apply tracking and make the text look crushed. You also have to take into account the resolution of the output device being used to avoid letters running together in the final output. Always examine the layout on paper before deciding on a close tracking setting.

In all cases what matters is that the tracked text looks good and is legible.

To summarise, tracking can be used:

» for special effects

» to copy fit

» to alter the 'density' of a block of text

» to compensate for the illusion of increased space in large point sizes

» Kerning

Tracking refers to the alteration of letter spacing for every letter in the font, *kerning* on the other hand alters the letter spacing of particular pairs of letters. Some pairs of letters have shapes that fit together so well that moving them closer improves the overall look of the text.

To kern a pair of letters use the Text tool to highlight the first letter of the pair and then use the ChangeBar to set an appropriate letter space. For example, the 'Av' pair in aviator looks too far apart using the default spacing. The solution is to select the letter A and set a letter space of -18%. The space between the v and i can also be decreased in the same way although not as much. You can adjust the spacing between any group of letters in the same way. Always remember that it is the space following each selected letter that is altered by the letter spacing control. You can set the tracking of any highlighted block of text and this facility can be used to kern any letter pair.

The most common use of kerning is within headlines at large point sizes. Just as the tracking is used to compensate for the illusion of increasing space as the point size increases, so kerning becomes more important at higher point sizes. PagePlus 3 will automatically kern particular pairs of characters when the point size in use passes a specified threshold. Auto-Kerning is turned on by default but you can disable it using the Spacing dialog box. You can also set the point size threshold above which auto-kerning is applied - 16 points by default. The only problem with auto-kerning is that it only works for TrueType fonts that include pair kerning information. Most of the standard TrueType fonts do include pair kerning data but it tends to be very conservative. For example, in Times Roman at 72 points the kerning applied to A and v is only 4%.

You can also use kerning to produce letter forms that are not available in a font such as the 'ae' diphthong - as in formulæ. In such cases you should always check that they are not actually available as special characters which usually look a lot better than a pair of kerned characters.

» Justification and alignment

Inter-word spacing is not specified as part of a font's definition except via the size of a space character. Even in this case there are a number of different widths of space character available - en-space (i.e. the width of an N), em-space (i.e. the width of an M) and so on. You can vary the default inter-word spacing just as you can the letter spacing. However, the way in which words are spaced also depends on whether or not the lines are to be justified. The reason is that text is justified to exactly fit between left and right margins by altering the word spacing. The simplest case of word spacing occurs in non-justified text.

There are three simple non-justified alignment types which use a very similar method of fitting words to a line. In each case words are added to a line using a fixed optimum space until the next word to be added would exceed the maximum line length. When this happens a new line is started and therefore a non-justified line is always shorter or exactly equal to the maximum line length. After a line of text has been filled in this way it can be aligned between the margins using one of four possible methods.

》 Left alignment
  Aligns the start of each line so producing a straight left-hand side and a ragged right-hand side.

» Right alignment
Aligns the end of each line so producing a ragged left-hand edge and a straight right-hand edge.

» Centered
Aligns the start of each line so as to position the line centrally between the margins. In this case both edges of a block of text are ragged.

» Justified
Aligns the start of each line with the left-hand edge and then inserts extra "padding" space in the line to make it end aligned on the right-hand edge. In this case both edges of a block of text are straight.

Justified alignment is different from the other three in that it actually inserts space to make the two edges of the text block line up. Padding space can be added either between words - inter-word spaces, or between letters - inter-letter spacing. Justified text usually looks good but there are potential problems. If the line is very short then a lot of space has to be inserted to justify it correctly and this space can make the line look very "loose". This is particularly noticeable where letter spacing is used to fit a single long word into a short line. There are various methods of improving justification but even the best typesetting method still occasionally produces silly results that can only be resolved by manual methods.

PagePlus uses a simple but effective technique involving the use of three inter-word space settings - minimum word spacing, optimum word spacing and maximum word spacing. When a line is justified words are added until the space between words falls below the specified minimum. When this happens the last word is moved to the next line to increase the inter-word spacing. It may be that this increase in inter-word spacing is too large to be acceptable. In this case the only way that it can be reduced is if part of the first word on the next line is moved back. This involves finding a suitable point in the word to add a hyphen so that it can be split across the lines. PagePlus 3 incorporates an auto-hyphenation feature which is triggered when the inter-word space goes above the preset maximum. You can adjust the maximum and minimum inter-word spacing by clicking on the Advanced button in the Spacing dialog box. The Advanced dialog box that appears allows you to set the

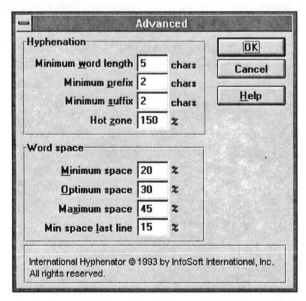

inter-word spacing and details of hyphenation.

As well as the Maximum and Minimum inter-word spacing you can also set the Optimum space to be used when a line is left, right or centre aligned. In this case each inter-word space is set to the optimum spacing unless this would trigger hyphenation, when it is allowed to fall to the minimum inter-word spacing.

The last line of any block of justified text is usually not justified but left aligned. This convention serves to mark the end of a paragraph and avoids having to justify a short line. You can set the minimum inter-word space for a last line independently. The reason is that space in a left aligned line can be lower without increasing the overall density of the text because of the space left at the end of the line.

If you would like to justify the last line or a single line of text then you can select the Force Justify alignment. This can also be used to create special effects such as a single line of right and left aligned text - see Tour Three and Chapter 10.

» Hyphenation

Hyphenation is a contentious technique of improving layout. There is no doubt that even when done well it lowers overall readability. In most cases you can avoid hyphenation in headlines by careful choice of point size and tracking. Where it is more difficult is if you are using narrow columns or the subject matter of the text has a tendency to include more long words than average. Newspapers and newsletters tend to suffer from short line lengths and scientific and technical documents tend to suffer from above average occurrences long words. In both cases hyphenation may be a solution - but increasing the line length is another!

PagePlus 3 includes an auto-hyphenation facility that works reasonably well. There are rules that can be applied to most languages to provide potential hyphenation positions without needing to know what the word means or how it is pronounced. In many cases this produces good hyphenation. In other cases it gives results you might not like.

For example, the words readdress and envelope will be hyphenated as read-dress and enve-lope. Which, even if you find them acceptable, are not easy to read.

Hyphenation		
Minimum word length	5	chars
Minimum prefix	2	chars
Minimum suffix	2	chars
Hot zone	150	%

You can turn auto-hyphenation on and off using the Spacing dialog box. Auto-hyphenation is on by default. You can also control the details of hyphenation using the advanced spacing dialog box. You can set the minimum word length for hyphenation. A word shorter than this will not be hyphenated. Minimum prefix and suffix set the smallest acceptable fragment produced by hyphenation. Finally the hot zone only affects text that is right, left or centre aligned and specifies the amount of space that can be left at the end of a line before hyphenation is used to reduce it. The hot zone is measured as a percentage of the current point size.

To set the language used for auto-hyphenation (to UK or American English) you can use the Tools,Preferences, General command. This also sets the language used for spell checking and thesaurus.

The best sort of hyphenation is manual - only a human has the intelligence necessary to find the best split for any given word. You can insert a discretionary or soft hyphen into a word using the Text,Insert Hyphen menu command or by typing a hyphen with the Ctrl key held down. A soft hyphen has no effect unless the word spacing in a line could be reduced by breaking the word concerned at a soft hyphen. Rather than going through and introducing soft hyphens in an entire text a much better approach is to look for *loose lines*, i.e. lines with excessive space, and placing a soft hyphen in the first word of the next line. This should cause the word to be split between the lines. The advantage of a soft hyphen is that if the layout changes so that the word no longer has to be split then the hyphen will not appear.

A word that contains a soft hyphen will not be changed by auto-hyphenation. This means that placing a soft hyphen in front of the first letter of a word provides a way of marking it as 'not to be hyphenated'.

» Leading

Inter-line spacing is commonly termed '*leading*', which is pronounced 'ledding'. This is a measure of the distance between lines of text. (The name comes from the strips of lead that typographers used to space rows of type.) The measurement is taken between the baseline of the lines of text, and is measured either as a percentage of the text's point size or as an absolute measurement in points. The advantage of specifying the leading as a percentage is that the same relative spacing is maintained irrespective of the point size you select.

The consideration of leading is fairly similar to that for inter-letter spacing. For most body text of around 10 to 14 points the default size of 120% is normally a reasonable size. However, if the text is much larger, as it probably would be for a headline, the lines may need tightening up (the leading reduced).

Like kerning, changing the leading can also be used for design effects or to allow more text into a particular space. However, it should be applied consistently to similar parts of the text throughout any design. For example, all your body text should have the same leading and all your headlines should have the same leading.

You can change the leading of text in PagePlus in increments of 1% by selecting the text, or highlighting specific lines within a text object with the Text tool, and then using the ChangeBar with the Leading property selected from the Properties Palette. Use the ChangeBar's scroll bar and the WYSIWYG display to achieve the appropriate look. You can also fill in the Leading text box in the Spacing dialog box if you want to change a number of spacing values in one go. Notice that if you specify absolute leading then the ChangeBar shows the leading in points rather than as a percentage.

PagePlus's approach of specifying leading as a percentage of point size is a reasonable one as long as you are happy setting the leading interactively and don't worry too much about what the actual setting is. You will often hear people with a traditional publishing background specify font size and leading as "x on y". So for example, you will hear a layout specified as "10 on 11 Helvetica", meaning 10 point Helvetica text with 11 point leading. If you want to accept this sort of verbal instruction then simply select the point size and set the leading using the absolute option in the Spacing dialog box.

» Paragraph spacing

A paragraph of text is a collection of lines terminated by pressing the Enter or carriage return key. When text is imported into a frame each paragraph is formatted according to the default text typography. As will become apparent, control of paragraph typography is fundamental to laying out documents that contain a lot of regular text. Paragraph typography is simply a matter of specifying font, point size, letter spacing, word spacing and leading, as already described, but there are two additional typographic controls concerned with the positioning of the entire paragraph - *paragraph space* and *space above*.

Paragraph space determines the amount of space left at the end of the paragraph before the start of the next. Space above sets the amount of space left before a paragraph starts. Both are measured as a percentage of the leading so 100% paragraph space leaves one line height after each paragraph. The space that you set after a paragraph is added to any space above set for the following paragraph. So for example, if you set 100% paragraph space and the paragraph following has 200% space above the total gap between the paragraphs will be 300%, i.e. three lines.

Why do you need to be able to specify both the space after and before each paragraph? The answer is so that you can automatically determine how different types of paragraph fit together. For example, it is usual for a subheading to be positioned closer to the paragraph below it than to the paragraph before it and by setting the paragraph space for the subheading to 20% and the space above to 75% the unequal spacing can be enforced. However, you do need to keep in mind that the 75% space above will be added to whatever paragraph space is set for the previous paragraph.

Paragraph spacing can only be set in the Spacing dialog box which appears when you use the command Text,Spacing.

» Indents and tabs

Another aspect of typography unique to paragraphs is the idea of an *indent*. It is a common device to indent the first line of every paragraph to make it stand out. Similarly you might want to set a narrower right and left margin on a block of text to mark it out as different. You can set both right and left

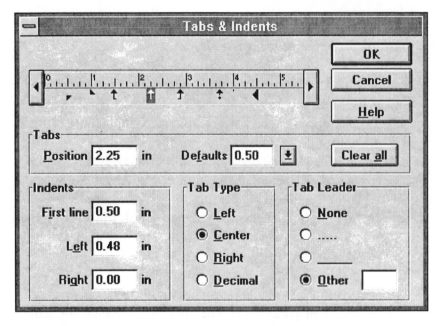

margins and set an indent on the first line of every paragraph using the command Text,Tabs & Indents to display the Tabs & Indents dialog box.

You can set a first line indent or a new left and right margin either by typing in new values into the text boxes or by dragging the markers on the ruler line.

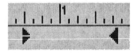

The left and right margins are indicated by arrows pointing inward. You can drag either arrow to set the margin positions but notice that you cannot move the arrows outside the frame that contains the text. This means that you cannot set a left margin less than zero or a right margin wider than the

frame width. The left margin marker can be moved as two halves of the arrow head. The top half of the arrow controls the position of the first line indent, if any, and the lower half sets the left margin for the rest of the paragraph.

As well as setting right and left indents you can also set paragraph tabs. A *tab* is an invisible marker that text jumps to when you use a Tab character. The idea is much the same as with the mechanical tabs that you can set up on a typewriter but it is much more flexible. PagePlus offers four types of tab:

✝ » Left tab - text aligns its left-hand edge on the tab

✝ » Right tab - text aligns its right-hand edge on the tab

✝ » Center tab - text is centred around the tab

✝ » Decimal tab - decimal points align on the tab

You can set any of these tabs by selecting the appropriate type and then clicking on the tab ruler. To adjust tabs you simply drag the existing tab symbols to their new position. To remove a tab drag the symbol off the bottom of the ruler. Changing a tab's type is a matter of selecting it and then selecting its new type. You can also enter an exact position for a tab in the text box while it is selected. In addition to the custom tab settings you can also select a regular tab spacing which always uses left tabs.

First column	left-tabbed	right-tabbed	center-tabbed	decimal-tabbed
Notice	how	the	different	1234.456
tab	types	cause	the	234.56
columns	in	this	table	12456.33
to	line	up	in	334.33
different	ways.	The	first	12.333
column	is	left	aligned	23456.222
the	second	is	left	1.2
the	third	is	right	2222.3333
and	the	fourth	is	2.3
centered	no	leaders	used	23433.44

Typically tabs are used to create small tables within text. In this case the left tab is the most useful because it produces columns with straight left-hand sides. Centre tabs produce columns with ragged right and left sides but centring looks better when the items in the column are small compared to the column heading. Decimal tabs make columns of figures easier to read and understand. The right tab is useful for tables of contents and other two column tables. Complex tables complete with rulings are much easier to create using TablePlus, see Tour Six in the next chapter and Tour Nine Chapter 10.

If a tab results in text being displaced a large distance it can be difficult for the eye to follow the line across the page. In this case you might like to select a *leader* character to be used to fill in the space. You can select one of the standard leader characters - most commonly a dot - or type in your own character.

Notice that paragraph indents and tabs are measured from the frame margins and so complete control over the paragraph typography involves setting the frame up correctly, see Chapter 6.

» Text effects

In addition to all the control that you have over the way that a font is laid out on the page you also have a certain amount of discretion over how it appears. You should already be familiar with the idea of bold and italic effects but it is worth pointing out that these effects are achieved not by modifying the normal font but by using separate fonts designed to be bold or italic. The reason for this is that simply thickening the lines in the normal font doesn't produce a bold font that looks good. In the same way slanting the letters in the normal font doesn't produce a satisfactory italic font. What this means is that usually when you install a new TrueType font you should also install a bold, an italic and sometimes a bold-italic version of the font. However, if a bold or italic font isn't available PagePlus will simulate one by thickening or rotating the letter shapes in the normal font. As well as simulating bold and italic fonts there are a number of other uses for modifications to the letters in a font.

You can, of course set any selected portion of text or a complete paragraph to bold, italic or bold italic  using the ChangeBar. In addition you can also set the strikethrough and underline properties. Both of these text properties are leftovers from the days when typewriters were the standard way of producing documents. Underlining and strikethrough are easy to implement text effects when you are using a typewriter. In most cases you should avoid the use of these two effects in body text - use italics, bold or even a font change instead. In headlines and captions you might find underlining useful but notice that you cannot alter the relative position of the line under the text.

There is one other text effect available as a permanent icon in the ChangeBar - Outline. By clicking on this button you can convert any TrueType font to just its outline. As with bold and italic effects this is really just a simulation of a true outline font and the overall effect produced depends very much on the font being modified. It is worth knowing that you can buy specially designed TrueType outline fonts.

There are three other text effects available in the Properties Palette which are extremely useful in creating artistic headlines, logos and banners.

» Character width
You can stretch or compress the letter shapes in any font by adjusting the character width. You can use this facility to create expanded or condensed fonts but it is much better to use it on single or groups of letters to create special effects.

» Slant angle
Individual characters in a font can be rotated through any angle. Negative angles slope the characters to the left and positive angles slope the characters to the right. You can use this to simulate italic or script fonts but its real purpose is to create special effects. Do not confuse slant angle with text rotation which makes the baseline slope.

» Advance
The advance property is more descriptively known as baseline shift. You can move the baseline up or down by any specified number of points. Positive shifts move the baseline down and negative shifts move it up. There are a number of uses of baseline shift including making up composite characters but the most obvious is in creating sub and superscripts.

As well as these specific text properties you can also assign text a colour, a fill pattern and a shading. Unless the text is in a fairly large point size, fill patterns and even intermediate tones are usually unsuccessful because of the very small areas to be filled.

You can, of course access all of these text properties in the Character dialog box that appears when you use the menu command Text,Character.

It is important to realise that all of these text effects can be applied independently of one another. For example it is quite possible to have expanded slanted outline text. You can even apply different effects to each letter of a caption or headline. In most cases you will also have to kern different portions of the headline to make the spacing more natural. Even without TypePlus - the optional typeface editor - you can create effective text art. By selectively applying baseline shift, slant angle, character width and kerning you can make words look like their meaning:

You should also keep in mind that you can use combinations of typographic effects, rotation and multiple copies of the same text object to produce text art. For example, by rotating a text object through exactly -45° (using the Status Editor) and then setting a character slant of +45° you can fit text to a 45° baseline. Add one copy in outline slightly shifted from another in black and the result is very effective. More such text techniques are discussed in Chapter 10.

Key points

» A font is a typeface family but the term is now commonly used to describe a particular typeface or style such as Times Roman bold.

» The most common unit of measurement used in DTP is the point (roughly 1/72 inch).

» Typography is the control of how letter shapes are placed on a page.

» It is better to use only TrueType fonts or Adobe fonts if you are using a PostScript printer. Changing printer can change a layout if you have used a printer specific font.

» Altering the letter spacing for a block of text is known as tracking and it is useful to fit text to a given space and to alter the density of the page. Changing the letter space between pairs of letters is known as kerning and it is used to improve the look of the text.

» You can also use word and line spacing to alter the density of text. Line spacing is also known as leading.

» Paragraph typography sets the text alignment (right, left, centred, justified or force justified), first line, left and right indents, tabs and paragraph spacing.

» There is limited control over the character shape and positioning within a font. Baseline shift and slant angle move a character with respect to the others. Character width can be used to stretch or compress the letter shapes.

» Avoid the 'typewriter' emphasis of underline and strikethrough. Use bold or italic instead.

Chapter 6

Frame Text

Controlling the look of individual lines of text is the first step towards making full use of PagePlus's DTP abilities. You could set an entire book length manuscript simply by selecting an appropriate font, point size etc. and manually positioning every paragraph. However, it would be a tedious task and it would have to be completely redone to accommodate even the smallest change. The most powerful aspect of modern DTP systems is their ability to quickly reformat a layout to take account of change.

In this chapter we look at ways of controlling the overall layout of a document. The main tools in achieving a more or less automatic control over document layout are frame text and styles both of which are discussed. The chapter closes with a tour which consolidates the ideas introduced in this chapter and the previous one.

» Frame text

So far all of the discussion of typography has been completely general in that it can be applied to free or frame text. However, free text and frame text are distinct and have different problems associated with them. *Free text* is normally used in small quantities to create impact or add decorative effects. *Frame text* is usually used in larger quantities and with fewer variations in typography. In this case the problem is ensuring regularity and consistency of style. Before we look at ways of controlling the typography of frame text we need to look a little more closely at how frame text can be created and manipulated and how it relates to free text.

A text frame can be considered to be a page in miniature. You can define margins and columns for a frame just as you can for a page. If you type free text directly onto a page then it will automatically fit between the page column guides. If you type text into a frame then it will fit between the frame column guides. The difference is that frame text will stay between the frame's column guides. Free text on the page isn't restricted in this way and its line length can be altered simply by editing its bounding box.

Another difference, and perhaps the most important one, is that frame text will flow into a frame and into subsequent linked frames. It helps to think of a frame as a container for text that will automatically fill up and then overflow into the next container until all of the text is used up.

A common misconception is to think of frame text as being a single object - it isn't. Each paragraph within the frame is a separate text object, as is the frame itself. This can complicate matters when you try to manipulate what appears to be a single object - i.e. the frame plus the frame text. If you click on a paragraph it will be selected and you can manipulate it in isolation from the other text in the frame. If you click a second time then the frame will be selected and you can edit - move or resize - it. If you edit a frame then the text that it contains is re-flowed to fit into its new container.

To create a frame all you have to do is draw one using the Frame tool from the ToolBox. A frame 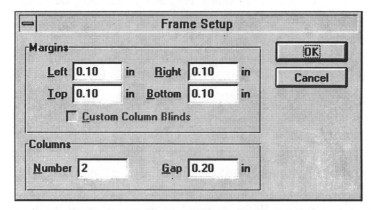 will also be automatically created if you import a text file without first creating or selecting a frame to be used to hold the text - see later. New in PagePlus 3 is the Frame Assistant which appears when you create a new frame and offers you choices about what to do next. If you click on Cancel you can continue to work with the frame directly.

A frame has column guides, a gap between columns and four margins. You can set all of these using the command Page,Frame Setup which accesses the Frame Setup dialog box.

You can also set the number of columns in the ChangeBar or via the Page,Frame,Columns menu command.

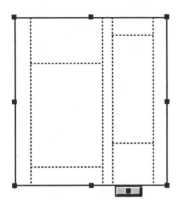

The column margins can also be set by interactively dragging the margin guides which are shown within the frame. If the margins are initially set to zero then you have to drag the corresponding frame bounding box edge - but do so avoiding the handles which are used to resize the frame.

As well as being able to set the right, left, top and bottom margins you can also drag the gap or gutter between the columns to produce an unequal division into columns of unequal width. This also works with the page column guides but you cannot drag the page margins. Also notice that you can drag each column's top or bottom margins independently of one another to produce unequal starting and finishing positions for the text. When text is flowed into the frame it fills the space between the margin guides.

If you do drag the margin guides then the Frame Setup dialog box will show the Custom Column Blinds box checked and you will not be able to enter top and bottom margins using it. To restore equal top and bottom margins simply uncheck the Custom Column Blinds box. (The margin guides are referred to as *frame blinds* hence the name.) There is no way to create columns of unequal width apart from dragging the guides.

You can set the defaults used to create a frame using the Tools,Defaults,Frame command. The defaults can be set either by selecting from the Frame Setup dialog box or by selecting a frame with the properties that you want to become the default before you use the command.

» Importing text

You can create frame text by typing directly into a frame using the Text tool but in most cases it will be imported from an existing text file. You can import text created by a wide range of word processors including Windows Write, Microsoft Word, WordPerfect, Ami Pro, WordStar or any text processor that can create ASCII or Rich Text Format files.

To import text you can either use the File,Import Text menu command or you can double click on the link button at the bottom of the text frame that you want to fill. If you are using the Frame Assistant you can also select the Import from WP option. No matter which route you choose you will see the same dialog box next.

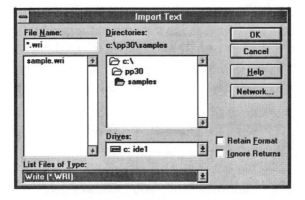

You can then select the word processor type and file that you want to load. Notice that if the word processor file doesn't end in the default extension offered simply type over it with the correct extension in the dialog box.

If you select the Retain Format box then the word processor text will be imported complete with as much formatting as PagePlus can translate. You may think at first that this is a good option because it preserves the work done in the word processor. In practice it generally turns out to be unhelpful because the formatting applied in the word processor is inappropriate and awkward to work with in PagePlus. It is generally much better to import the text without formatting but in any given case you can experiment with both options.

A particular problem with importing word processor files is that some include carriage returns at the end of every line which turns each line into a separate paragraph. The solution is to check the Ignore Returns option.

Imported text is always placed in a frame. If you import text by double clicking on the link button at the bottom of a frame the new text is stored in that frame. If you use the File,Import text command then what happens depends on what is already on the page. If there is a single frame on the page then the text will automatically be flowed into this frame. If there is more than one frame on the page then you have to select one before using the File,Import text command. If no frame is selected then a frame that uses the page guides as a template, that is with the same columns and gap width, is created between the page margins.

That is, if you are importing text to a page:

》 If there is a single frame the text will be flowed into it.

》 If there are multiple frames you have to select one of the frames before importing the text.

》 If there are no frames a default page frame will be created to hold the text.

This default page frame is an important facility if you are trying to create a very regular document because, as we shall see, PagePlus will automatically create as many default page frames as are needed to hold all of the text. At this point you might be thinking that the best way to create a regular document is to use text frames placed on the master pages. However, this doesn't work because the text doesn't flow into frames placed on the master page. The reason is that the master page frame is repeated on every page complete with its contents. In other words, its contents do not change as you move through a document.

» Autoflow

After dealing with importing text into a single frame, the next question is what happens when the first frame is full? In general PagePlus will always try to find or create sufficient frames to hold all of the text.

If there are already additional pages in the document then, for each page in turn, PagePlus will ask you if the text should be flowed into any empty frames that it contains. If any of the extra pages do not contain any text frames then you will be asked if the file should be autoflowed onto the page. If you click on Yes then a default page frame will be created. If there aren't enough extra pages then you will be asked if it is OK to create sufficient pages, together with their default frames, to hold the text. Notice that this implies that text will not be autoflowed onto any page that contains only text frames that are already used. In short:

» If empty frames exist on subsequent pages then PagePlus asks if the text should be flowed into each one.

» If there are no subsequent pages with empty frames PagePlus asks if the text should be flowed into default frames on any pages that do not already have used text frames on them.

» When there are no more pages suitable for flowing the text PagePlus will ask if it should create additional pages complete with default frames.

» Organising flow

The rules for flowing text into frames are fairly simple but it is clear that there are two possible ways of controlling layout using text frames.

» Create an empty document consisting of the required number of pages and text frames and then flow the text into these existing frames.

» Create a single or double page layout, using master pages, without text frames and allow PagePlus to create new pages automatically, complete with the default page frame.

The first approach is better in cases where the text layout of each page is different and the second is better where the text layout of each page is the same.

You can of course use the trick of placing as many empty text frames in the layout as required and then relying on PagePlus to create enough default page frames to hold the remainder. For example, if you set up a 3-column first page, then place a single column frame on it, then when you import text it will fill the single column frame on the first page but thereafter it will fill newly created 3-column default page frames.

If all this sounds complicated then remember that you can always edit the layout after the text has been imported to change it to anything you want it to be. What we are discussing is how to set things up so that you get as close as possible to the desired layout without having to do any extra work. That is, by preparing master pages to have the correct margins, columns and gaps we can rely on PagePlus to create as many pages as necessary, complete with default page frames to accommodate the imported text.

» Manual linking

When text is flowed into a frame you have the option of creating a linked chain of frames - either from existing empty frames or from newly created page frames. If you opt not to do this, or if you later change your mind, then it is very easy to manually create a chain of frames. Each frame in a chain displays the name of the file that was used to create it and its position in the chain is displayed in the ChangeBar when the frame is selected. You can also move to the next frame in the chain by clicking on one of the arrow buttons in the ChangeBar. Double clicking takes you to the first or last frame in a chain.

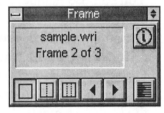

You can edit or add to the chain of frames using the link button at the bottom right-hand corner of each frame. If you click on this button the cursor changes to an image of links in a chain. If you then click on another frame this becomes the next frame in the chain. Notice that this also implies that all of the frames that used to follow the frame that you have relinked are no longer part of the chain.

"Of course" said Sharon in a disappointed voice "it's entirely possible that nobody will recognize me. After all..." she eyed the cartoon rabbit "...I'm merely a thinly disguised pastiche on one of literature's

If you simply click anywhere on the page then the link is broken and not remade to another frame. The text that used to flow in the lost tail end of the chain is still present and ready to be reflowed if you manually create a chain large enough to hold it.

If you create a frame while another frame is selected they are automatically linked. This is the method that the Frame Assistant uses to allow you to create a set of linked frames. If you select the option "Add more frames" then the frame tool is retained and the frame that you have just drawn is selected. When you draw subsequent frames, even if they are on other pages, they are automatically linked into a chain.

You can use manual linking to alter the chain of text frames created when the text was first imported. Each frame that becomes unlinked becomes an empty frame ready to be re-used. There is no way to unlink the text from the first frame in the chain and return it to an empty frame, other than by deleting each individual paragraph of text. It is easier to delete the frame, re-create it and re-import the entire text.

» Editing frame text

One of the most difficult features of PagePlus to get used to is the way that frame text is still treated as a collection of individual text blocks. When you import a file each paragraph, i.e. a number of lines ending with a carriage return, is converted into a text block. You can select each text block within a frame and set its typographic properties, spacing, font, etc., and edit it. If you click on a text block with the Text tool selected then a cursor appears and you can edit the text 'in place'. If you double click then the whole block is transferred to WritePlus where you can proceed to edit it.

Once you have a text block selected within a frame you can manipulate it much like any free text block. If you drag either of the side handles then the left and right paragraph margins are altered. If you drag the top handles then the leading is changed. You can think of this as the text simply altering its layout to fit the new bounding box that you have created for it. However, unlike free text, the frame text maintains its position among the other text blocks. Notice that there is a difference between resizing the bounding box of a text block and resizing the frame. Also notice that you can only drag the frame margins when the frame, and not the text block, is selected.

The way that text blocks act as independent entities that happen to find themselves confined by a frame gives you a great deal of power and flexibility in creating a layout. It can also be a cause of silly mistakes unless you make sure that you know exactly what it is you are working with. When you click on a frame make sure that you have actually selected it by looking for the frame button at the bottom right-hand edge. If you don't see the frame button then you have selected a text block within the frame. Clicking a second time then selects the frame.

» Moving frame text

As well as being able to resize the bounding box, you can also drag a text block. However, what happens depends on where you drag it to. If you drag a block out of a frame then it becomes free text. This is a very useful trick because it allows you to 'pull' headlines out of imported text. You can also convert free text into frame text by dragging it over the frame. When the left-hand edge of the free text aligns with the same edge of the frame then the cursor changes to show you that if you release the text it will be added to the frame.

Another way to convert frame text to free text and vice versa is to use the F4 key. When moving a block of frame text pressing F4 will make it become free text. When moving free text over a frame pressing F4 will cause it to become a block within the frame.

When you convert free text to frame text how the text is inserted into the sequence of blocks depends on the exact position you drop it onto the frame and the shape of the current cursor. When the text block is positioned so that the cursor is also over another block the flow before symbol will appear and the second block will be highlighted. When this happens the text block that you are dragging will be inserted after the highlighted block. If you want it inserted before the

 highlighted block press F2 which toggles the insert after cursor to an insert before cursor. When you release the block it will be flowed in with the rest of the text.

The same technique can be used to alter the order of the blocks. Simply drag the block to its new position and select the flow before or after cursor. You should practice moving blocks using some sample text.

If you drag a text block up or down the column but without moving the cursor onto a second block then the move up/down cursor appears. If you release the block while this is visible the paragraph spacing is changed. If you try to move

 a block so that it comes before the current first block you will find that you only ever see the move up/down cursor by default - to see the flow after cursor press F2.

Always remember that you can move smaller text selections using Cut and Paste. This is also the only way to move text from one block to another. If you want to keep a text object as free text at all times then it is worth selecting the Keep as Free Text option in the Spacing dialog box. With this option checked free text ignores any frames that it might be dragged over.

» What is a text block?

Although it is convenient to identify a text block with a paragraph this isn't actually the case. A text block can contain line breaks and if you edit a text block you will find that you can press Enter and create multiple paragraphs that are all treated as a single text block. It is only when text is imported that each paragraph is converted into a separate text block. Notice also that paragraph spacing and indents apply to all of the paragraphs that are part of a single block. However, it is an advantage to restrict each text block to a single paragraph within frame text.

To start a new text block you have to click or double click with the text tool on something other than text. The reason is that if you click or double click on text then it is assumed that you want to edit that block rather than to create a new one.

> This is a single text block even though it contains more than one paragraph.
>
> This is another paragraph but it is part of the same text block

In many cases the only way to create a new block within an existing sequence is to first create the block as free text outside the frame or as the final block. In either case the block then has to be dragged to its final position.

» Text preparation

You can edit frame text after it has been imported but it is very important to realise that any changes you make are not made to the text in the file that you imported. That is, when you import text it is read in and stored within the .PPP document file. When you load the document at a later date the original file is not used - just the internal copy of the text.

This has important implications for text preparation for PagePlus. You can use a word processor to prepare text but after it has been imported you cannot use the word processor again on that text unless you are prepared to re-import it and so lose any changes you may have made within PagePlus.

As PagePlus 3's own WritePlus is as good at editing text as most word processors - it has a spelling checker, thesaurus, search and replace and a word count - you could simply decide to live with the imported version of the text and not worry about keeping the external file up to date. This is the best approach if you can use it but if the changes have to be made available in other formats then your only choice is to avoid making any changes in PagePlus and always return to the word processor to work with the text. Notice that you cannot use OLE links between a text object and your favourite word processor because PagePlus always uses WritePlus to edit any embedded text.

» Managing frames using styles

The most common problem with frame text is setting the typography for all the paragraphs in the frame. For example suppose you wanted to change the point size for all of the text blocks in a frame - how can this be achieved easily? The answer is that you can use the Text,Text Style command to apply and create *paragraph styles*.

Each object - graphics or text - in a layout can be associated with a named style, a collection of property settings. A paragraph or text style is simply a named set of fonts and other typographic settings.

There are a number of ways of creating a style but the most direct is to use the Text,Text Style,Palette menu command.

If you use this command with a text object already selected you are taken straight to the Text Style Palette dialog box.

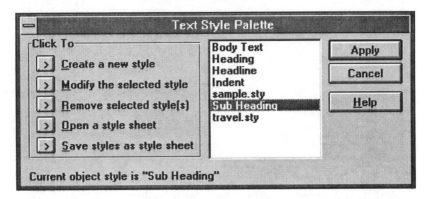

You can use this to remove or update an existing style or create a new one. Clicking on the Create a new style button displays an additional part to the dialog box, allowing you to define the new style by selecting specific property values. You can give a new name to the style and use the three buttons to define character, spacing and tab attributes.

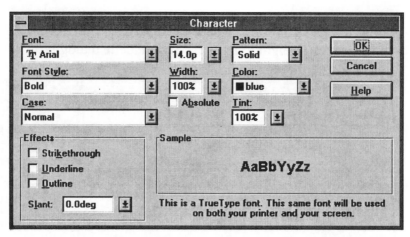

If you click on the Character attributes button the Character dialog box appears allowing you to select font, point size, bold, italic etc.. If you click on Spacing and Alignment then the Spacing dialog box, discussed in the previous chapter, opens allowing you to specify the remaining aspects of typography. Finally the Tabs and Indents button leads to the Tabs & Indents dialog box which was also discussed in the previous chapter.

Once you have a selection of styles defined they are saved along with the document. If you want to use the same set of styles in the future you can use the Save styles as style sheet button in the Text Style Palette dialog. A style sheet stores all of the styles that you have defined and can be read into any other document using the Open a style sheet button in the same dialog box. If you need to create documents that fit into a house style then it is vital that you make use of the style sheet facility to make a common set of styles available for any new document.

Notice that the styles defined in the style sheet are merged with whatever styles have already been defined in the document. You will be prompted before any existing styles are overwritten. If you make changes to a style sheet by saving an update then any documents that make use of the style sheet are not automatically updated. You have to re-load the modified style sheet for it to have any effect.

» Applying styles

The quickest way to apply a style is to select the Style icon from the Properties Palette and then select the style's name from the drop down list. You can also apply a style using the Text Style Palette dialog box by clicking on the Apply button.

Using WritePlus as your text processor has the advantage of allowing you to apply named styles to each paragraph. Simply select the one you want from the drop down list of styles. You can also see the current style applied to any paragraph listed at the side of the text.

» Updating and using styles

Applying a style is easy but there are number of less obvious considerations. The most important fact to keep in mind about styles is that if you alter the definition of a style all of the objects to which the style applies are also changed. This provides a very easy way to make global changes to a text layout. When you import a file without formatting into a frame every text block is assigned a style with the same name as the file but ending in .sty. If you import with formatting no style is applied. The properties assigned to the imported text are set using the Tools,Defaults,Text command. However, you can change the format of every text block either by assigning a new style or by updating the existing style.

If you want to update the existing style then all you have to do is select one of the text blocks and change its properties in the usual way. Each time you change a property you can update the style by clicking on the small tick icon that appears in the top right-hand corner of the ChangeBar. Clicking on this produces the AutoApply dialog box.

The AutoApply dialog box gives you three choices. You can decide to make the change you have made to the selected text object affect only that object without altering the style itself. Alternatively you can let the change affect not only the selected text object but all the others have the same style (i.e. update the style). Or you can keep both the original style and a new one by giving the altered style a name of its own.

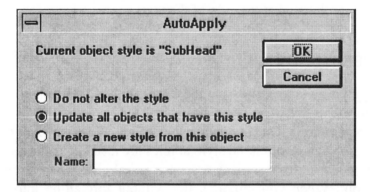

If you want to change more than one aspect of a style then it is easier to select an object that uses the style, change as many of the properties that you want to alter in the usual way, and then use the Text,Text Style,Update command. This displays a box which asks you to confirm that you want to proceed with updating the style to which you have made alterations, warning you that this will change all the other objects that use the same style.

To summarise:

» To change one aspect of a style edit an object that uses the style via the ChangeBar and click on the tick that appears in the top right-hand corner.

» To change a number of aspects of a style edit an object that uses the style and then use the command Text,Text Style,Update.

Alternatively,

» use the Text,Text Style,Palette command and define each property using the dialog boxes.

When working with frame text you are likely to make a great deal of use of all of these operations. It is generally a good idea to define styles for the main part of the text, traditionally called Body Text, and for each of the heading types. When the file is imported the first task is to substitute the Body Text style for the default style that it has been assigned. The next task is to assign the appropriate heading style to each of the heading lines. Only after this has been done should the properties of individual text items be changed to deviate from the applied styles where necessary.

If you make the maximum possible use of styles to control the typography then you will find it very easy to make sweeping changes throughout the layout, confident that the changes are made consistently.

» Managing pages

In many cases the extra pages needed in a multi-page document will be added automatically when you import text - however, there are still occasions when you will need to add pages manually. You can add, remove or jump straight to any

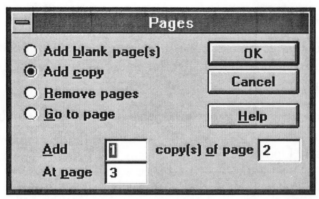

page using the Pages dialog box, which appears either when you double click on the page number box at the bottom of the screen or when you use the Page,Pages menu command.

You can use this to add or remove any number of pages from the document. How this works has already been discussed in connection with master pages but as well as adding blank pages you can also add complete copies of specific pages. Pages added as blanks simply have the same page size, margins and columns as the previous right or left page as appropriate.

If you opt to add a copy of the page then everything on the page - frames, graphics and, in some cases, text will be copied. Notice that if you make a full copy of a page that contains the first text frame in a linked chain then the text in the frame will be copied. If you choose to copy a page containing an intermediate frame in the chain then only the empty frame will be copied.

You can also use the Pages dialog box to go to any page in the document by referring to it by its number as an alternative to using the page movement buttons at the bottom of the screen.

» Templates

The best way to create a complex document like a folded booklet is to first set up the right and left master pages and a set of appropriate styles. Having gone to this much trouble it is clearly worth keeping the design so that it can be filled with text again and again. PagePlus allows you to do this by saving the document as a template. Simply use the command Save As and select Template in the dialog box. A template is saved along with all pages, styles, frames and defaults. You can use a template simply by loading it - use File,Open and select Template in the dialog box. You can then use the document in the normal way and when you save it you will be prompted for a name. A template is nothing more than a complete PagePlus document saved using a different naming scheme so that you are less likely to overwrite it and so lose it.

» Tour Four: a folded booklet

A common production method for a small booklet is to use a physical paper size twice as big as the desired page size. By turning the physical page on its side it is possible to print two of the smaller pages on each side of the larger sheets. Arranging pages on large sheets to make production easier and cheaper is called *imposition*. However, the layout of such a booklet is a good example of the ideas concerning frame text, autoflow, and styles introduced in this chapter.

The metric paper size A5 is obtained by folding a sheet of A4 in half and so it is an ideal booklet page size. However, if you want to print a booklet on Letter size paper 8.5 x 11 inches then all you have to do is enter a custom page of 5.5 x 4.25 inches. For this tour we will use a standard A5 page size.

As the booklet will be assembled by folding, the right and left margins have to be varied to keep a wider margin on the fold side of the page. This means we need to set up a right and left master page. If you are working with A5, or any metric page size, then it is better to work with a centimetre ruler. The reason is simply that most positions on the page will correspond to an exact division on this ruler and so the snap grid can be used. If you are working with a page size measured in inches then select an inch scale or inches divided into tenths. If you find that the snap grid seems to make it more difficult to position objects to the page boundaries then the chances are that you have used one system of measurements to set up the page and then changed to another for the rulers.

● If you are using the A5 metric page size use the command Tools,Preferences,General to select rulers graduated in centimetres or millimetres.

Once the rulers are correct for the page size you can define the layout for the the right and left page in one go by defining a pair of master pages with mirrored margins.

● Click on the page number box or use the command Page, Goto master page. Next double click anywhere on the

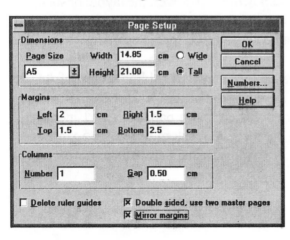 blank page to display the Page Setup dialog box for the Master Page. Select the page size and type in the margins as shown. Also click on the Double sided and Mirror margins boxes.

Notice that for the right master page the left margin is larger than the right margin. A margin of 1 cm is about as small a margin as it is safe to work with - most printing equipment cannot print any closer to the edge of the paper than this. If you examine the left master page you will see that, as expected, the right margin is larger.

Most booklets need some sort of page numbering and as PagePlus supports automatic page numbering it makes sense to define a page footer on each of the master pages.

● Goto the right master page by clicking on the arrows next to the page number text box. Click on the horizontal ruler to create vertical guides to extend the margins. Next click on the vertical ruler to create two horizontal guides just below the bottom margin.

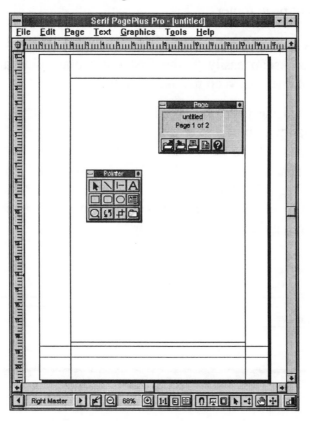

● Drag the guides to position them but make sure that snap is on. If you are using the A5 page size then the two horizontal guides should be set to 18.8 cm and 19.5 cm from the top of the page.

If you find the guides difficult to position then make sure you have the correct rulers showing and snap turned on. The guide closest to the bottom margin can be difficult to position because it is attracted to the margin guide. The solution to this problem is to zoom in on the bottom margin by clicking on the Zoom In button on the Status Bar. This allows you to move the guide closer to the bottom margin's position without it being snapped into place.

The next step is to add the text and a single ruling line to form the right page footer.

● The line can be drawn using the 45 degree line tool and it should snap easily to the first horizontal guide and be positioned between the margin guides.

● To add the text, click with the Text tool near the lower horizontal guide and enter

Page

● Next use the Text,Insert Page Number command. The page number will show as # while you are editing the text. Finally place the free text's bounding box between the margin guides below the ruling.

The page number footer text has the wrong format - it would be better in a sans-serif font like Arial and it needs to be right justified. Instead of simply modifying its format it is better to create a specific style.

● Select the text and using the ChangeBar set it to Arial 12 point, and right align it in the usual way.

● With the reformatted text still selected, use the Text,Text Style, Palette command and click on Create a new style in the dialog box that appears. This leads to an extended dialog box where you can type in the new style's name - RightFoot. Clicking on OK without making further changes means that it will be based on the current object.

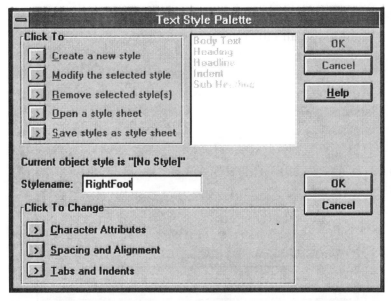

This completes the design of the right master page. Of course if you wanted a more elaborate page you could add a page header and any other embellishments - but notice that at this stage you should only add details that you want to appear on every right page.

Now it is time to create the left master page. The easiest way of doing this is to move a copy of the page number text onto the left master and then align it using suitable guides.

● Select the page number text on the right master page and use the command Edit,Copy to copy it to the clipboard.

● Move to the left master page by clicking on the left arrow next to the page number box. Use the command Edit,Paste to paste the page numbering text onto the left master page.

● Extend the page margins and add two horizontal guides as for the right master page. The horizontal guides should be set to exactly the same ruler positions. Draw the horizontal line and position the text's bounding box using the guides.

● The final adjustment is to change the text alignment from right to left and to create a new LeftFoot style. In this case it is easier to use the ChangeBar and to click on the tick that appears in its top right-hand corner. This displays the AutoApply dialog which you can use to create the new style.

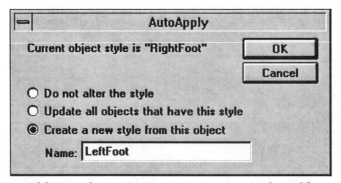

You could save these master pages as a template if you are likely to create many folded booklets using this page numbering style. In practice it would also be useful to save any text styles that you create as a booklet style sheet.

If you would like to see the right and left master
pages as they will appear when the booklet is
opened then select the facing pages view, either
by clicking on the facing pages icon or using
the command Page,Views,Facing Pages.

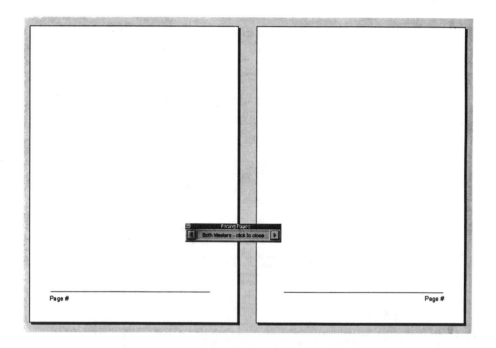

The next job is to leave the master pages and import some
text. You will notice that a text frame has not been included
on either of the master pages. It is a common mistake to think
that all the repeated elements of a page frame have to be
included on the master pages. In the case of the text frames
that will hold the imported text this would be a mistake. The
regular layout on each of the booklet's pages is going to be
achieved by allowing PagePlus to autoflow the imported text
into default page frames. Each default page frame takes its
layout from the margins and column guides on the right and
left pages as appropriate. This takes account of differences
between the right and left pages.

In this example we will load the readme file that is supplied with PagePlus - you should read the contents of this file anyway so turning it into a booklet is not a bad idea! This should be stored in the directory **\pp30\program** and it should be called **ppreadme.wri**. If you can't find this file then any text file, for example **sample.wri**, will do.

- Leave the master pages and select page one of the layout. You will find that you already have a right page one and a left page two in your layout.

- Use the command File,Import text and select the name of the text file you are going to import, i.e. **ppreadme.wri** in the **\pp30\program** directory.

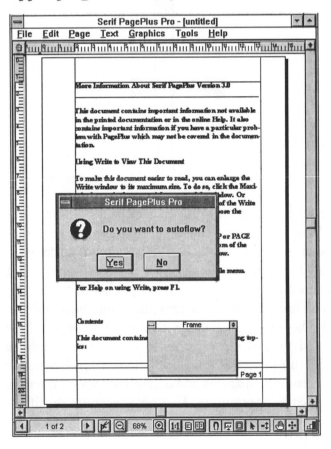

● PagePlus will create a default page frame on page 1 and then ask you if you want to autoflow the rest of the text. Answer Yes and repeat the answer when you are asked if you specifically want to flow the text onto page 2. After this you will see page after page created until you reach page 20.

At this point you will have 20 pages of autoflowed text with correctly laid out right and left pages complete with page numbers. Notice that a folded booklet has to have a total number of pages that is a multiple of four. The reason is that each A4 sheet that will be used can hold four A5 pages, two on each side. If after autoflowing you end up with a number of pages that isn't a multiple of four then you can adjust the paragraph styles and other details of the layout until you do have a multiple of four - or accept blank pages in your publication!

As long as the text was imported without formatting each block will have been assigned the style ppreadme.sty. This now needs to be modified

● Use the command Text,Text Style,Palette to modify the style ppreadme.sty to use 10 point Times Roman text with 120% spacing and space above set to 10%. Apply this to the text.

● The main heading is the first line of the text so apply the style Head (supplied by PagePlus itself) to this.

● Then go through the text and identify any block that should be a subheading and apply the style SubHead to it.

With these changes the booklet shrinks to 11 pages so remove all of the pages after page 12. You can modify the Head and SubHead style definitions to whatever you think suits the tone of the document - in this case the defaults are appropriate. If you look through the pages you will also find lines that have been added as rulings. These have been generated as part of the importing process. If you want to keep them you may have to reposition them. Alternatively you can just delete them. By working your way through the text you will find a number of additional types of paragraph style that you need. In particular, you will need a number of styles that use indents and tabs.

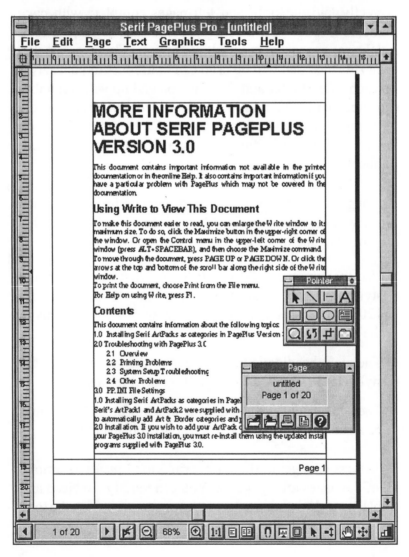

You can save the final result as BOOKLET.PPP. You also might like to save the styles as a booklet style sheet.

Of course for a real booklet you may want a different number of pages, you might want a front and back cover, embedded pictures, multiple columns etc. but you can achieve all of this using techniques discussed in this book.

» Printing the booklet

Now you have a completed 12 page booklet the next problem is to print it. There are two possible ways that you might want to print the booklet depending on how you are going to produce multiple copies of it. If you are going to send it to a print shop you will need to print each page onto a large sheet of paper - A4 is a good choice - complete with crop marks, file information etc.. The printer will take 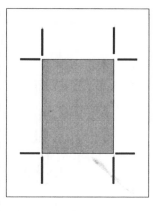 these masters and use them to put together a composite printing plate that prints a number of pages at a time. See Chapter 8 for more information.

The alternative is that you want to produce the booklet yourself in small numbers using your own laser or inkjet printer. In this case you have to print two A5 pages on a single sheet of A4 turned sideways into landscape mode. Notice that this isn't quite as simple as you might think because the order in which the pages have to be printed out is not page number order. For example, in the case of a four page booklet the first A4 page would have page 1 and page 4 and would be folded so that page 1 was on the outside front and 4 on the outside back. The second would have page 2 and page 3 and would be folded so that 2 was on the inside front and 3 on the inside back. To see why this is just think about how the paper pages are folded to give you the booklet.

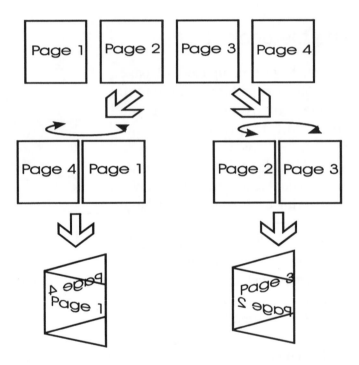

PagePlus will correctly print the pages onto sheets of paper that are twice as large. All you have to do is use the Print command and select A4 paper. Click on the Options button and select Print As Booklet in the Options dialog box that appears.

When you print the booklet the pages will come out in the correct order for folding. Unfortunately most printers only print on one side of the sheet at a time. To produce a booklet that you can fold you need to print page 1 and then, after turning the paper over and putting it back into the printer, you

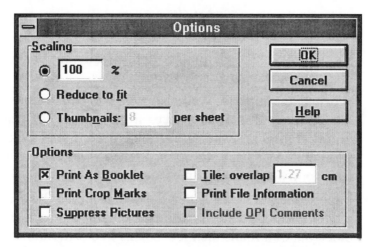

need to print page 2 and so on until the booklet is complete. You can select which page to print using the Print dialog box. Unfortunately there is no print all odd and then print all even option which is what you would really like. You may feel that printing each side of each sheet in turn is too much trouble in which case print each sheet once using only one side of the paper and use these as masters for photocopying.

» Going into production

If you want a long run of a booklet then you will need to take a step into the world of traditional printing methods. This is the subject of Chapter 8 where we look at how DTP interfaces with mass production printing methods.

Key points

» Frame text is used where a large amount of text has to be organised into columns or multiple pages.

» A frame has many of the same properties as a page, specifically columns, gutters and margins.

» You can create unequal columns and margins by dragging on the gutter and margin guides.

» When text is imported you can opt for it to be autoflowed into as many frames as it takes to hold all of the text. Empty frames on existing pages are used first and then additional pages and frames are added. You can create and modify a chain of frames manually.

» Imported text is stored within the document file. You can move blocks of text within a frame. If you drag a text block out of a frame then it becomes free text. Similarly if you drag free text into a frame it will be added to the text flow.

» Styles are the best way of controlling the formatting of text blocks.

» You can create a style from an existing object or define one by selecting all of the properties to be applied.

» Styles can be updated from existing objects.

» Each page in a document can be individually set up with regard to page size, margins, columns and gutters.

» You can copy any page with or without the objects it contains to create new pages.

» Master pages used in conjunction with default page frames make regular documents easy.

» Templates are documents, complete with empty pages and styles, that can be used as the basis for creating other documents.

Chapter 7

Graphics and OLE

Text may be the largest component of most documents but graphics are often the most noticeable. A failure to use graphics correctly can ruin an otherwise good layout. Fortunately graphics are in general a lot easier to control in PagePlus than text. One reason for this is simply that there are fewer things that you can do to them to alter their appearance! Another is that PagePlus also supports OLE (Object Linking and Embedding) which is an easy and convenient way of importing graphics so that the link to the package that created them is still maintained. OLE is very powerful - and is not restricted to graphics but lets you work with many external objects - but it does have practical limitations and you need to understand these to get the best from it.

» Types of graphics

Graphics are usually imported into PagePlus after being created using some other program. While PagePlus does have some good internal graphics tools they are really only suitable for simple designs, underlinings and boxes. If you want to include a picture or complex drawing then it will be created by some other package and imported - either directly or via OLE.

All graphic files fit into two broad categories - *bitmaps* (paint-type graphics) and *vectors* (draw-type graphics). The difference is the way in which the information relating to the artwork is stored. In a bitmap graphic the data is stored in a file by way of defining thousands, even millions, of pixels (small dots) that make up the artwork dot by dot, line by line. Each pixel is set to a particular colour and this is how the image is built up. Vector graphic files store information by way of defining what lines and shapes exist, where they are, how large they are, and what colour they are. You can think of a vector graphic file as being a list of instructions about how to draw the image.

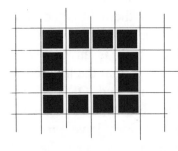

A bitmap representation of a square would be something like the drawing shown here. Of course in a real bitmap drawing there would be many more smaller dots.

A vector representation of a square would be something like: "Starting from a point 1 inch from the left and 1 inch down move and draw to the point 1 inch to the right. Next move and draw to a point one inch below, then move and draw to

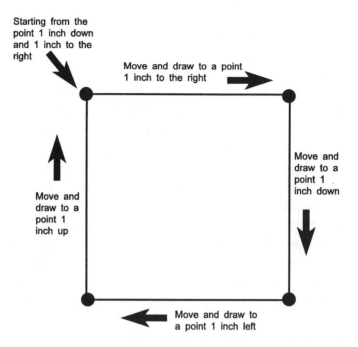

a point one inch to the left and finally to the point 1 inch up."
Notice that you cannot see the vector representation in the
same way that you can 'see' the bitmap. To make a vector
representation into a picture the instructions have to be
obeyed and a drawing created.

Once you recognise the essential difference between bitmap
and vector graphics you can easily appreciate their different
properties and behaviour. A bitmap graphic has to store the
state (i.e. colour) of thousands of pixels and this takes a lot
of space on disk and in memory. Also, the resolution of a
bitmapped graphic is more or less fixed to the number of dots
per inch (dpi) used to create it. You can scale bitmapped
graphics by adding or subtracting dots but this is a tricky
business and the result can look very poor. By contrast, vector
graphics take very little space to store and they can be scaled

simply by redrawing the picture using as many dots as required.

This makes it sound as if vector graphics are the obvious choice but they have their limitations. You cannot scan in a photograph or drawing as a vector because this would imply that it was converted to a set of instructions to draw the picture. There are tracing packages which can convert a bitmap to a vector representation but they don't work very well and need a lot of human intervention. Vector formats are slow to display because they have to draw the picture whereas bitmaps can simply be read in ready for display. Vector formats are also more complicated and this means that they often don't display as expected. Bitmaps, being simple, are more robust as long as you use them with understanding. Notice that it is quite easy to convert a vector format to a bitmap of a specified resolution but, as already discussed, conversion in the other direction is much more difficult.

To summarise:

» Bitmapped graphics take a lot of storage space and cannot be easily scaled without loss of fidelity.

» Vector graphics take very little space and they can be scaled very easily.

» Bitmapped graphics are robust and can represent pictures that are scanned in.

» Vector formats tend to be temperamental and they are really only suitable for artwork drawn using the computer.

There are programs that can be used to create vector or bitmapped graphics. Bitmap based programs tend to be called painting programs and vector based programs are called drawing packages. However, this naming convention isn't hard and fast. A bitmap painting program is included with Windows - Paintbrush - but there is no standard drawing package supplied.

» Graphics file formats

There are a great many graphics types or *formats* used by different applications but only a much smaller number can claim to be standard and not all of these work very well! PagePlus 3 can export and import a graphic using any of the following formats:

Windows Metafile (.WMF)
Windows Bitmap (.BMP)
Encapsulated PostScript file (.EPS)
Computer Graphics Metafile (.CGM)
Tagged Image File format (.TIF)
JPEG compressed (.JPG)
AutoCAD (.DXF)
Corel Draw (.CDR)
Draw (.DRW)
Graphics Interchange Format (.GIF)
Photo CD (.PCD)
Targa (.TGA)
WordPerfect graphics (.WPG)
Paintbrush (.PCX)

Each one of these has its advantages and disadvantages and so if you have a choice it is worth knowing something of their characteristics. However, in many cases you will not have a choice as the graphic will be supplied in only one format! Some of these formats are standard in the sense that they are used by many different programs. Some are proprietary and used only by one or two applications.

Each of the standard formats has a number of variations that are used either for special purposes or by particular applications - these varieties are usually referred to as *flavours*. What this means is that in some cases the only way to discover if an application will work with PagePlus is to try it out.

There are six vector formats supported by PagePlus. Three of these are standard and widely supported:

>> WMF - vector

Windows MetaFile format is the native vector format used by Windows. Its main advantages are that it can be cut, copied and pasted via the Clipboard from one application to another - and it tends to work! For simple drawings it is always the best choice. However, WMF is a fairly primitive vector format and it does sometimes fail to work properly if the drawing is very complex. WMF also has the advantage of being very standardised.

>> CGM - vector

The Computer Graphics Metafile standard is supposed to be internationally defined - but the specification is so vague that different applications implement many different flavours of CGM. It works well only for simple images and where you have verified that the specific application's CGM files can be read correctly by PagePlus.

>> EPS - vector and bitmapped

Encapsulated PostScript format uses the PostScript language stored in a file. EPS files will only print on a PostScript printer but they are very robust and generally work. You cannot see an EPS file on the screen so to allow the graphic to be positioned a low resolution (TIF) bitmap is generally included in the file header. It is this low resolution bitmap image which displays on the screen and which is used to print to a non-PostScript printer. If an EPS file doesn't have a bitmap header then it will show on the screen and print on non-PostScript printers as a cross. EPS files can include high resolution bitmapped images but it is more common to use EPS for vector drawings. Unless you are using a PostScript printer or sending output to a bureau don't use EPS format.

Three of the vector formats are proprietary but they are very important because of the widespread use of the products that they belong to - Corel Draw, AutoCAD and Micrografx Draw:

》 CDR - vector

This is the native format used by Corel Draw, a well known illustration package. Corel Draw is available in a number of different versions. At the time of writing the latest version is Corel 5 which was released just before PagePlus 3. As a consequence PagePlus will only read files created by Corel Draw 4 or earlier. If you are using Corel Draw 5 then the solution is to save your drawings in Corel Draw 4 format - an option you can select in the Save File dialog box.

Corel Draw is a very complex package that is capable of producing very sophisticated effects. Indeed often they are so complex that printing them out proves to be a problem! Don't expect PagePlus, or any other program for that matter, to cope with the full complexity that Corel Draw could throw at them. It should work with reasonably simple drawings.

》 DXF - vector

DXF is the native format used by AutoCAD, the most commonly used design package. It has also been adopted by most of its competitors in the drafting/design world. DXF is reasonably well defined and you should have few problems with it. Notice, however, that it is a fairly simple drawing format and not really suitable for general illustrations.

» DRW - vector

This is the native format used by Micrografx Designer and its related products. It is a complex format not unlike CDR but overall it is more stable and tends to work. Again, you can really only expect it to work well for simple drawings.

There are eight bitmapped formats supported by PagePlus and six of these are widely used standards:

» BMP - bitmap

Windows BitMaPs are Windows own native format for bitmapped images, just as WMF is the format for vector drawings. A BMP image can be transferred between applications using the Clipboard. BMP is a fairly limited format but PagePlus uses it to good effect and, in general, it is faster to import a BMP image than any other format.

» TIF - bitmap

Tagged Image Format is the closest thing to a workable standard for bitmaps that exists. Unfortunately there are a rather a large number of TIF formats and it is a complex and sophisticated standard. The common flavours of TIF are - Class B - black and white images, Class G - grey scale images, Class P - colour images using a palette of up to 256 colours, and Class R - TrueColor RGB images giving photographic quality. As well as these basic types there are also a number of different forms of data compression that can be used to reduce the amount of space the file takes to store. The only compression options in common use are no compression, LZW or packbits compression and PagePlus seems to support all three formats.

It isn't possible to test PagePlus with all possible flavours of TIF file and all possible compression schemes but in principle it will read G, P and R formats with or without compression.

» PCX - bitmap

PCX is one of the oldest and most common bitmap formats used on the PC. PCX files are stored using the extension PCX or occasionally PCC. The format has developed over the years and there are a number of versions in current use. Version 2.5 is the oldest and uses a fixed set of 16 colours. Version 2.8 allows the 16 colours to be picked from a larger set. Version 3.0 allows 256 colours to be picked from a larger set. The very latest PCX format works with 24-bit TrueColor images - which are of photographic quality. In tests PagePlus appears to work with all types of PCX files including 24-bit TrueColor - but, as is always the case, its success depends on the application which created the PCX file.

» GIF - bitmap

This is a standard file format used to transmit images over telephone lines. It was introduced by the CompuServe network and it has the advantage of being simple and well defined. Its limitation is that it is restricted to 256 colours selected from a larger set. In practice GIF tends to work reliably and it makes a good interchange format.

» PCD - bitmap

Kodak's Photo CD process takes standard 35mm colour film and converts it into digitised files stored on CD-ROM. The format used is PCD. An image stored in PCD format can be read at a number of different resolutions ranging from a tiny thumbnail image that can be used to scan through libraries of images to a large full colour format that can be used in high quality publishing. The Photo CD format is rapidly becoming the standard for image libraries issued on CD. The standard is well defined, has no variations to cause problems, and tends to work reliably.

» JPG - bitmap

JPG is a format defined by the Joint Photographic Experts Group (JPEG) and it addresses a different problem to the other image formats described. JPG attempts to store an image using as little disk space as possible without noticeable loss of quality. An image stored in JPG format can take ten times less storage than one stored in TIF or PCX format and looks just as good in use. The only problem is that reading in a JPG image can be slow. As it is well defined and has no variations it tends to work reliably.

There are also two less common proprietary formats:

» TGA - bitmap

This is a format introduced by a video card manufacturer - Targa - to allow the storage of true colour images. Today there are better and more widely supported true colour image formats.

» WPG - bitmap

This is the native format used by the WordPerfect suite of programs. Its main advantage is that there are large clipart libraries available in this format targeted at WordPerfect users. It is a simple format that tends to work.

» Which format?

This wide range of file formats is bewildering and in practice the only way to discover if one application can save a file in the correct format for PagePlus is to try it and see. In general, for vector images you should use WMF or, if you are working with a PostScript printer, EPS format. For bitmaps use BMP format for simple images and either TIF or PCX for scanned images. Of course you may not have a choice if the graphics are supplied in a given format. For example, if you are using a Photo CD library then you will naturally use PCD format.

It is a good idea to choose a drawing and painting package to work with PagePlus and try to use them as a team. Discover which formats work by trial and error. If you find that using a particular facility results in an imported image that doesn't look right or crashes the system then avoid using that feature. Slowly you will learn what works and what doesn't and you will be able to avoid much of the frustration of the graphics file format muddle we find ourselves in.

Perhaps the most important advice is:

» Always save a PagePlus document before importing a picture. Although it is rare PagePlus can crash even while you are just browsing the picture files that are available.

» Importing pictures

Importing a picture is simplicity itself. One route is to use the File,Import Picture menu command in which case you may see the Picture Assistant, although this can be disabled if you prefer.

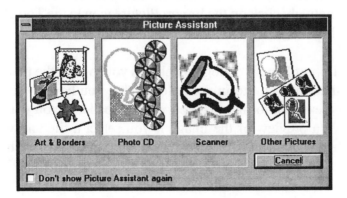

The Photo CD and Scanner buttons in the Picture Assistant are simply short cut ways of reading in a Photo CD file or activating a TWAIN scanner that is connected to your machine. For more details of scanning see Chapter 8. Here we are concerned with the other two buttons.

If you click on Art & Borders then you will see the Art & Borders dialog box. Art and borders are just pictures stored in a special menu for your convenience when you install PagePlus. Working with art and borders is exactly the same as for standard pictures. They are nothing more than images stored in .WMF format but in a special location and with an easy to use classification that helps you find what you are looking for.

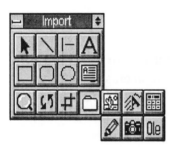

If you have followed the tours in the earlier chapters you will already be familiar with another route to the Art & Borders dialog box, which is to click on the Import Picture icon in the ToolBox and then double click on the first icon in the flyout, the Art & Borders icon.

Similarly there are two routes to the Import Picture dialog box. After using the File,Import Picture command click on the Other Pictures button in the Picture Assistant. Alternatively click on the Import Picture icon in the ToolBox and then single click on the Art & Borders icon.

The Import Picture dialog box allows you to pick the picture file that you want to import. Notice that you have to select the type of file format that you want to load and you will be shown a preview of the image if you select a file and wait while PagePlus performs any conversions necessary to show

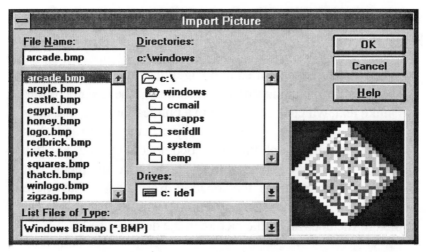

it. The preview option is very useful but it can also be a problem. If you click on an image accidentally and then pause for a moment you could have a very long wait while it is converted for preview. Another danger is that if you accidentally click on a damaged or incompatible image file then PagePlus can crash trying to prepare the preview. The safest way of avoiding the preview is to locate the file that you want and then double click on its name. This is equivalent to clicking on the file to select it and then clicking on OK to load it.

Once the file has been selected PagePlus usually takes a few moments to convert the file into a suitable form. This delay can be a few minutes for a large colour image. After this is over the cursor changes to a cross-hair and you can place the picture on the page. You can do this in one of two ways. You can drag using the cross-hair to create a bounding box for the picture to fit into or you can simply click at the intended location and allow PagePlus to size the image for you. Of course once the picture is placed on the page you can move and resize its bounding box in the usual way - so the initial placement isn't final.

» Picture links

When a picture is imported into PagePlus, information relating to where the picture is stored is recorded in the document file. Unlike text, which is stored within a publication, a picture does not normally become a permanent object in the design and it has to be re-imported each time the document is opened. For this reason, you must be sure not to delete or move any pictures in your publication from the location from which they were originally imported. Also any editing you do to the original picture file does affect the picture in the document.

You can store a picture as part of a PagePlus document by inserting it as an OLE object. Whether a picture is linked or embedded is determined by the Tools,Preferences,Picture command. This displays the Picture Preferences dialog box.

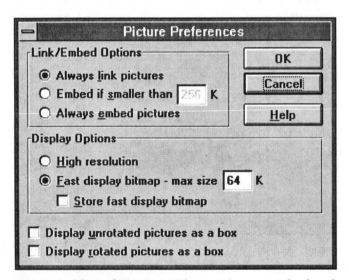

You can use this to force PagePlus to always embed a picture or embed it only if the file is smaller than a specified size. Of course the main problem with embedding a picture is that it increases the size of the document and for this reason you may not want to embed large picture files.

If a publication file is opened and a picture cannot be found, because it has been moved or deleted, you will be prompted to redefine the location or filename to be used. You can discover which picture files a document is using via the menu command Tools,Fonts & Pictures.

» Picture size

Changing the size of a picture is a very easy operation but unless you understand how picture size affects the final printed result then you are likely to be disappointed. How images behave when you scale them depends on their type - vector or bitmapped.

If you have imported a drawing in vector format, e.g. EPS, WMF or CGM, then sizing has little effect, except perhaps to introduce distortions due to a change in aspect ratio (height to width). The biggest problem with scaling a vector drawing is to do with line widths. If the drawing uses very fine lines and you print it to a 300 dpi laser printer the lines may be too narrow for the printer to resolve. In the case of a vector drawing a line is never lost because it is too narrow - it is simply printed at the narrowest that the printer can manage. This can make very fine lines look thicker than they actually are in the drawing. What is worse, when the drawing is printed for final production on a higher resolution printer the lines that were reasonably thick in the low resolution proofs suddenly become vanishingly thin because the output device can render them correctly.

Fine lines are a problem in vector drawings but if you are using a bitmap format, i.e. BMP, PCX or TIF, then you have to be much more careful. The problem is that when the bitmap is printed its image has to be built up using dots. The number of dots available depends on the resolution of the printer and ranges from 75 dots per inch (dpi) for a low resolution dot matrix printer to between 300 and 600 dpi for a laser printer and 1200 dpi or more for an imagesetter.

When the bitmap is printed its resolution has to be converted to the resolution of the output device. This is discussed more fully in the next chapter but what it is important to realise at this stage is that the ratio of the image and the printer resolution is an important factor in output quality. For example, if the picture is 150 dpi and the printer is 300 dpi four printer dots will be used to make up one single picture dot. For some types of picture it is important to keep the printer resolution an exact multiple of the picture resolution. For example, if you are working with a 300 dpi printer then acceptable picture resolutions are 300, 150, 100, 75 dpi and so on but not arbitrary resolutions such as 173 dpi. How crucial this is depends on the type of image that you are working with. It is vital for black and white images and dithered grey level images (see Chapter 8) but not important for true grey level or coloured images.

In practice the only way to make sure that you haven't resized a picture inappropriately is to print it out at and look at the result. If there is a banding - called a *moiré pattern* - then you should change the size of the image.

To help you keep a picture to multiples of the printer resolution you can use a constrained sizing. Select one of the corner handles of the image and start to drag it to resize the image. Once you have started the resize operation, press and hold the Ctrl key. This constrains the picture size to give exact ratios of the currently selected printer resolution. Notice that if you press the Ctrl key before you start to drag the handle, you simply copy the image instead of resizing it. Using this method you will find that there is a smallest size that you can make the picture. This corresponds to the point where the picture resolution matches the printer resolution.

If you want to constrain picture resizing so that the height and width of the image are kept in proportion begin dragging the corner handle and then hold down the Shift key. Notice that you can also rotate and reflect any picture. In some cases the rotation operation can introduce distortions.

Once again it is worth pointing out that you do not have to match printer and picture resolution if you are working with vector format drawings or true grey level images. However, the only test to see if scaling an image has introduced patterning or other artefacts is to look at a proof print. What is important is that you know that slight changes in image size can result in large changes in image quality.

» Cropping

When you import a picture you can think of its bounding box as a frame that is used to determine its size and position in the page. Normally when you drag or resize the bounding box the picture is moved or resized to fit it. However, sometimes you need to alter an image so that only part of it shows in the bounding box. This is generally referred to as *cropping* the image.

You can crop an image in PagePlus by using the Crop tool. This works much like the usual selection tool but when you alter the size of the bounding box using this tool the picture is not resized to fit it.

This provides a way of changing the size of the bounding box to show only part of the whole picture. To determine which part of the whole picture is on display drag the picture using the crop tool. This gives the user the impression of dragging the image behind the bounding box - rather like sliding a photo around inside a frame. Notice that you cannot drag the bounding box to a new position using the crop tool.

The crop tool can be used on text objects - although its usefulness in this respect is limited. If you resize the bounding box of free text using it you can then move the text around to show only a given portion.

» Controlling graphics

As well as importing pictures, you can also use PagePlus's tools to draw simple graphics objects - boxes, circles and lines. Controlling the way that these display and print is just a matter of assigning properties to them using the ChangeBar and the Properties Palette as described in previous chapters. However, you can control the graphics properties more directly using dialog boxes and you can create graphics styles that group graphics properties in the same way that text styles group text properties.

All graphics objects have two sets of properties - fill and line. The command Graphics,Fill displays the Fill dialog box which you can use to set all of the fill properties.

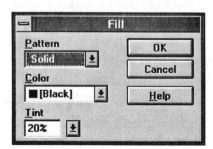

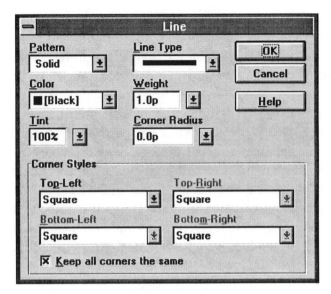

Similarly the command Graphics,Line displays a dialog in which you can set all the properties of lines.

The line and fill properties control everything relevant to the way a graphics object looks, except of course its size and position. You can group line and fill properties into named styles which can then be applied to a graphics object with one command. To create or modify a graphics style simply use the menu command Graphics,Graphic Style,Palette. This displays a menu which can be use to create or modify a named style.

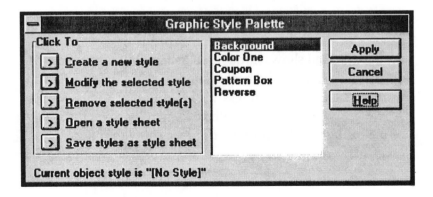

The shortcut way of getting to the Graphic Style Palette dialog is to double click on the Styles icon in the Properties Palette when a graphics object is selected.

The Graphic Style Palette works in exactly the same way as the Text Style Palette except that you can only set fill and line styles via the Line and Fill dialog boxes discussed earlier. You can also create or modify graphics styles by clicking on the tick icon that appears in the corner of the ChangeBar after you change any graphics property. If you use graphics styles in the same way as text styles you should have no problems. Notice that graphics styles are saved in style sheets and merged when you load a style sheet.

» Picture frames

The frame that surrounds a picture can be assigned a range of graphics properties. It behaves as if it was a graphics rectangle in the sense that you can set its fill colour, line colour, fill tint, line type etc.. You can do all of this using the ChangeBar and Properties Palette in the usual way. However, as the picture overlays the frame exactly in most cases you will not see any effect of changing the frame's line or fill properties.

The frame acts as a background to the picture and what you can see of the fill that you assign depends on how much of the background shows through. In general bitmapped images do not allow any of the background to show through and so in most cases it is pointless to try to colour them. Vector drawings, on the other hand, do not generally cover the whole of the background and so the fill does show through.

In the case of bitmapped images there is a way to allow the background to show and that is to set a border using the command Graphics,Picture - or by double clicking on the information icon in the Properties Palette. This displays the Picture dialog box which allows you to control many aspects of the way a picture is displayed.

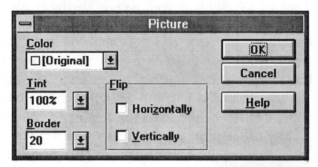

By increasing the border percentage, the background colour, fill, pattern and tint become visible. You can also add special effects by setting the colour, density and type of the line surrounding the picture. Notice that if you select a line colour, tint, type and line pattern the line might still not show unless you also select a non-zero line weight! The final touch is to round the corners of the frame.

Notice that setting properties for a picture frame is exactly the same as setting properties on any of the graphics objects, square, rectangle, circle, etc., that you can create with PagePlus's own tools. You can also draw extra lines and shapes to augment an imported picture. In this case you might have to determine which object is in front of another - see later.

» Colour control

As well as being able to set the background colour of the frame, you can also set its foreground colour. If you select the foreground colour of an imported graphics object then exactly what happens depends on the type of the image - as in the case of the frame colour. The principle is that each colour used in the picture is converted to a brightness value and then this is used to set the foreground colour. In the case of grey scale pictures this results in the black portion of black and white images being converted into whatever colour you select. In the case of colour images all of the colours are replaced by a shade of the selected foreground colour. The simplest way to see what this looks like is to actually try it. To set the foreground colour of a picture use the command Graphics,Picture which displays the Picture dialog box.

You can also set the colour and tint directly using two commands that are only available at Professional level, Graphics,Picture,Color and Graphics,Picture,Shading or by clicking on the equivalent icons in the Properties Palette. Picture Color is on the left and Picture Shade is on the right.

You can use the foreground colour setting in conjunction with a background colour for special effects. In most cases it is a matter of trial and error to see what the overall effect is. This said, there is one important use for the foreground and background colour settings used with pictures and this is to set spot colours, see Chapter 9.

In the case of vector drawings the control of colour extends beyond setting a foreground and frame colour as you can actually set any colour used in the drawing to any colour you can use in PagePlus. If you use the command Tools,Color Mapper while a vector drawing is selected you will see the Color Mapper dialog box.

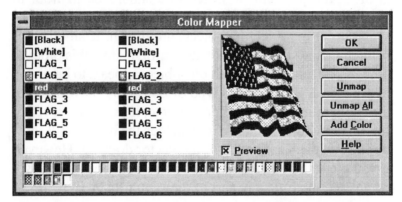

While the Color Mapper can be used to create artistic effects, its main purpose is in controlling colour in spot colour printing. This is explained, along with other matters of colour management, in Chapter 8.

To summarise:

» A picture's frame has line and fill properties just as if it was a box graphic.

» Bitmaps do not allow the frame to show through so its fill and line properties are only visible if you set a border size greater than 0%. You can alter the foreground colour of a bitmap.

» Vector drawings do allow the frame to show through and so adjusting the fill colour allows you to modify the picture's background colour as well as foreground colour.

» You can reassign every colour in an imported vector drawing using the Color Mapper.

» In front and behind

When you are working with multiple graphics objects there is often the problem of which one should be in front of another. This idea of in front or behind simply corresponds to the order in which the objects are drawn. If an object is behind another then it will be drawn first. How this order of drawing affects the way that one object appears to be on top of another depends on the type of object and how much of the background it leaves. For example, if you place a vector format drawing in front of a bitmap then the bitmap will show through as the background of the vector drawing. However, if you place the bitmap in front of the vector the bitmap will completely obscure any part of the vector that it overlaps.

As graphics objects are drawn in the order in which they are created, an object you are just creating will be in front of all other objects already on the page. To change the order you simply select an object and use the Send to back or Bring to front icons that appear when you click on the Wrap Palette

 icon in the ChangeBar. Alternatively you could use the Edit,Arrange menu command.

If you are only trying to arrange a pair of graphics objects then selecting one of them and sending it to the back or front usually is sufficient. However, if you are trying to arrange a set of three or more overlapping objects it may be necessary to select each one in turn and send it to the back in order to establish the order in which they should be drawn.

» Alignment

In most cases it is sufficient to use guides to align objects but occasionally it is worth knowing that PagePlus has an alignment command that will align any number of objects. Having selected a number of objects that you want to align, use the Edit,Align Items command (again only available at Professional level) which displays the Align Items dialog box.

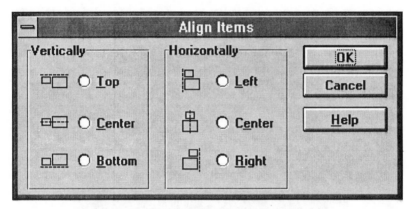

You can then select a horizontal and/or vertical alignment for the whole group. Notice that it is the bounding box of each object which is aligned. You can use this to align a group of objects after placing one of them accurately.

» Wrap

A page layout is determined by the way text flows in frames and by how it avoids or runs over picture items and even other text objects. This is controlled by the Wrap icons in the ChangeBar. If you select an object and then click on the first wrap icon, text will not avoid it. If you select the second wrap icon then a wrap outline appears. Any text that overlaps with the object will avoid its wrap outline.

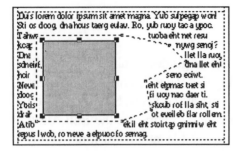

You can edit the wrap outline by dragging its handles or nodes to produce the shape that you require. You can add extra nodes by clicking on the wrap outline.

New in PagePlus 3 is the ability to select between an external or an internal wrap. You can also opt for the wrap outline to be made to follow the outline of a picture as closely as possible. How well this works depends on how much contrast the picture has. What you can rely on is that any picture that consists of a shape on a white background will give a very close wrap outline. You can control the type of wrap outline that PagePlus generates using the Tools,Wrap command which make the Wrap Settings dialog box appear.

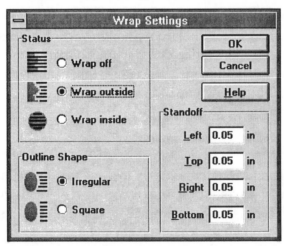

By selecting the appropriate options you can set wrap off or on, and define internal or external and regular versus irregular wrap outlines. Also notice that the Wrap Settings dialog box allows you to set the Standoff. This is the initial distance between the object's bounding box and the wrap outline that appears. You can set this to ensure that text automatically keeps a minimum distance from an object. The Standoff settings also control how close an irregular wrap outline approaches the picture object's boundary.

You can set Wrap on for any object including text but text also has an additional wrap property as text is the object that actually does the avoiding! Each text block can be told either to ignore or to avoid an object's wrap outline. By default text blocks are set to wrap but if you select a text block and click on the Wrap off icon then the text block will not wrap around any object, even if it has wrap on.

》 Text wrapping is an interaction between two objects - the object that has the wrap outline defined and the text block which will take notice or ignore the wrap outline.

If you use the Tools,Wrap command while a text object is selected you will see a slightly different version of the dialog box. In this case the additional choice is to select Text will wrap or not. Also notice that the wrap icons in the ToolBar change their meaning depending on whether or not a text object is selected. If a text object is selected they set the Text will wrap

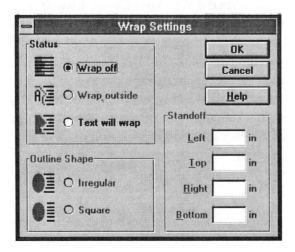

property instead of Wrap on/off. Notice that this means that to set wrap on for a text object, i.e. to make other text avoid it, you have to use the Tools,Wrap Settings menu command.

It is very easy to use text wrapping to create imaginative and well integrated layouts. You can even use invisible graphics objects to force text into particular shapes. Simply draw a rectangle, set its line thickness to 0p, its fill colour to clear and switch wrap on and you have a wrap outline that can be used to shape text but without any visible graphics object involved. See Chapter 10 for an example of text wrap in action.

Perhaps the most important thing to realise and remember about text wrap is that it can be applied to any object that you can place on the page. You can define a text wrap for any picture, any imported OLE object including tables (see the next section), for free text and even around frame text. However, remember that you can only set wrap on for a text object using the Tools,Wrap Settings menu command.

» OLE and the Clipboard

OLE can be used via the Windows Clipboard to insert objects created by other applications into layouts. Using the Clipboard to transfer objects between applications is quite easy. All you have to do is start the other application, select the data or object to be transferred, and use the command Edit,Copy. Nearly all Windows applications have this menu command. This transfers the object to the Clipboard. Next you go back to PagePlus and use the command Edit,Paste or Edit,Paste Special.

The difference between these two commands is that Edit,Paste inserts the object on the Clipboard as data while Edit,Paste Special can be used to insert it as an OLE object. To understand the distinction we will have to look a little more closely at how an OLE object behaves.

An OLE object has many of the properties of a standard PagePlus object. It has a bounding box, an optional wrap frame and it can have a range of graphics properties assigned to it - fill colour, line type etc.. The difference between it and other objects is that PagePlus cannot edit its contents. The reason is simply that the contents of an OLE object belong to another application and PagePlus only knows enough about them to display the object, not to edit it.

If you want to edit an OLE object it is necessary to return to the application that created it. To do this all you have to do is double click on the object or use the Edit,Object command with the object selected. After a few moments' wait while the application is started you will see its menu and window with the object already loaded for editing. Once you have finished, selecting File,Update or File,Exit returns you to PagePlus.

In other words, an OLE object has a link between it and the application that created it. If you choose to paste data into PagePlus not as an OLE object then the data is simply inserted as a standard internal PagePlus object. Of course this isn't always possible and in some cases PagePlus will insist on pasting an OLE object. Even if you use Paste Special you will be offered a choice of pasting in the object from the Clipboard as an OLE object or as a simpler type of data.

The main problem with OLE when used with other applications is that the level of implementation varies widely. For example, you can copy a section of an Excel spreadsheet

and paste it into PagePlus as an OLE object but it displays as
unformatted text. You can paste an entire spreadsheet and in
this case it displays as a bitmap picture. The only way of
discovering if OLE is a useful way of transferring data
between an application and PagePlus is to try it and see.

 If you want to create an OLE object from scratch
then you can use the command Edit,Insert Object
or click on the OLE Icon in the toolbox which
displays the Insert Object dialog box.

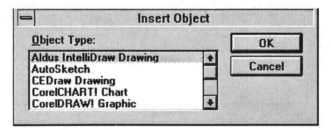

All of the OLE supporting applications installed on your
system are listed here. When you select one of these the
application is started. When you have finished creating the
object exiting the application returns you to PagePlus and the
object will be placed on the page.

Notice that you can use OLE to embed graphics files within
a PagePlus document so that you don't have to worry about
keeping track of the necessary files. In general it isn't possible
to load existing files into an OLE object that you have created
using the Insert Object command - but it can be done using
a different method.

To embed an existing graphics file simply load it into the
application that created it, select all of it and copy it to the
Clipboard. Then transfer back to PagePlus and use the
Edit,Paste Special command to paste the graphic as an OLE

object. After this you can edit the OLE graphic by double clicking on it. Of course, there is no connection between the OLE object and the original file used to create it. Some applications, such as Paintbrush, do have commands that allow you to load a file into a new OLE object and in this case you can use the Insert OLE object command. You will find an example of using OLE in this way in the next tour.

OLE is also used with all the Serif mini-applications. In other words, it is used to embed tables created using TablePlus, pictures created using DrawPlus and PhotoPlus, and word art created using TypePlus. These work in  exactly the same way as general OLE objects, the only real difference being that you can insert them by clicking on the special icons in the toolbox. All OLE objects are external to PagePlus and this sometimes causes difficulty with colour matching and spot colour printing in particular. Most of these problems can be solved using PagePlus 3's Color Mapper, see Chapter 8.

You can also copy the entire Windows desktop to the Clipboard by pressing the Print Screen button on your keyboard. Individual windows can also be copied to the Clipboard by pressing Alt-Print Screen which copies the current window.

You can also use the Clipboard to apply a particular format to an object already in PagePlus. For example, if you copy a text object to the Clipboard, you can apply its style (range of properties) to other text objects by selecting the text object to be changed and then selecting Edit,Paste Format.

» Graphics sources

One of the main problems confronting DTP users is where to get good quality artwork from. In the main there are only three sources of good artwork. You can scan in photos or illustrations, you can draw your own, or you can use clipart.

Clipart is the term used to describe pieces of artwork, either scanned images or created in a graphics package, which are stored as graphics files ready for use. There is a variety of clipart available for the PC, some in colour and some in black and white, and in many file types. The PagePlus ArtPack contains 500 pieces of clipart in the Windows Metafile format. The PhotoPack provides a range of images in Photo CD format. Other applications that you already have - drawing packages, word processors and even spreadsheets - may have clipart bundled with them, and of course you can buy clipart on its own. Check adverts in the computer press for clipart suppliers if you are searching for a specific piece of artwork. Using PagePlus, and many other packages, clipart can often be modified to suit your needs, by cropping, rotating, framing, etc.. In most cases it needs to be customised by editing using a suitable graphics package.

» Using external graphics packages

It is possible that you might be able to do everything you want using nothing but PagePlus and Paintbrush. However, most DTP users find that a more advanced graphics package is needed. If you are using mainly screen captures and scanned images then you need an image editor such as Serif's PhotoPlus. This allows you to convert from one graphics format to another, perform picture corrections such as adjusting colour, brightness and contrast and create photo effects. If you want to combine these facilities with those of a full painting package consider programs such as PhotoStyler and Photoshop, the market leaders, or PhotoFinish which is a good budget package which works well with PagePlus.

If you want to originate sketches, plans or illustrations you need a vector drawing package. Choosing one is difficult because of their relatively high price and the large range that is available. The market leader is Corel Draw 5 and its earlier versions, Draw 3 and Draw 4 are also available at a lower cost. This package comes with a customised version of PhotoFinish, so it serves as a drawing and a painting package. Its drawbacks are that it is a very big program - running it from CD-ROM is advisable - and some of its more advanced features do not always work reliably. If you are looking for a budget drawing package Serif's DrawPlus is well worth considering. It is easy to use with PagePlus and includes some advanced features such as gradient fills.

It is worth knowing that you can use PagePlus to create vector and bitmap graphics using its File,Export as Picture command, as explained in Tour Five.

» Tour Five: an OLE graphics object

The aim of this tour is to produce a logo for use on letterheads, invoices and other company stationery or for incorporating into quotes, flyers, adverts and so on. It demonstrates the idea of using other software in conjunction with PagePlus 3.

Before you begin on the tour itself start Paintbrush and use the command Options,Image Attributes to set a default size of image of 640 by 480 pels (i.e. pixels). Then start PagePlus or, if you are already using it with a document on the screen, save your work and select File,New to begin a new design.

The size of the page and its margins, etc. are of no great importance for this particular design as the page is merely used as a design pasteboard for the business logo, to be used in other documents rather than as a finished layout. You can therefore accept the page set-up defaults.

It is helpful for this design, however, to position a vertical guide on the page, approximately 4 inches from the left of the page (3 inches from the margin). This partitions off a narrow area to be used for the logo.

» Opening another package using OLE

As discussed earlier in this chapter, PagePlus's OLE feature allows you to share objects with other OLE supporting packages. In this tour we will use Paintbrush - the standard Windows bitmap editor - to place an existing bitmap graphic file on the page.

● To access Paintbrush from PagePlus using OLE, select the Import picture tool and then click on the OLE icon from the flyout that appears. The Insert Object dialog then opens.

Insert Object	
Object Type:	OK
Microsoft Graph	Cancel
Package	
Paintbrush Picture	
Serif TableEdit	
Serif TypePlus	

● Select Paintbrush Picture from the Insert Object dialog and click on OK. The cursor then becomes a cross-hair indicating that it is ready to paste an object. Click near to the top left margin of your page to indicate where you want the OLE object to be pasted. Paintbrush then automatically opens ready for use.

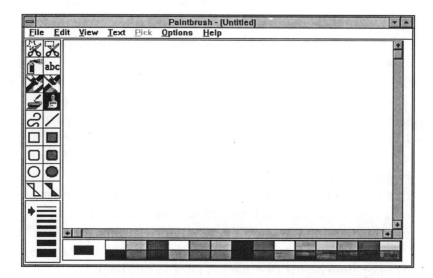

● From the Paintbrush menus at the top of the window select Edit,Paste From. The Paste From dialog then opens allowing you to import an object into Paintbrush.

Other applications may not have a command equivalent to Edit,Paste From and in this case you would need to transfer the existing file to the Clipboard and paste it into PagePlus using the command Edit,Paste Special. Once pasted into PagePlus you can edit it in Paintbrush by double clicking on it.

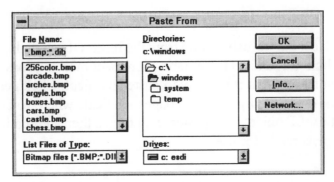

- Using the directory field select the directory **C:\windows**. From the File Name list you can then double-click on **arches.bmp** to import this graphic.

The arches.bmp file is included in Windows 3.1 but not in later versions of Windows or in Windows for Workgroups. If you have upgraded from Windows 3.1 to a more recent version this file will, by default, not be removed but if your original Windows is a more recent version you will not have this file available. In this case you can do a simple drawing of an arch (a truncated ellipse will do) in Paintbrush to provide a suitable graphic to export and manipulate. Alternatively a substitute bitmap is provided in the file c7_arch.bmp on the Companion Disk to this book.

- Now select File,Update, followed by File,Exit & Return to PagePlus[untitled].

- Though the picture is now in PagePlus it is very small, so click on the picture to select it and drag on the bottom right handle, with the Shift key held down to keep its original proportions, until the graphic takes up the area in the top left corner of your page defined by your guides.

● Assume that you now decide you want to alter the OLE object in Paintbrush. Double-click with the Pointer tool on the object. You are then returned to Paintbrush with the object loaded and ready for editing.

● Select the Paint Roller tool from the Paintbrush's tool palette which is at the left side of the screen and click on the white colour from the colour palette at the bottom of the screen. Position the cursor above the dark blue 'archway' areas in the graphic and click. These areas then become white.

● Select File,Update from the pull down menu at the top of the screen to make these changes to the linked picture in PagePlus. Then select File,Exit & Return to PagePlus to return to PagePlus with the object amended.

Notice that the original graphic file Arches.bmp is not affected by the changes you have made. If you want to check, load Paintbrush using the Program Manager and open Arches.bmp. If you had imported the graphics file instead of working with it as an OLE object the only way that you could have changed its appearance would be to edit the original file. In other words, OLE uses embedding to make a copy of the graphic which is stored in the PagePlus document file.

» Cropping the object

The OLE object on your page has a great deal of white space to the right and at the bottom of the picture. You need to remove this by cropping it.

● First set snapping off by clicking on the Snap icon on the StatusBar so that the button is out.

● Then, click on the object to select it and select the Crop tool from the ToolBox.

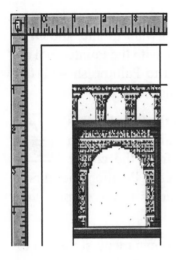

● Now drag inwards on the bottom right handle of the object. As the handle is dragged inwards part of the picture (in this case the white space) is removed. Drag the handle in until it is right at the bottom corner of the picture. If you go too far with the crop tool you can drag back out or set the object back to its original state by double-clicking on it.

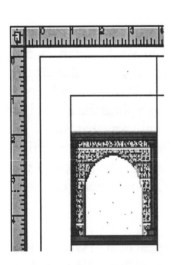

You may need to select the Pointer tool to resize your object to the right width. Set snapping on to make the object as wide as the area from the left margin to the vertical guide.

● Now select the Crop tool again if it is not already selected. Drag the top centre handle of the object inwards to remove the top set of arches from the graphic.

● Make sure that the snapping is off when you do this so that you can drag the cursor precisely.

》 Adding the text

● Select the Text tool from the ToolBox and drag the I-beam cursor from the left margin, just above the picture, to the vertical guide.

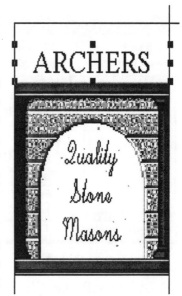

- Type in:
  ARCHERS
- Use the ChangeBar to set the font to Times New Roman, the size to 36 points and the alignment to Center. You can reposition the text precisely above the picture, using snapping.

- Create the other text objects by dragging across the graphic from the left margin to the vertical guide with the Text tool.

- Type in:

  Quality
  Stone
  Masons
- Use the ChangeBar to make the text 40 points in size, Script font and centre align it. You can then position the text precisely, in the archway, using the Pointer tool.

» Saving the logo as a single object

In order to use this design as a logo for use in a publication it must be grouped together and saved as a single graphic.

- Select all the objects on the page. This is best done by either dragging the Pointer tool around the entire design or by selecting Edit,Select All. Each individual object then becomes surrounded by handles.

- Now select File,Export as Picture... which opens the Export as Picture dialog.

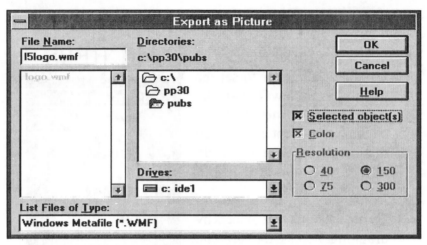

- Make sure that the Selected objects box is selected.

- By default the file will be saved into the directory **C:\pp30\pubs** but you can specify an alternative if you wish. When you have made your selections, type in t5logo.wmf in the filename field and click on OK. Your icon is then saved in the appropriate directory as a windows metafile (.WMF). You can also export icons as Bitmaps (.BMP) or Encapsulated PostScript (.EPS) files.

You may be a little surprised at the choice of WMF format used to save the graphic as Arches.bmp is most certainly a bitmap and WMF is a vector format. The reason for choosing WMF rather than BMP format for export in this case is simply that the text included as part of the logo is a vector graphic. If we had selected BMP format then this would have been converted to a bitmap and, as a result would have lost its ability to be rescaled without loss of quality. Of course saving the graphic as a vector format doesn't convert the original bitmap into a vector drawing - it is simply included in the vector file as a bitmap. That is, when you rescale the WMF file the text is re-scaled to the new resolution without loss of quality, but the bitmap component still suffers from all of the problems inherent in bitmaps.

If you were to choose to export a graphic as a bitmap then you would also have to select the resolution to be used to convert any vector elements it may contain. To do this you need to know the size that the graphic is likely to be used at and the resolution of the printer. Notice that you can also convert any object into a picture without saving it to disk using the Tools,Convert to picture command.

» Retrieving and using the logo

The design is now finished and you can save your work as a standard PagePlus publication file (.PPP) if you want to. However, having exported the graphic as a .WMF file this isn't essential. If you don't save your work as a .PPP file then you will not be able to modify the design in the future.

The logo you created as a WMF file can be retrieved into any PagePlus publication, if you wish, in just the same way as you would import any other PagePlus object. For example if you wanted to create a compliments slip using the logo simply import it, scale it, and add the necessary text

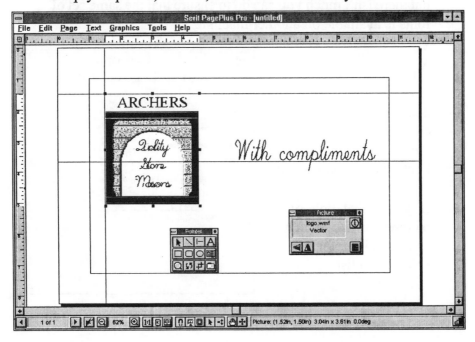

- The first step in using the logo in this way is to select the Import Picture tool from the ToolBox and then double click on the Art & Borders icon to open the Import Picture dialog. Here specify the directory and filename you used to store t5logo.wmf.

- Once imported you can size and crop the image and assign properties to the frame.

» External resources

If you import pictures and use linking then they become part of the external resources needed to create a document. If you then copy the document to another disk or another computer it is important that you remember also to copy the external resources used by the document. However, copying the picture files along with the document usually isn't sufficient. PagePlus remembers the location of the document files as well as their names. This means that if you move picture files PagePlus will not be able to find them and it will ask you to supply their new location. Fonts are also an external resource but there isn't much you can do to ensure that the same set of fonts is available on another machine.

To find out what external resources are used by a document you can use the command Tools, Fonts & Pictures which displays the Fonts & Pictures dialog box.

If you select any of the pictures or fonts then its exact details are shown just below each list.

Fonts & Pictures

The following fonts & pictures are used in your publication:

Close

Fonts:
BriemScript
Script
Times New Roman

BriemScript is a TrueType font.

Pictures:
logo.wmf

c:\pageplus\logo.wmf

If you have imported and linked a picture and want to convert it to an OLE object then all you have to do is cut the picture to the Clipboard and then use Paste Special to insert it as an OLE object. This is one way to ensure that PagePlus can always find the pictures that you have used.

» The power of OLE

In this tour we have explored using OLE to access graphics. It is worth remembering that OLE lets you link to many other types of data - figures in a spreadsheet, records in a database and so on - and it therefore widens the scope of any one application. In Chapters 9 and 10 we will return to OLE in the context of creating tables using Serif's mini application TablePlus.

Key points

» There are two different types of graphics formats - bitmap and vector. Bitmaps are simple, easy to use and fast but they are not scalable. Vector drawings tend to be complex and slow to work with but they are fully scalable.

» When you import a picture it is normally linked to the document. You can opt to have the file embedded but this makes the document file larger.

» You can apply many of the standard properties - line width, fill etc. - to a picture. You can also colour a picture.

» The order in which graphics objects are drawn affects which appears to be in front. You can alter the order using the Send to back or Bring to front icons.

» Groups of objects can be automatically aligned on the page using the Edit,Align items menu command.

» Text wrap can be set on or off for any object. Each text block can be individually set to take notice of wrap outlines or ignore them.

» Objects from any Windows application that supports OLE can be embedded but the effect that is produced varies greatly.

» The Export as Picture command can be used to turn any group of objects into a single graphics object that can be imported or embedded.

Chapter 8

<u>Pre-press</u>

The final stage in preparing a document is to transfer it to paper. You might think that this is just a matter of using a print command and waiting for the output. At best it can be this easy but in most cases you need to understand how the output is produced to get the result you intended.

If you are going to make use of a printing press to produce the final product in bulk then you need to think in terms of producing output suitable for the press. You might be able to use a laser printer but for the highest quality results you need to make use of an imagesetter - a high resolution output device. This leads us to consider the whole business of preparing material for the press, or *pre-press* as it is often called. In this chapter the focus is on using printers - how their resolution and other characteristics affect reproduction, using an external bureau for film or bromide, and colour printing in both spot and process colour.

» Resolution

All output devices have a maximum working *resolution*. Most printers work by printing black dots on paper and their resolution is measured as the maximum number of dots to the inch, or dpi, that they can produce. For example, impact or dot matrix printers can work at 75 dpi to around 150 dpi, laser printers work at 300 to 600 dpi and so on. Sometimes the horizontal resolution will be different from the vertical resolution. For example, some laser printers produce 600 dpi horizontally but only 300 dpi vertically, but in most cases the horizontal and vertical resolutions are the same.

There are two confusing factors with regard to printer resolution. The first is that some printers claim to be able to print dots at, say, 300 dpi but the dots are very large and overlap so reducing the effective resolution. Some 24-pin dot matrix printers fall into this category. Laser printers and ink jet printers are currently the only low cost output devices that can claim a true 300 dpi resolution.

The second factor is the use of various resolution enhancement methods. These increase the effective resolution by shifting dots slightly where possible to produce smoother curves than a basic 300 dpi resolution would suggest. Most modern laser printers use some sort of resolution enhancement to boost 300 dpi to look more like 400 dpi.

The quality and type of output that you can produce really does depend on the resolution of the printer. What you find acceptable is very much a matter of personal taste and that of the intended audience. It is perfectly possible to produce acceptable results using nothing but a dot matrix printer but for external consumption something better is usually required.

The following is a rough guide to the resolution required for typical types of work:

» Black and white text with line illustrations - 300 dpi preferably with some sort of resolution enhancement.

» Continuous tone photographs - 600 dpi minimum.

» Spot colour work with tints - 300 to 600 dpi.

» Process colour - 1200 dpi minimum.

» Grey tones

The most important thing to realise is that all printing processes are restricted to monochrome. That is, ink is either applied to the paper or it isn't. For example, a laser printer usually prints black dots on a white paper. This is fine for solid black text but what about tints? How can a printer that works with full black dots produce an area of grey? The answer is that the density of black dots is varied. When the output is viewed at a normal distance the eye averages the number of dots in a given area to see an even grey tone.

This sounds simple enough but in practice there are lots of problems. The first problem is the reduction in resolution. If you have a 300 dpi laser printer then a pure black and white image looks reasonably sharp but if you want to print five grey levels you need to use a 'super dot' built out of a 2 by 2 cell of basic dots. In this scheme all the basic dots are used as follows:

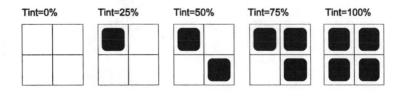

This means that to print 5 grey levels you have to accept a drop in resolution from 300 dpi to 150 dpi. If you think that this is an acceptable drop in resolution consider the situation when you need to represent 256 grey levels, the number usually considered to be the minimum for photographic reproduction. This needs a super cell of 16 by 16 basic dots which reduces the resolution of a 300 dpi laser to a quite unacceptable 19 dpi. Even if you consider the higher resolution offered by an imagesetter, 1200 dpi say, the need to represent 256 grey levels soon reduces the resolution to a just acceptable 75 dpi.

» Optimum screens

The second major problem with using a variable dot density to print grey levels is that the pattern of dots can become visible to the eye as a regular banding across the image. The solution to this problem is to vary the arrangement of dots used to break up the patterning across the image. Notice that for most of the grey levels you can choose from more than one possible super dot pattern.

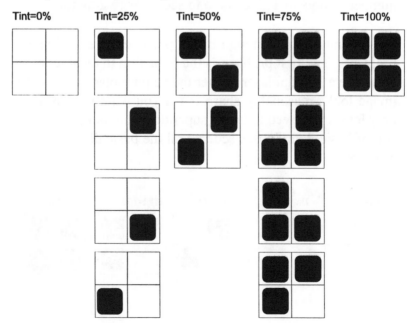

By choosing which pattern is used it is possible to minimise the patterning. How dots are assigned to the grey levels within a continuous tone image like a photograph is called *screening*. This terminology comes from the days when photographs were converted to a pattern of dots by the use of a mechanical process involving a screen with holes in it. Whenever you print a grey tone on a printer a screen is used to convert it to a pattern of dots.

Some DTP packages give you a choice of type of screen but as printer technology has improved most now rely on the optimised screens that have been defined for each type of printer. For example, all PostScript printers have a predefined set of optimum screens that PagePlus will simply make use of. You will, however, still find some paint and drawing applications that offer a choice of screen method. In most cases it is better to use the printer defaults. It is also important that you do not use a paint package to screen a grey level image before you import it into PagePlus - always let PagePlus perform the screening.

» Screen density and angle

Even if the choice of screening method has been removed, you can still choose some of the characteristics of the screen used. In particular most printers allow you to set the *screen density* and *angle*. The default screens used by most printers arrange the dots into lines and so screen density is measured in lines per inch (lpi). The screen angle is simply the angle that the lines make with the horizontal.

It may seem sensible always to choose the highest resolution screen but this isn't the case. The higher the screen resolution the smaller the number of dots used in each super dot and so the smaller the number of grey levels that can be printed. For example, if you are using a 300 dpi printer then using a 150 lpi screen implies working with a super dot made up from 4 printer dots. In other words, the screen may be a fine one but in combination with a 300 dpi printer it can only represent five different grey tones. In most cases this would be unacceptable. If you reduce the screen resolution you can represent more grey levels. In other words, you can trade resolution for the number of grey tones that can be represented. In practice there will be a best choice of screen resolution but this will depend on printer resolution and on the number of grey tones that that image actually contains. For simple images without large areas of slowly changing tones you might be able to increase the screen resolution without loss of quality - however, you can only discover this by trial and error. The ideal solution to the problem is to use an output device that has a high enough basic resolution for you to select a high resolution screen that represents enough grey tones for all images.

The relationship between printer resolution, screen resolution and number of grey tones is quite simple:

$$\text{Grey levels} = \left\{ \frac{\text{printer resolution in dpi}}{\text{screen resolution in lpi}} \right\}^2 + 1$$

It is useful to have a table of common values for reference:

	Printer resolution		
Screen	300 dpi	600 dpi	1200 dpi
50 lpi	37	145	577
60 lpi	26	101	401
100 lpi	10	37	145
120 lpi	7	26	101

A standard 300 dpi PostScript printer defaults to a 60 lpi screen giving 26 grey levels and a 1200 dpi imagesetter defaults to 100 lpi giving 145 grey levels. Some printers don't tell you directly what line screen they are using but prefer to use descriptions like 'photographic quality screen' and so on. For example, a 300 dpi LaserJet set to photographic quality uses a 37 lpi screen giving 65 grey levels.

As well as selecting a screen density, you can also select an angle if you need to. If you find that the screen pattern is interfering with the image content - i.e. a horizontal stripe is being made into a patchwork by vertical screen lines - then you can change it. In some cases, the LaserJet family of printers for example, screen angle doesn't apply because they use a type of screen that doesn't produce a pattern of lines.

» Selecting a screen

There are no facilities within PagePlus to select the screen used to print grey tones. Instead you have to make use of the general Windows Printer Setup commands. Exactly what you can alter depends on the printer type. In many cases you will not even find a reference to the screen density - just general descriptions such as 'high quality'. You also need to know that the terms *dithering* and *half tone* are also used to refer to the type of screening process used.

For example, if you want to select a screen for a PostScript printer then you would use the File,Printer Setup command within PagePlus to take you to the standard Windows Printer Setup dialog box.

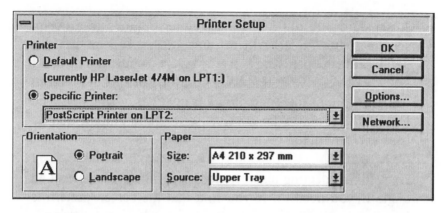

In nearly all cases the part of the setup that alters the screen is kept well out of the way. In the case of a PostScript printer you have to click on the Options button, and then on the Advanced button in the dialog box that appears, to reach the Advanced Options dialog box where you can at last set the screen resolution (Halftone Frequency) and angle (Halftone Angle). Notice that all PostScript devices, including high resolution imagesetters, use the same set of Printer Setup dialog boxes.

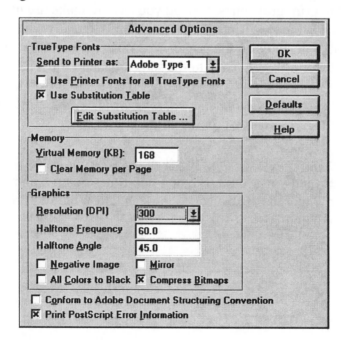

In the case of a LaserJet you have a simple choice of screen density, in the box titled Dithering, and a separate control over the overall density of print. All you can really do is select a setting by trial and error - keeping in mind that the Coarse setting will be able to reproduce more grey levels.

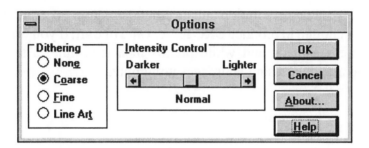

» Pre-press output

Producing output suitable for use with a printing press isn't a difficult task. For simple black and white output you might be able to use a 300 dpi laser printer and paper masters, often referred to as Camera Ready Copy (CRC). The paper printouts can sometimes be used as masters in a plateless printing process something like photocopying. However, for the highest quality, and for long runs, the paper masters are photographed and the negatives are used to create plates. You don't really need to worry about how the plates are made or used but it does help to keep in mind that the paper output will be photographed.

Before you print the paper masters make sure you clean the printer and then run off a few pages of something else to make sure everything has settled down again. If you are using a laser printer then it is better not to use a new toner cartridge because it takes a few hundred pages before a cartridge works well. Some people use special high quality paper when producing paper masters but this isn't always necessary.

What matters is the degree of contrast between the black and the white when viewed by reflected light. That is, judge the quality of the output by placing it on a solid surface in front of an even source of light such a north facing window. Look out for paper blemishes and printer smudges.

A 600 dpi or a resolution enhanced 300 dpi laser is certainly good enough to produce CRC for text and line art. If you want to include black and white photos then it is time to start thinking about using an imagesetting bureau.

» Using a bureau

There is a lot of mystery surrounding the use of an imagesetter via a bureau. Much of this is caused by the lack of understanding of the technicalities of the process by the people running the bureau. If they are Mac based then they will often tell you that they cannot process PC output. The chances are that they probably can but why argue - there is bound to be another bureau which understands better!

The key fact to keep in mind is that most imagesetters are nothing more than PostScript output devices that write high resolution output to film rather than to paper. As Windows has a PostScript driver you can most certainly send output to a PostScript imagesetter. The only complication is that instead of being connected to the output device directly you have to send the output to disk and then send the disk to the output device.

If you are working with one of the many Linotronic imagesetters then the simplest way of creating suitable output is to install it as a printing device. For example, if the bureau uses a Linotronic 330 simply use the Control Panel to install it as another printer. If the bureau uses an Agfa or some other imagesetter than follow the same steps but select the appropriate driver. In some cases the bureau will provide you with the required printer driver if you ask.

Click on the Control Panel icon in the Main Program Manager group, click on the printer icon that appears and click Add in the Printer dialog box that appears. This displays a long list of printer types which you can scroll through until you find a number of Linotronic models listed. Select the correct model and press the Install button. If you already have a PostScript printer installed you will not even have to find the Windows setup disks because the Linotronic is just a variety of PostScript printer and will use the same drivers.

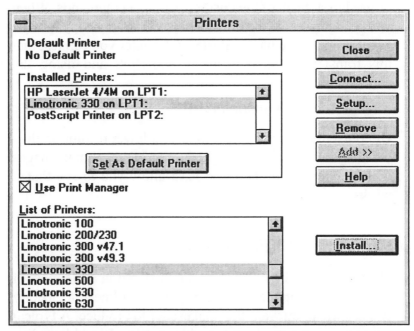

Once the Linotronic is installed the next step is to press the Connect button and select FILE: in the Ports list within the Connect dialog box that appears.

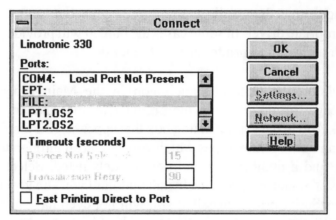

After this when you print to the Linotronic you will be asked to specify a filename to be used for the output. This file will be used to store all of the PostScript output commands. When you send this file to the bureau they will simply copy it to the Linotronic. If you have a PostScript printer you can test that this transfer works by starting MS-DOS and using the command:

COPY *filename* PRN

Of course the laser printer will have a lower resolution than the imagesetter and so the reproduction of any bitmap images will be poor but it should at least allow you to see that it works.

» Specifying imagesetter output

Once you have the PostScript output stored in a file most of the work is complete. However, you do still need to specify exactly what you want the imagesetter to produce. A typical imagesetter can produce bromide or film. Bromide is like photographic printing paper and it is used as CRC by the printer. You can think of bromide as the high resolution equivalent of paper.

If the printer can accept film from you then it will cost you a little more to produce initially but, as it cuts out the photographic stage later on, it will probably save you at least an equivalent amount on the printer's bill. An imagesetter can print your output onto large sheets of film on request but you also have to specify a few extra details. The film can be printed as a positive or as a negative. Which you need depends on which one the plate making process uses. A more complex question is 'emulsion side up or down'. Film, unlike paper, can be viewed from both sides but one side is the side that is printed on - the emulsion side. If you hold the file so that what is printed on it is readable then the emulsion side of the film will either be up or down. Hence the rather longer term 'right reading emulsion side up/down'. You can get a clearer idea about the way that this works by trying it with an old photographic negative. To change from emulsion side up to down involves mirror reversing the output. Which one you need again depends on the plate making process used. So when you send a file to an imagesetter you should specify film or bromide and, if you specify film, you should also state whether it should be positive or negative and emulsion side up or emulsion side down.

This seems straightforward enough but there is a very simple way that it can go wrong. The imagesetter has controls that the operator can use to turn a positive print into a negative and to mirror reverse it. The trouble is that the Postscript printer driver also gives you the option to convert the output to a negative or mirror reverse it. Suppose you click on the Negative Image option then the file will print as a negative without the imagesetter operator having to intervene. But if you have asked for a negative print the chances are that the operator will also select the negative image option with the result that a positive is printed! The same problem can occur with 'emulsion side up/down' if you mirror reverse the output and then the imagesetter does the same thing!

There is no 100% sure way of avoiding this problem but it helps to include a description of what the file contains and what you want. For example, if you have created an output file without selecting the Negative image option or Mirror reverse then your instructions to the bureau might be something like:

● File called *filename* containing 3 A4 pages to be sent to film negative, emulsion side down. The file is positive and not reversed.

What is important is that you make it clear to the operator what the file contains and what you want produced. If you use the same bureau regularly they will soon get to know how you work and then mistakes are only likely to happen if you do something out of the ordinary.

» Pre-press screens

If you are preparing output to be used by a printing press then you need to take account of the characteristics of the printing process in selecting a screen. Suppose, for example, that you are using a very high resolution imagesetter to produce film. You may think that the finer the screen the better, but this isn't the case if you create dots that are so fine that the press cannot reproduce them. In this case the result will be a smudge of ink rather than a smooth grey tone. It is vital that the screen density is selected to provide a balance of grey level and resolution while still being less than the maximum resolution of the press. How do you find out the maximum lines per inch (lpi) that a press can work with? You have no choice but to ask the technical department at the printers you are thinking of using.

There is also the type of paper to be considered. Even if the press can print the fine dots they may run together if the paper is very absorbent - this is called the *dot gain*. For example, 150 lpi produces a good sharp image on glossy paper but a smudged mess on newsprint. Again, you have to ask your printer for advice. PagePlus also contains some default settings for different types of paper when printing full colour, see the section on process colour later in this chapter. For example, a low cost booklet and pamphlet printer who is not using plates and is working with low quality paper might recommend no more than 85 lpi. For higher quality work on glossy paper 120 lpi might be the upper limit.

» PostScript and fonts

There is a particular problem with using PostScript printers in that their native font format is Adobe Type I. PagePlus and most other Window applications have a natural affinity for TrueType fonts and so something has to be done about matching the two types of font. The solution to the problem is to be found in the Windows advanced printer setup.

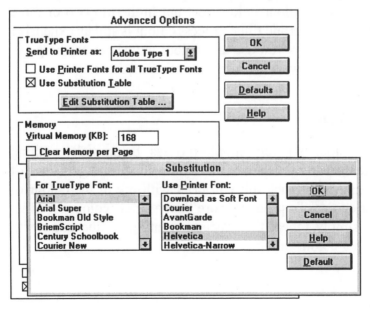

To reach the appropriate dialog box use the command File,Printer Setup, click on the Options button and then on the Advanced button. The Advanced Options dialog box allows you to edit the font substitution table. This specifies exactly how each TrueType font will be treated. If there is an Adobe font that matches the TrueType font then it will be used in place of it. For example, Arial is an almost perfect match for Helvetica and so it is usual to use the Helvetica Adobe font built into every PostScript printer in place of it.

If there isn't a suitable Adobe font then you can opt to have the TrueType font downloaded - select Download as Soft Font. If you are sending the resulting file to an imagesetter this entails the disadvantage of increasing the size of the file.

» Colour printing

Although most DTP is still black and white, colour is beginning to be more common and PagePlus 3 is good at handling colour. However, you need to know that there are two different methods of printing in colour - *spot* and *process colour*. Spot colour is low cost but limited to two or three specific colours and tints. Process colour is still an expensive process but you can use any colour anywhere on the page. PagePlus can work with both printing methods.

» Spot colour

Spot colour is a very simple process, being really nothing more than an extension of black on white printing. Instead of printing with black ink you print with ink of the colour of your choice. To produce more than a single colour on white you simply repeat the process, printing on the page with another colour of ink.

When you create a spot colour document using DTP you simply specify the colour of each component of the page. When you print the document you can either opt for a composite (all colours printed to the page) or for separations (only one colour printed on the page). The spot colour separations are, of course, used to create plates suitable for applying that colour to the printed page. Notice that when a spot colour separation is created it is printed in black and white - it is only when the ink is applied to the plate that the actual colour is determined.

For example, you could draw a logo using spot red and prepare a separation for a red plate accordingly. At the last minute, however, you could change your mind and print the spot colour as blue by specifying a shade of blue ink. In other words, what affects the final printed result is the ink used to print each of the separations. This is a powerful advantage because it allows us to avoid the problem of accurate colour representation on a monitor screen.

Instead of having to select the spot colour by looking at it on the screen there are books of colour standards, complete with names and reference numbers. For example, the Pantone library, as used in PagePlus, is the best known and in this system colours are specified as Pantone Red 1283 and so on. Although there will be some attempt to show a Pantone colour accurately on the screen this doesn't matter very much because you should have chosen the colour on the basis of a sample in a colour book and the printer will select the appropriate ink to the exact specification.

» Knockouts and traps

Spot colour is a simple process but it brings with it a number of new problems. The first is that you do not normally print spot colours over each other. The reason is simply that the inks will mix and produce an unpredictable colour. In addition mixing spot colours can load the paper with too much ink and result in runs and smudges. The solution to this problem is known as *knockout*. Spot colours are generally set to knockout, that is remove, colours that they are positioned over. So if you draw a spot red square with a spot blue circle in the middle then the spot blue circle will knockout the red, leaving a white hole in the red separation where the blue ink will be printed.

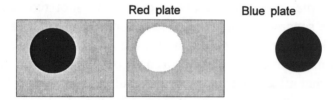

In nearly all cases spot colours should be set to knockout rather than overprint. The only exception is black which is such a strong colour it can overprint any other colour. For example, if you have a great deal of black text on a yellow background then setting black to overprint will make the finished job easier to print because there is no need to align the two plates exactly.

Knockouts cause a problem for accurate registration of the plates. If the press is 100% accurate then each spot colour would fit into its knockout perfectly. However, no printing process is 100% accurate and so there are bound to be slight shifts between the plates. This usually produces thin white lines around spot colour objects caused by the paper showing through. The solution to this problem is to alter the size of the knockout slightly to allow the inks to overlap enough to accommodate slight shifts in the plates. This is called *trapping*.

Spread trap
light foreground into
dark background

Choke trap
light background into
dark foreground

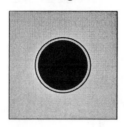

There are two sorts of trap - a *spread trap* where the object is made to overlap the background and a *choke trap* where the background overlaps the object. The difference is all a question of which ink is darker. If you use a spread trap for a light object on a dark background and a choke trap for a dark object on a light background then the shape of the object will hardly be changed.

» Spot colour in PagePlus

All you have to do to make use of spot colour in PagePlus is to make sure that you only assign a small number of colours as line and fill colours. Obviously if you use a great many colours then the number of separations that would be needed grows to the point where the spot colour process is uneconomical. This specifically means that you cannot import full colour pictures and expect them to print in full colour. Pictures that you import for spot colour work have to use a limited number of colours and you have to further assign them to spot colours within PagePlus.

After you have completed your design you have to print spot colour separations with one plate (or print-out) being used per colour. Use the File,Print command in the usual way but select Color Separate in the Print dialog box.

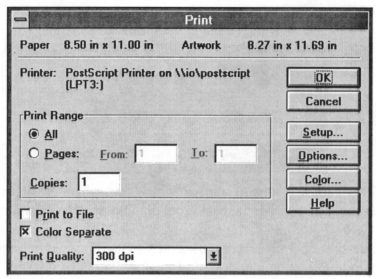

You can control the usual aspects of printing such as which pages to print and use the Setup button to select the printer, the paper size and so on. If you click on the Options button you can also select crop marks and file info. When you are printing separations, file info and crop marks are usually essential to allow the printer to identify and align the plates. If you click on the Color... button you will see the Color Separations dialog box which lists each colour used in your design.

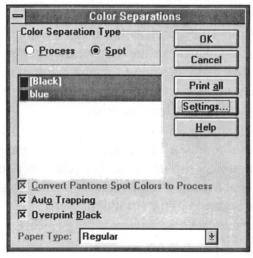

To print a spot colour separation you have to make sure that the Spot option in the Color Separation Type box is selected. As this point the list of colours is probably the most important information concerning your design. Each colour that you have used in your design will be listed. In most cases you will be surprised to see colours that you didn't think you had used listed and some that you thought you had will be missing! The reason is that when you import pictures sometimes their colours are added to the spot colour list and sometimes they are not. The exact way that this works is described later. It is a good idea to use the File,Print command and the Color Separations box while you are creating the layout just to see what colours are actually in use. If you do this you can keep track of the colour list and make corrections as you go. There is nothing more frustrating than trying to locate which object is using a colour that you never intended to use! A good tip is to actually print the "rogue" plate and see what is on it. You can select which plates you would like to print individually or click on the Print All button.

What other options there are depends on the type of printer you are using. You will only be offered all of the options if you are printing to a PostScript printer. The OverPrint Black option should normally be selected unless you have a good reason to want black knocked out of the other plates. As black is most often used for fine details and complex shapes such as text overprinting it reduces the alignment problems with very little loss of print quality. The only situation where you might want to knock out black is if you are using very large areas of black over another very strong colour. In this case the colour quality of the finished print would be improved, and its drying time reduced, by knocking out black. In such cases you generally have to speak to your printer and ask for advice in the early stages of design.

If you are using a PostScript printer, or if you are sending your output to a PostScript imagesetter then you will be able to use PagePlus's *autotrapping*. This is a simple but effective facility that applies a slight spread to text and graphics objects. There are some adjustments that you can make to the trapping applied but in nearly all cases it is unnecessary to do so. If you do want to adjust trapping then click on the Settings button. You can only alter the size an object has to be before trapping is applied and what the maximum size increase is. Clearly increasing the size of a small object is a bigger distortion than the same size increase applied to a larger object.

» Spot colour and imported objects

When you apply a colour to an object within PagePlus the colour that you use is known by its name (e.g. Peach) and by its actual colour value as defined by the mixture of Red, Green and Blue (RGB) needed to make it. When you import a coloured object the range of colour information available to PagePlus varies. Bitmaps only supply RGB colour information and not colour names. This is a problem because even if you import a bitmap which uses a single colour that looks like Peach there is no way that PagePlus can be sure that the RGB value specified is actually the same as the colour it calls Peach. The difficulty is that there is no general agreement on what names to give to colours.

Vector drawings do generally contain the names of colours used but even here this is unlikely to be of much help to PagePlus. For example, what an external drawing package calls Peach might not be the same colour as PagePlus refers to as Peach.

The difficulty of identifying colours by name is very important to the spot colour process because each plate is identified by name only. Indeed the actual colours used in a spot colour process are a matter for the printer and out of the hands of the DTP user! For example, you may create a design which uses a particular shade of blue but the actual colour used is determined by the ink that the printer uses for that plate. Many DTP packages consider spot colour to be an unimportant process and leave the problem of printing imported objects unsolved. PagePlus 3 provides colour assignment of both bitmaps and vector drawings to enable you to include imported objects within a spot colour layout.

» Spot colour assignment to bitmaps

A bitmap can contain an arbitrary range of colours and no colour naming information is included at all. This makes it impossible to assign a number of spot colours to a bitmap because there is no simple way to refer to the colours that it contains. The only sensible way of dealing with the problem is to assign a spot colour as the foreground colour of the image. This technique has already been described in Chapter 7. Use the Graphics,Picture,Color command to assign a colour and the Graphics,Picture,Shading command to assign a tint if you want to. The bitmap is converted to a monochrome, i.e. foreground colour on white, image which will appear on the foreground colour's plate. For simple bitmaps this is usually sufficient and it even works well with scanned in images as long as you select the foreground colour carefully. Notice that if you don't assign a colour to a bitmap then it will not appear on any of the spot colour plates.

» Spot colour assignment to vector drawings

A vector drawing generally does include named colours. The problem here is the matching up of the names used in the external package that created or edited the vector drawing and the colours used in PagePlus. If you simply import a vector object and go directly to print separations you might be surprised to see that there are more colours in use than you expected.

For example, if you create a layout in yellow text on blue then you might expect the sample ArtPack image of the sun, i.e. Sun3.wmf, to also appear on the yellow plate but if you use the File,Print command and examine the colours that have been used you will find that there is an extra colour called SUN3_1. This is a default name created by PagePlus for the unnamed yellowish colour used in Sun3.wmf. If you print spot colour separations the yellow text and the yellow sun will appear on different plates.

To allow you to match up the colours used within a vector object and the spot colours used in the design, PagePlus provides the Color Mapper. If you select a vector object and use the command Tools,Color Mapper you will see a list of the named colours, including any that PagePlus has had to name, listed. You can then assign each colour used by the vector object to a spot colour used in your design. You can also see what the effect of this assignment is in the preview display at the right of the dialog box. If the redraw time for the preview is too long then you can disable it and view the final result when you have completed colour mapping.

For example, to make the picture Sun3.wmf print correctly on the yellow plate the colour mapper would be used to map the colour SUN3_1 to the standard colour YELLOW.

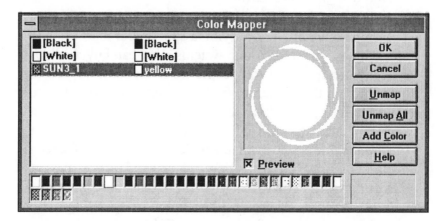

Following this you will find that the spot colour separations only list blue and yellow plates as required. In other cases the number of colours that need to be mapped can be quite large.

Notice that you might find you need to use the Color Mapper on imported graphics objects that are created by TablePlus, TypePlus or DrawPlus. Although if you restrict yourself to simple colours - red, yellow and so on - you will find that they are recognised as the same colours within PagePlus without the need to use the Color Mapper.

» Controlling spot colour

As already mentioned the spot colour process is mainly concerned with what you call a colour rather than its actual colour. The colour that results in the final print is determined solely by the colour of the ink that the printer uses for each plate. This raises the question of how to specify to the printer what colour you want them to use. If the actual colour isn't critical you can resort to describing it in words or supply a colour sample clipped from something printed. The colour sample approach works well as long as your printer is prepared to spend time matching it to ink colours and you do not mind slight colour shifts.

The only sure way of specifying a spot colour is to use one of the many standard colour systems. You can buy a colour swatch corresponding to specific inks. This allows you to look through the swatch to find the colour you want to use and specify it precisely as an ink number or code. The best known of these standard colour systems is the Pantone colour library and this is also available in PagePlus as a set of screen display colours. You can use any colour standard you like but it is important to check that your printer also uses the same colour standard. There is little point in spending time specifying a colour as Pantone Blue 72CV only to discover that this means nothing to your printer!

If you are going to use the Pantone system then it is worth using Pantone colours in your design. The screen representation of these colours isn't going to be accurate enough for you to be certain what the finished print will look like but it is close enough for you to get a feel for the overall composition. You can add spot colours to the colour palette using the command Tools,Defaults,Colors which displays the Edit Colors dialog box.

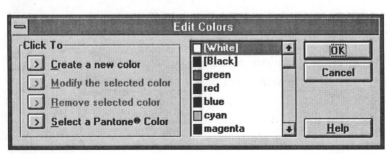

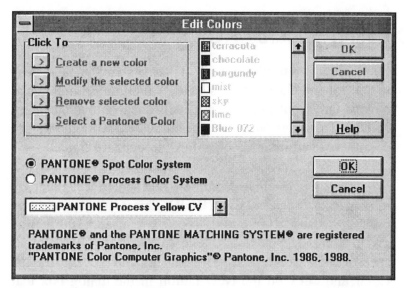

If you click on the Select a Pantone Color button you can select Pantone standard colours from the drop down list.

Once you have selected suitable spot colours - most designs will only use one or two spot colours - you can apply them to objects using the ChangeBar and Properties Palette as usual. To make life easier you might like to remove the non-spot colours from the colour list. The Pantone Process Color system has a slightly different purpose and is described in the section on process colour.

» Spot colour tints

Although it should be obvious, it is worth pointing out that you can use tints with spot colours in exactly the same way as with a grey level. Many DTP users tend to think of a spot colour as something that they can only use at 100% but a screen can be used to create intermediate tones. You can make use of this to increase the apparent number of colours in spot colour design.

» Creating colours - RGB and HSL

Spot colour is a useful process. It is easy to understand, easy to control and cheap. It does have its limitations though and beyond three spot colours it is usually cheaper to move to full colour. To understand the difficulties of working in full colour we need first to look at how colours are created.

When a colour is created on the VDU screen it is made by mixing Red, Green and Blue (RGB). This is called an additive process because 100% Red, 100% Green and 100% Blue gives white. If you would like to see how RGB colour specification works then use the command Tools,Defaults, Color and click on the New button in the dialog box that appears. You can then use the Custom Color Selector to select any colour you want. If you look at the three boxes labelled Red, Green, Blue you can see how any colour is made up of these three primaries. You can also type in RGB values and see what colour this corresponds to. The three boxes labelled Hue, Sat and Lum are an alternative way of describing colour using Hue (i.e. colour), Saturation (i.e. amount of colour) and Luminance (i.e. brightness).

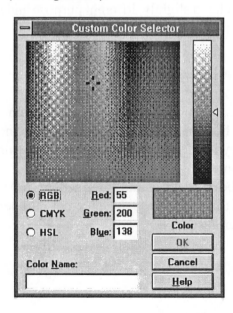

» Process colour

To create any colour on paper using inks we need to use a subtractive process because the page is viewed in white light and we see the colours that are reflected back, i.e. not absorbed. The three inks used in full colour printing are Cyan, Magenta and Yellow (CMY). Mixing 100% of each colour gives black. However, the black that is produced is a sort of muddy brown due to impurities in the inks. To print a true black, a black ink is included as another printing stage even though in theory it isn't really needed. This results in there being four basic colours: Cyan, Magenta, Yellow and blacK (CMYK).

Given that you have four colours at your disposal you would think that the problem of translating from an RGB colour specification to a CMYK specification would be easy. Surprisingly, however, there are RGB colours that cannot be produced using CMYK.

The biggest difference between spot colour and process colour is that in process printing the inks always overprint - they have to mix to produce intermediate colours. In this case a separate screen is used for each of the process colours. Each screen is set at a different angle so that the four screens fit together without creating a visible pattern of dots. The default screens are usually set at 45° for black, 75° for magenta, 90° for yellow and 105° for cyan. These then fit together in such a way that the dots of different colours print in a tiny rosette pattern.

Altering the screen angles is a dangerous business because it is very easy to create a regular patterning, a moiré pattern, which ruins the image. While it might be easy to experiment with grey or spot colour screens, colour screens are another matter. Stick with the defaults unless you know exactly what you are doing. However, you can still select the screen resolution in lines per inch and this is just as important, if not more so, for colour work. You need to make sure that you do not exceed the resolution of the press and take account of the absorption of the paper, i.e. the dot gain.

» PagePlus and process colour

You can only create process colour separations using PagePlus if you are printing to a PostScript printer. As you are almost certain to need to produce film using a PostScript imagesetter to achieve the resolution necessary for process colour this isn't an unreasonable restriction.

To create a process colour layout you simply choose any colour you want to use from the colour palette except the Pantone spot colours - and even these can be converted to process colour if you select the Convert Pantone Spot Colors to Process box in the Color Separations dialog box. You can even create new colours using the Custom Color Selector. As process colours overprint there is no need to worry about overlapping objects.

Once the layout is complete you can print it in the usual way but to produce process colour separations you have to select the option Process in the Color Separation Type box. As with spot colour you can select any or all of the possible four separations - C, M, Y or K - to print. Unlike spot colour, however, you can also select the screens to be used. If you click on the Settings button the Color Separation Settings dialog box is displayed. This looks like a very complicated and intimidating dialog box, and indeed it is, but most of the time you can ignore it. The default settings work well enough in most cases.

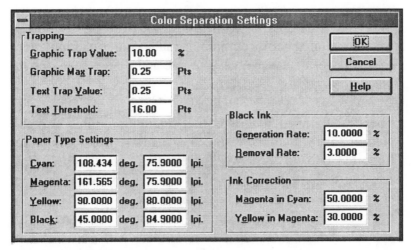

If you select the type of paper that is going to be used, PagePlus will make use of its knowledge of the available printer resolutions to set up four suitable screens - lower resolution for more absorbent low quality paper and higher resolution for better quality paper. If you select custom paper then you can enter values for the screens' resolution and angles yourself.

» Black generation

If you are going to make very much use of process colour via PagePlus then you need to understand one more technicality, *black generation*. The inclusion of the black ink in process colour causes something of a problem. The reason is simply that you don't need it as any RGB colour can be converted to CMY without the use of black. Equal proportions of CMY give a sort of warm brown-black which in most situations would be better replaced by the cold black produced by black ink. The question is, if every RGB colour that you use in PagePlus can be converted to CMY how is the black plate to be generated?

There are a number of solutions to this problem and many were developed before computers made colour manipulation easier. PagePlus takes a very simple and direct approach to black generation.

The first thing to realise is that PagePlus is able to treat colours that you apply within it differently from colours in imported objects. Within PagePlus there are two different ways to create a black tint. You can start by assigning the colour black and then setting a tint between 0 and 100%. In this case PagePlus will recognise your use of black and it will appear on the black separation. However, if you create a custom colour by mixing equal proportions of RGB the result will look like a black tint but it will not appear on the black separation. Instead equal proportions of CMY will be used to generate the tone.

So, for colours that you assign within PagePlus:

» The colour black and its tints are used to generate the black plate.

» Equal mixtures of RGB look black or grey but they are not transferred to the black plate.

Using these rules you can determine how black is produced for internal objects but this doesn't work for imported or OLE objects. The reason is simply that the colours within an external object are specified as RGB values and PagePlus has no way of telling if equal proportions of RGB were generated as black or if they were intended to be a warm brown colour mix.

One approach would be to simply ignore the problem and not to worry about black generation for external objects. There is a good reason why you cannot do this. There is a limit on the amount of ink that paper can accept without causing problems with drying and smudging. In most cases you cannot apply 100% Cyan, Magenta and Yellow ink to produce black without the result being a mess! Usually the amount of ink in any area of the page has to be kept down to 200% to 250% but it does depend very much on the type of paper and on the press.

The solution to the problem is to remove a specified percentage of the grey component to the black plate. The grey component is simply the largest equal percentage of CMY in a colour because mixing equal proportions of C, M and Y produce a shade of black.

For example, suppose that 100% of the grey component is to be removed to the black plate and the inks about to be applied were:

C	M	Y	K
20%	50%	30%	0%

In this case the grey component is 20% and all of it will be removed to the black plate. The resulting ink applied to the paper is:

C	M	Y	K
0%	30%	10%	20%

Notice that by removing all of the grey component the total ink applied has been reduced from 100% to 60%.

You can control the proportion of the grey component removed to the black plate by clicking on the Settings button in the Color Separations dialog box. You can set a percentage of the grey component to be generated on the black plate and the percentage to remove from the C, M and Y plates. For example, if you set the Generation Rate to 100% then all of the grey component will appear on the black plate. If you also set the Removal Rate to 100% then all of the grey component will be removed from the C, M and Y plates. In practice this would produce an image with strong cold blacks but very washed out colours. A common solution is to generate a higher proportion of black from the grey component than you remove from the C, M and Y plates. This produces clear blacks but without reducing the overall colour saturation too much.

Unfortunately there is no easy way of deciding on appropriate settings except by trial and error. Increasing the generation rate makes the blacks in images colder and decreasing the removal rate increases the warmth and depth in coloured areas. If you generate too much black without removing enough then the result can be over-inking.

Start from the default settings and make small adjustments as you become familiar with the results produced by the type of images and the printing process you are working with. It is a matter of learning what effect changes have. If you are serious about working with process colour then you could try to calibrate your entire production line. By scanning in a colour test strip, or by converting it to Photo CD, you can produce a colour separation and test print. By adjusting the black generation parameters and colour correcting the scanned image you can establish the range of settings which work.

It is worth commenting that process colour is a difficult technique to master and there is a great deal of mythology surrounding it. In most cases PagePlus's default settings are a good starting point to work from, in conjunction with advice from your printer.

» Colour accuracy

The colours that appear on your screen are in no way accurate. To see this for yourself, select a nice shade of blue and then adjust the monitor's colour contrast. The 'blue' can be made anything from washed out slate grey to purple. Even a carefully adjusted monitor is little help in allowing you to judge the finished effect of mixing inks on paper. There are books of process colour samples, much like spot colour samples, but you still can be surprised at the finished result, unless you have a colour proof made.

PagePlus includes Pantone Process colours and it is important not to confuse these with Pantone Spot colours. The spot colours correspond to inks of the same name which produce the same colour as displayed in the Pantone colour sample booklet. The Pantone Process colours on the other hand are simply set proportions of CMYK that produce the colour in the Pantone Process colour sample book. You can think of them as a pre-printed test of the colour so that you have a rough idea of the finished result.

Colour control and correction is the most difficult area of DTP and new programs and methods are still being developed. If you are worried about the exact colour rendering of your layout then produce colour separations to film and ask your bureau to produce a Cromalin print. This is a photographic process which recombines the CMYK separations and lets you see a reasonable approximation to the final paper print. The main problem with a Cromalin is that it is expensive and still not 100% accurate.

The complication is *colour correction*. All scanning devices, monitors and printing presses introduce *colour bias*. This has to be removed if the finished product is going to be free of colour casts. This is very similar to the problem of getting back colour photos from the processor which are too red or blue. In the case of colour correcting separations the job is more difficult because you cannot see the finished results until they are printed. Sophisticated packages can allow for a range of colour corrections from scanner colour casts to ink contamination. PagePlus allows you to adjust ink contamination in the Options dialog box just below the Black Generation setting, but if you want to make colour corrections to images then you need a special image editor such as ImagePro or Photoshop.

As long as you are not trying to produce colour photo reproductions of glossy colour magazine quality, then you should be able to use PagePlus to create process colour separations. If you need this extra quality then an alternative is to allow a specialist pre-press bureau to add the colour photos to your layout. In this case simply select the Suppress Pictures option in the Print Options dialog box. You then have to supply the photographic originals for the pre-press bureau to separate and manually paste into the film. You can also opt for OPI (Open Pre-press Interface) comments to be inserted into your PostScript output in place of the images. You supply the bureau with this PostScript file on disk and they scan in and separate the photographs storing the result in place of the comments. The file is then sent to film in the usual way.

If you really want to keep control and minimise costs, then the only solution is to use an advanced image processing package such as PhotoShop or PhotoStyler to scan in and separate the image into a CMYK TIF file. This is a "flavour" of TIF file that specifies colour as proportions of C, M, Y and K rather than RGB. That is, the TIF file has the black generated already and PagePlus will not change this when producing separations. Using CMYK TIFs means that you can bring the full power of these specialist packages to bear on producing the best possible CMYK separations.

» Page marks

The page size that you set up in PagePlus often doesn't correspond to the physical page size used by your printing device. If you are using the output from your printer as the finished product then this can be a problem. However, when it comes to producing CRC and film for a printing press it is important that your physical page size is bigger. The reason is simply that you need to include marks outside the layout area that the printer can use to align the printing plates. In most cases you need at least an extra inch around the layout area for crop and registration marks. *Crop marks* show how the paper needs to be trimmed to produce the final page size and *registration marks* (or alignment marks) are used to align each of the separations. If you are producing paper CRC via a laser printer then it is worth knowing that the accuracy of alignment that you can achieve is limited because of the uneven stretching of the paper as it passes through the heating rollers. This one reason why colour separations generally have to be sent to film.

To make PagePlus add crop and registration marks simply select the Crop Marks box in the Options dialog box. It is also a good idea to add information about how the separations were made alongside the crop marks by selecting the File Information box, also in the Options dialog box. You can add your own custom registration marks by drawing lines, circles and so on using the predefined colour called Register. This is an equal mix of 100% C, M, Y and K and so anything you draw using it appears on each of the separations.

Notice that when you are sending a layout to an imagesetter it is important to set a physical page size, using the Printer Setup dialog box, that is large enough to take the layout page and its crop marks. Ask the bureau that you are going to use what is the largest page area their machine can handle. Don't make the physical page size much bigger than it needs to be because this simply wastes film. Many bureaux charge for film by a fixed page size - usually A4. If your layout is on A5 then it is usual to select A4 film to accommodate the crop marks. A4 can be printed on A3 or A4 "extra" which is slightly larger than A4 to accommodate crop marks. If your layout uses a full A3 sheet then print to A3 extra to make sure that there is room for the crop marks.

» Image input

If you are planning to use photographs within your layouts then you will either need a scanner or you will have to use a bureau or the Kodak Photo CD process. The whole subject of scanners is tricky because manufacturers tend not to explain exactly what their scanners can do. A scanner can work at a given resolution in dpi, much like a printer, but unlike a printer you can alter the effective resolution of a scanner by scaling. For example, if you have a 100 dpi scanner then scanning in a photo at twice the size that you want to use it and then scaling it within PagePlus gives an effective resolution of 200 dpi. You can see that scanner resolution isn't quite as fixed as printer resolution.

In general if you have an original that you are going to reproduce, scaled to a different size and at a given screen resolution, then you need to scan at a resolution given by:

$$\text{scan resolution} = \frac{\text{picture height}}{\text{original height}} \times \text{screen resolution}$$

For example, if you have a photo 5 inches high by 4 inches wide and plan to reproduce this so that its height is only 2 inches using a 100 lpi screen, then you need to scan in the original at 125 dpi. This is, of course, a minimum scan resolution that will produce a picture file with a resolution that just matches the screen resolution. In practice it is advisable to scan at 1.5 or 2 times the minimum resolution to allow for changes. Notice that using a much higher scan resolution can actually reduce the quality of the final image and certainly wastes disk storage space.

The exception to this 'lowest scan resolution is the best' rule is when you are scanning line art. In this case always scan at the highest possible resolution so that you are certain of recording any fine lines.

As well as spatial resolution in dpi you also have to take account of grey level resolution. Many early scanners were '1-bit' scanners which means they could only distinguish between full black and full white. If you are planning to scan photographs you need a scanner that can work at 256 grey levels (sometimes called an 8-bit scanner) with a spatial resolution of at least 300 dpi. Some 1-bit scanners use a special trick to give the impression that they can scan grey levels. This involves screening the image and storing it pre-screened. If you try to use one of these image formats in PagePlus it is vital that you optimise scaling for the printer resolution, otherwise the built-in screen will be distorted. If at all possible try not to use limited grey scale resolution scanners. True grey level file formats can be rescaled without too much worry.

Scanning in line art can also cause problems when you rescale it. If you scale it without regard to the printer resolution then fine detail can be lost in an unpredictable way. At one scaling it will be visible but a slight change in the size of the image can make the detail vanish. It is possible to scale line art to non-optimum printer sizes to good effect but only by trial and error.

Colour scanners bring with them another level of difficulty. Until recently moderately priced scanners could only manage a maximum of eight tones of Red, Green and Blue, i.e. 512 colours. These produce acceptable, but not professional, results. Now there are affordable 24-bit scanners, that is offering 256 Red, 256 Green and 256 Blue tones, making a total of over 16 million distinct colours. With patience and calibration these can produce excellent results. If you need top quality results then send the colour photo to a bureau and let them scan it for you. Colour scanners all suffer from colour errors that make their output too blue or too red. You need a colour editing/scanning package such as PhotoFinish or PhotoPlus to colour correct the results before they can be used.

» TWAIN scanners and PagePlus

Until very recently every scanner supported its own particular interface standard that needed special software drivers for each program that wanted to use them. As a result most scanners worked with the scanning program that was provided with them and that was all. The TWAIN standard has largely overcome this problem. TWAIN defines exactly how a scanner should work and any TWAIN scanner will work with any application that supports it. PagePlus supports a TWAIN scanner. All you have to do is install the scanner and its software. When you next use PagePlus you can select the Scanner option in the Picture Assistant or use the command File, Import Picture, Scanner if you have disabled the Picture Assistant. PagePlus will automatically find the

TWAIN driver and start the standard TWAIN SCAN dialog box running. Exactly what the SCAN dialog box looks like depends on the scanner you are using - it is part of the TWAIN implementation and not PagePlus. It usually gives you some way of previewing the scanned image, selecting a sub-area, altering the brightness and contrast and so on.

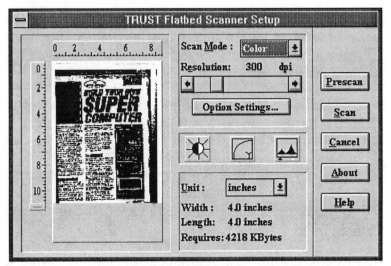

If for some reason you have more than one TWAIN device installed you can select which one is used for scanning via the Tools,Defaults,Scanner Source command.

In most cases it is probably better to use a separate image editing package to scan and edit the resulting image rather than rely on getting it right first time. An image that you have scanned directly into PagePlus can, however, be edited using PhotoPlus.

Key points

» The output resolution that you need depends on the type of graphics you are printing. Continuous tone images need at least 600 dpi or more.

» Grey tones are created using screens. The higher the screen resolution the smaller the number of grey tones that can be represented. Screen resolution is measured in lines per inch (lpi).

» The easiest way to send output to an imagesetter is to install the appropriate Windows printer driver.

» Spot colour is the simplest type of colour printing. It uses named colours and one printing pass per colour. A screen can be used to create spot colour tints. Imported images may have to be colour mapped to spot colours already used in the layout.

» Process colour can reproduce any colour using a combination of Cyan, Magenta, Yellow and blacK (CMYK). Four matched screens are used, one for each colour.

» Colours specified using Red, Green, Blue (RGB) have to be converted into CMYK. This is difficult because there is no unique way of generating the black ink needed to print any given image. PagePlus uses a simple black generation and removal method for imported images.

» When using a scanner for image input it is important to take account of any scaling that may be used. Scanning at too high a resolution can produce distortions. True grey and colour images can usually be scaled without problems. Black and white and dithered images should only be scaled to double, treble, etc. their actual size.

Chapter 9

Practical Production

Pre-press and production can seem bewildering to the beginner. There are so many choices to make and each choice affects what is possible within the design. In practice these choices are not independent of one another and issues such as page size, colour process and printing method have to be considered together. In this chapter we look at three sample layouts - a spot colour advert, a process colour A5 flyer and a spot colour A3 book cover. Each of these layouts is "real" in the sense that it went through the complete production cycle and was actually used, appearing in a magazine, in the product box of PagePlus 3 and on the cover of this book.

» Tour Six: a spot colour advert

As an example of the pre-press production process this tour creates a half page spot colour advert - for this book! This advertisement created in PagePlus has actually appeared in a magazine so this isn't a theoretical exercise. The production process is typical of creating a spot colour advert for off-the-page sales.

» Page size

To create an ad for a magazine you need to know the size allocated to the type of ad. You usually do this by asking for production, or mechanical, details. In this case the size was specified as 91 mm by 265 mm. Enter this as a custom page size using the Page Setup dialog box.

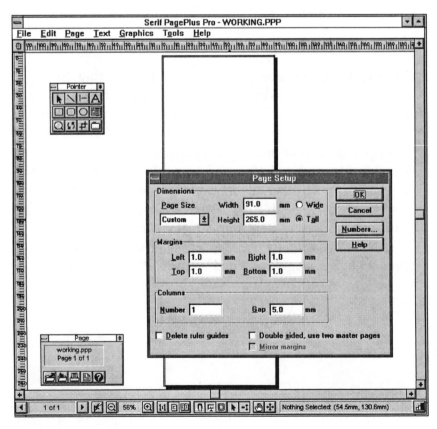

Sometimes you will be told that the size includes 'no-bleed'. *Bleed* is when the layout is allowed to spill over into the margins for special effects and *no bleed* is when there is going to be white space around the page. This advert was specified as no bleed - it was not to exceed the area allocated to it. Margins of 1 mm were set to act as guides for a box outline around the entire ad.

When this custom page size is printed it will be centred on the paper loaded into the printer and there will be plenty of space for crop marks, registration marks and whatever else you want to appear off the edge of the layout. As the page size is specified in millimetres, this is also the scale suitable for the rulers and snap grid.

» Image import

If you have any graphics or text that already exist as files on disk then it is usually a good idea to import them at an early stage. For one thing this gives you a chance to print them out to see if they work! If you adopt a cautious attitude then you will discover what the output looks like as you go along and avoid having to completely redesign everything when you find it doesn't work at the end.

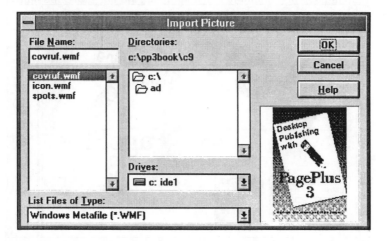

In this case the only prepared object was an early draft of the cover of this book, drawn using PagePlus and then exported as a picture in WMF format. Use the File,Import Picture command and the Import Picture dialog box to import your graphics.

Of course you don't have access to the WMF file for the cover of this book but it isn't difficult to put together something similar using PagePlus. Simply use a rotated rectangle and add some lettering. Select all of the objects in your design and use the Export as Picture command as you did in the previous tour for the logo.

» Adding a flash

In working out a layout it is often better to position the large or critical objects first. In this case the book cover and the word NEW rotated through an angle are positioned at the top of the page. It is also time to start to allocate the spot colours. As the actual colours used will be determined by the magazine printing the ad, there is no need to resort to accurate Pantone colours - a simple Red will do just as well.

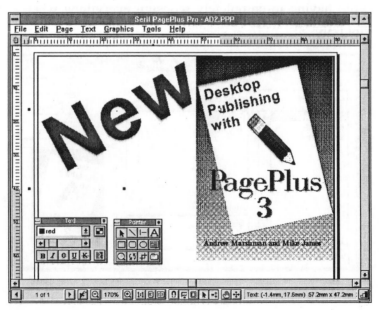

» Adding a coupon

In many cases the most difficult part of any advertising layout is the coupon - the section of the advert that is supposed to be cut out and returned to order goods. Coupons can vary from elaborate graphics to simple text but they nearly always involve rulings of some sort. In this case the rulings are so regular that they look like a table and TablePlus, which is included in the PagePlus Professional Suite and is also available as an add-on, is the best tool to use. Even when the rulings are not so regular TablePlus is still the quickest way of creating a coupon because you can merge and split cells to create a less regular table. The alternative is to draw the table using line and box drawing tools and this can be slow.

To run TablePlus simply click on the Import Picture icon in the ToolBox and then on the TablePlus icon. This opens the table editor application and you can start creating the table. TablePlus is easy to use but it has some limitations. You can't set text properties such as bold or italic on part of a text item and there is very little point in assigning

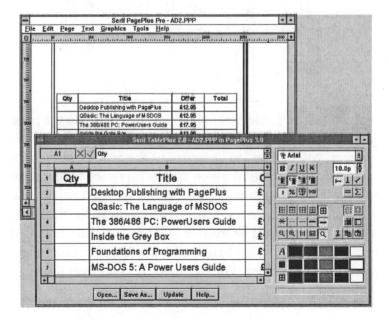

spot colour. This is because the table is treated as an OLE object in PagePlus and all spot colours in OLE objects appear on the black separation. Even with these limitations TablePlus provides a much more convenient way of creating the table than any alternative.

The quickest way to learn about TablePlus is to try using it. Like PagePlus, it has a HintLine that tells you what everything does. You can select individual cells or groups of cells by dragging with the pointer. You can set a border for each cell or group of cells to make regular or irregular rulings. Changing the size of each column or row is done by dragging on the column or row dividers. You can merge cells and split them apart again as required. The size of the entire table, number of rows and columns is controlled by the resize icon which displays the Edit table size dialog box.

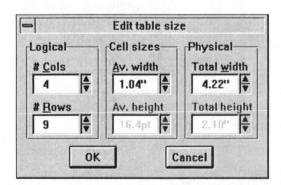

When you close TablePlus the table is inserted into the page and you can treat it in the same way as any other object. However, you do need to be aware of the problems inherent in scaling a table to fit a given space. It is very tempting to design a table using a reasonable point size and reasonable width rulings and then use scaling to make it fit the available space in the layout. The trouble is when the table is scaled every aspect of it - font height and width and ruling height and width - are scaled. For example, if you crush the table horizontally you will discover that all the vertical rulings are narrower than the horizontal rulings and the font is distorted. To avoid such distortion you should always scale a table with the Shift key held down to maintain its aspect ratio. (Remember you have to start to drag a handle before you press the Shift key.)

If you drag a handle to rescale the table and hold down the Ctrl key then the table will be kept to a multiple of its actual size i.e. 1:1, 2:1 and so on. Ideally you should use a table object at the exact size that it was created in TablePlus. Only in this case will the fonts and rulings be exactly the size you selected. However, this advice is too restrictive because it throws away the huge advantage of being able to scale a table to fit the available space. So in practice you should try to make the table fit the space as closely as possible without scaling and then use scaling sparingly to fit the table exactly. Also try to keep the horizontal and vertical scaling as equal as possible.

» The name and address box

You may not think of a name and address box as a table - but this is by far the easiest way to create one! In this case the table has two columns but in the first three rows the cells are joined together to make one. Only in the postcode row does the fact that there are two columns become clear. The rulings are generated automatically and take account of the joined cells.

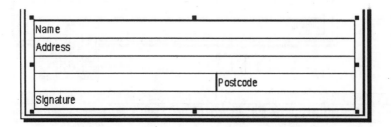

» Adding credit card boxes

After two uses of the table editor you might expect the row of empty boxes used for credit card details to be another table. This is where choosing the correct tool for the job makes a great deal of difference. The boxes have an uneven spacing so it is much easier to draw them using a square drawing tool. To make it easy what you do is draw one square and then copy it to the Windows Clipboard. Pasting gives you two squares that can be aligned to form a short row. Next copying both squares and pasting gives you a group of four. The rest of the row of boxes can now be assembled by repeatedly pasting the group of four. The snap grid helps in positioning them accurately.

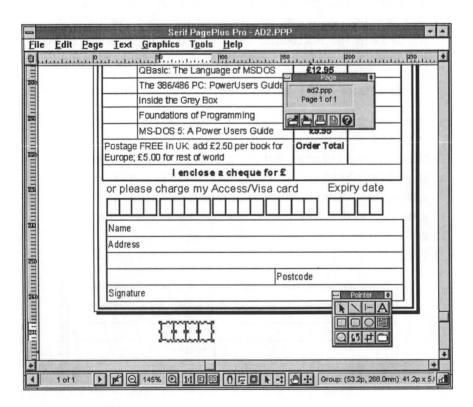

» The main text

Returning to the top of the advert, it is time to add some body text. This could be done by importing text that had been prepared using a word processor but often in small ads it is preferable to type the text from scratch. In this case it was thought a good idea to make the text flow around the flash as well as the picture. This is just a matter of using the Tools,Wrap settings menu command and then selecting Text Wrap in the dialog box. The wrap outline can then be edited to the correct shape. The body text was typed in as free text - there is no point in using frame text because there isn't enough to autoflow!

The final step is to add a small banner headline in red, the remainder of the text, and a box with a 1 point line around the entire page.

» Production

Once the layout is complete it only remains to print it. As two colours are used in the advert, two spot colour separations need to be printed - black and red. If you examine the layout you will see that neither colour overlaps the other and their placement relative to one another isn't critical. That is, there is no need to worry about the lack of traps and there is no real need to print to film as long as the resolution of the output device is high enough. As the spot colours are all used at 100% and there is only one small picture with few grey tones, 300 dpi laser print output is likely to be adequate. In fact a LaserJet 4 was used giving 600 dpi resolution and better quality in the graduated fill in the image of the book's cover.

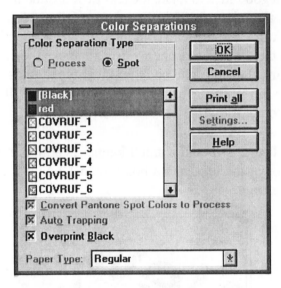

The first problem that arises is that when you select Color Separate in the Printer dialog box and then click on Colors to set the type of separations to Spot you will see a long list of colours that you haven't used! A moment's thought should tell you that they come from the imported picture. The solution to the problem is either to use the Color Mapper to reduce all of these colours to red or black, or to use the command Graphics,Picture,Color to set the foreground colour of this image to black. As we are not attempting to print spot colour within the image (this would require printing to film to ensure accurate registration) setting the foreground colour to black solves the problem.

As long as the magazine is happy about accepting paper CRC then printing the two separations, complete with crop and registration marks, is all that is necessary. If they want bromide or film then printing to a file is the only extra step required. However, you also need to ask the bureau what type of imagesetter they are using. In this case there is no need to specify a physical page size larger than the standard A4 used by the Linotronic driver.

Black   Red   Composite

» Tour Seven: a full colour flyer

This layout was used as the in-box advertising sheet for this book - so you are likely to have seen it already! The objectives of the layout were two-fold. The first was to include a colour photograph to demonstrate how well PagePlus handles process colour and the second was to include a range of techniques to show how flexible the process colour option is.

» The photo

The photograph was taken from a collection of wildlife shots supplied on a Photo CD by Corel. The licensing terms of this library are that you can use any photo in a design or publication as long as you don't redistribute the photograph in another library. This is an increasingly common form of licensing agreement. Do make sure, however, that any photo you use, be it in Photo CD format or scanned in from an original, isn't covered by a licensing agreement that involves a royalty payment. Obtaining permissions or complying with licences is one of the biggest DTP headaches so using a library with a simple "buy and use" condition may restrict your choice but at least it lets you concentrate on the layout!

The Photo CD image can be used in a number of resolutions, ranging from 92 x 128 to 2048 x 3072. The higher the resolution the larger the image file and the longer it takes to load and manipulate. So the question is which resolution to use? Given the overall layout is going to be on A5 and the image is likely to be no more than 4 by 4 inches it is easy to work out the sort of resolution that will be required, assuming that the resolution of the final output is known. As an imagesetter will have to be used to produce film and the final design is to be printed on art paper, the screens in use will be approximately 120 lpi. At 4 by 4 inches the lowest image resolution acceptable is **480 x 480, i.e.** 4 x 120 dpi=480 dots.

To be on the safe side the Photo CD image was read in at 1536 x 1024 because this allowed it to be cropped to the central area, i.e. the tiger's face, giving a final resolution of 950 x 980, i.e. roughly twice the minimum resolution.

The image could have been read directly into PagePlus but this would have resulted either in a link being made to the Photo CD or the entire image being embedded into the file. Given that the image has to be processed it makes more sense to first load it into PhotoPlus, crop it and save it onto the hard disk in TIF format. The Open File box in PhotoPlus allows you to see a thumbnail of the original image.

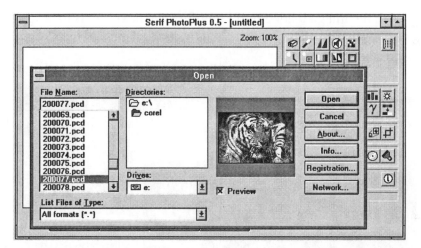

When you click on Open you will see another dialog box giving you a choice of resolutions - both spatial and colour. As already discussed, the spatial resolution needs to be 1536 x 1024 and it is obvious that we need more than a 16-colour or grey scale image. But are 256 colours enough or does it have to be TrueColor? A TrueColor image

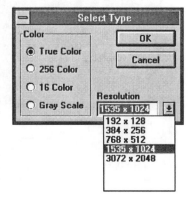

uses 24 bits to represent the colour of each pixel, i.e. each pixel can be set to any of 16,777,216 colours. The only disadvantage of using TrueColor is that the disk file that results is usually large and the image is slow to load and manipulate. A 256 colour image is one third of the size of a TrueColor image but it only uses 256 colours selected from the palette of over 16 million. As long as the range of colours within the image are not a complete spectrum of every possible colour, then a 256 colour image is often as good as a TrueColor image. In this case the file size for a TrueColor image - around 2.5 MBytes after cropping - isn't too big to use and so it is simpler not to use a 256 colour image.

With the image loaded into PhotoPlus the next step is to crop it. This is very easy and just needs a steady hand and the Crop tool.

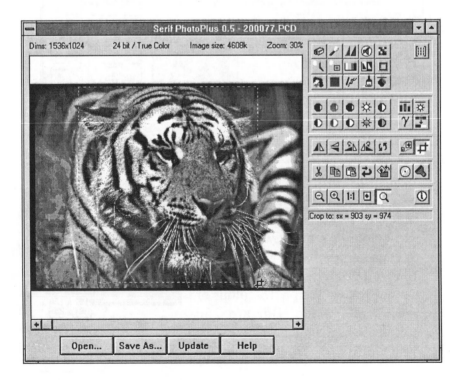

As the image is from a Photo CD library it is reasonably safe to assume that there are no colour biases and the image can be used "as is" without further processing. The next step is to save the image as an LZW compressed TIF file on your hard disk and import it into PagePlus in the usual way.

After placing the tiger on the page a black box was added to create a border. This gives you the opportunity to compare the difference between the black generated within an imported object and a true black as applied to an internal object. Also notice the guides that have been added to allow the alignment of other objects with the edge of the photo.

» The text

Compared to preparing the photograph the rest of the layout is fairly standard. A tint box at the top of the page is used as a background for the first two lines of text. These were made to fit between the vertical guides by interactively altering its point size and width. Fitting text in this way is a very difficult task in any other DTP package because they generally lack PagePlus's interactive way of changing properties.

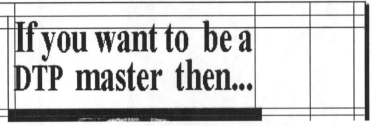

The final settings were 70 point Times New Roman with its width reduced to 70% to produce the tall thin look. Notice that it is important to remove the tint box's outline.

The text at the bottom of the page is equally straightforward. The first two lines are set in Arial, a sans serif font to contrast with the serif font Times New Roman. The only adjustment is that manual tracking has been applied to the "k" and "T" in "DeskTop".

The final two lines of text are set in Times New Roman with a fill of 100% white against a red tint panel. The actual red produced in the finished product was considered unimportant as long it was a strong pure colour.

» The flash

The star-shaped flash is a simple design created using TypePlus. A single star shape in yellow plus a red shadow was used to hold three text items in red. The only difficult part is in positioning the two curved text lines to fit within the star while maintaining the same circular curvature around the centre of the star. This was achieved by interactively shifting the text, sizing it and stretching it horizontally to change the curvature. As the layout is using process colour there is no need to worry about matching the colours used within the flash to the ones used within the main document. However, the red has the same RGB components and so will look the same as the red in the main document.

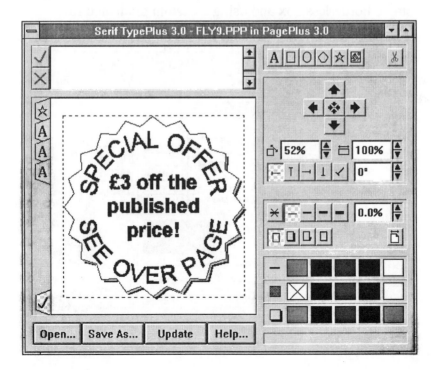

» The logo

The final step is to import and position the I/O Press logo which, although originally created using a drawing program, was available as a WMF file. Notice that the background colour of the logo is white and this does not allow the tint panel to show through.

» The reverse of the flyer

The reverse side of the flyer is a simple design which could just as well have been rendered using spot colour. Given that it uses four distinct colours it is unlikely that this would have been any cheaper than the four-colour printing used in process colour. The background to the page is graduated from blue to a light blue. The fill lightens rapidly so that the black text is readable. Maintaining sufficient contrast when text is placed against a tint box or graduated fill is always a problem.

The graduated fill was created using DrawPlus by drawing a single borderless box and using a custom graduated fill.

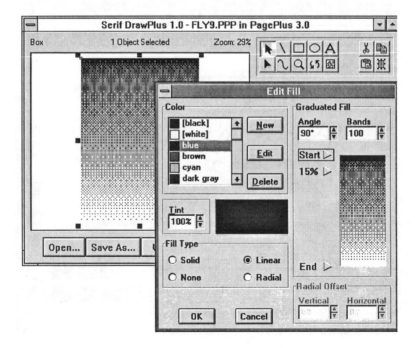

The exact starting and finishing tint values can be adjusted by trial and error to produce the desired effect. More difficult is choosing how may steps or *bands* the fill should use. A graduated fill is created by drawing individual rectangles each filled with an appropriate tint. If you have too many bands then the WMF file is large and takes too long to print. It can also cause some printers to fail to print the fill at all. If you have too few bands the fill looks "steppy". To work out how many bands to specify you need to consider the size of a single band. In this case the rectangle will be scaled to 8 inches vertically. If you want a single band to be no bigger than about 1/10 inch then you need 80 bands in the original rectangle. Rounding this up to 100 to reduces the band size to 0.08 inch which what was used in the final print.

Another way to look as this problem is to notice that 100 bands scaled into 8 inches gives a band density of 12.5 bands per inch. This should be compared to the imagesetter resolution of 120 lines per inch. If you try to print more than 120 bands per inch then you will fail because this is beyond the resolution of the imagesetter. On the other hand 12 bands per inch is well within the resolution of the imagesetter. This said it is has to be pointed out that using graduated fills is always a risk in the sense that you cannot be sure if the fill will look smooth or "steppy" until you see the film!

The remainder of the back page is straightforward, consisting of a catalogue of features and techniques. The two stars were created using TypePlus and rotated within PagePlus to the complementary angles required. The Headline text is set in red outline. All of the text apart from the two column bullet points is free text set between the page margins. The bullet points are in a two-column frame and use a technique described in Chapter 10 to make the bullets line up.

The name and address box is a TablePlus object and the credit card and signature boxes are drawn using the PagePlus Box tool. Notice that all of boxes are set to a white fill to increase the contrast.

Finally, it is worth saying that as a design - rather than as a sampler of techniques which is what was intended - the back page is an example of the overuse of DTP features with too many text styles and embellishments.

» Production

Process colour always needs the high resolution and accuracy of film so the final print had to be sent to a PostScript imagesetter. However, before this a large number of paper test prints were produced using a 300 dpi PostScript laser printer. This can at least check that the layout works even if it doesn't allow you to see the effect of the higher resolution. In most cases 300 dpi laser printer output looks darker than high resolution imagesetter output. Also notice that if your test print crashes the laser printer this doesn't mean that it will not print on an imagesetter. Laser printers often run out of memory when printing complex designs so any error messages that hint that the laser printer has run out of resources isn't as worrying as other types of problem. If, however, you can make your designs print to a standard PostScript laser printer there is no excuse for an imagesetter failing!

To produce the flyer a bureau running an Agfa imagesetter was used. The standard Agfa 9000 printer driver, supplied with Windows 3.1, was used to print the two pages to a file. As the design is on A5, the print was made to A4 sized paper to ensure that there was space for the crop marks and file information. This file was then sent to the bureau by modem, but it could just as easily have been sent on disk, for printing to film. The front page, the only colour critical component, was also proofed by requesting a cromalin.

When the film arrived the film for the back page was acceptable but the cromalin revealed that the tiger image lacked colour saturation and contrast. The solution was to use PhotoPlus to increase the contrast of the original image and send the result to film for a second time. This produced an acceptable result and these films were used to print the flyer.

If you look at the finished colour print you will notice that the black at the edges of the photo are browny as opposed to the solid black of the border. The browny tones really are 100% black and the effect is due to the difference between CMY black and pure blacK as described in Chapter 8. In this case the contrast of the photo would be improved by moving more of the grey component to the black plate, making the black darker and colder. However, this would have required yet another complete cycle of films and cromalin and would have been expensive in money and time.

» Tour Eight: a book cover

This tour demonstrates how to handle a large spot colour layout. The design is larger than A4 and so needs to be printed to A3 film. The book cover in question is currently wrapped around this book - so you have no difficulty in seeing the finished result!

» Setting the page size

For this design page size is more difficult than usual because the finished work has to wrap around the completed book. That is, it is the front cover, spine and back cover in one. You can create such large layouts using a page for each component and rely on the pre-press facilities at the printers to assemble the film for you but it is cheaper to do the job in one.

The first problem is working out the size of the cover. This book uses a page size of 156 mm by 234 mm so the whole cover has to be 234 mm tall and twice 156 mm wide plus the space needed for the spine. The only way to find out how much space to leave for the spine is to ask the printer after determining the paper type and the number of pages. Although printers do have access to tables that tell them the spine size for any number of pages, most do it by getting together the required number of pages and measuring! In this case the spine size is 15 mm making the page width 327 mm.

With the page size of 327 mm by 234 mm established, the next step is to position guides that divide the page into front, back and spine. The first guide should be set at 156 mm and the second at 171 mm. Although not necessary, setting 15 mm margins around the page serves as a reminder not to use the area too close to the edge.

» Importing the picture

The tiger photo used on the process colour flyer appears again in the cover design. In this case, however, the image has to be monochrome because the cover is in spot colour. Although there are a range of colours and effects that could be used, a simple grey level image is achieved by setting the foreground picture colour to black. An alternative way of achieving the same result would have been to use PhotoPlus, or another image editing package, to convert the colour image to grey scale.

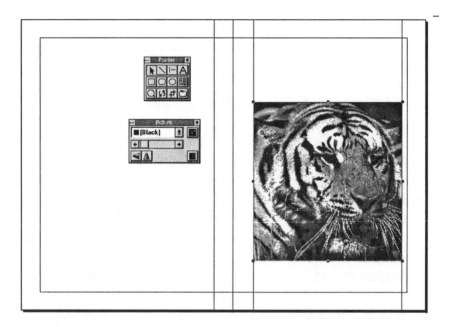

» The text

Nearly all of the remainder of the layout is text. The titles are sized interactively to fit between the guides inserted along the edges of the picture. As the point size is so large 5% tracking is applied to draw the text together. The front cover text is all yellow on black.

The back jacket text is white on black and it is loaded into a frame. Notice that as white always comes free in a spot colour layout this cover can be printed using just yellow and black, i.e. it is a two-colour printing job. The bullet points are loaded into a separate two-column frame which has been adjusted to produce equal columns of five bullet points each. The spine text is simply rotated and placed between the guides.

» The logos and barcode

The two I/O Press logos are the same WMF file used in the process colour flyer. The only change is that the Color Mapper has been used to change black to white and white to black. The barcode of the book's ISBN number is a TIF file created using one of the many barcode generating programs. The ISBN number is typed into the barcode program which writes the TIF file to disk.

» Production

As only two colours are used, the production of the film is just a matter of printing a spot colour separation. All of the imported images have been colour mapped to black and white so there are no nasty surprises waiting. The only unusual feature is that the film size has to be selected as A3 to accommodate the crop marks and file information. A particular problem with this sort of oversized layout is printing proofs using a laser printer. A4 paper is too small so you have a simple choice between printing a mosaic of pages which you have to stick together or using the Scale to fit option to print a reduced size version.

A final tip is that it is usually a good idea to make the background box 10% larger than the cover page size - that is add a 10% bleed. This makes sure that the black extends right up to the edge of the cover in case there are any misalignments. The same reasoning says that you should keep well away from the right and left edges of the cover and position any objects well to the centre of the spine. If you follow these guidelines then any errors in sizing the cover or the spine, or in applying the cover to the book, will be less apparent.

» Typical costings

One of the surprises awaiting you at the point where DTP meets the outside world of traditional printing is the wide range of charges you will encounter for the same services. In all cases it pays to shop around.

Often you can make use of laser printer output and so save the cost of film or bromide but if your layout includes spot colour that has to fit together accurately, photographs or process colour you will need film or bromide.

Most bureaux charge by the page for bromide and film. Typical prices are £5 to £9 for A4 film and £4 to £7 for A4 bromide. Larger sizes are often have to be quoted for but typically A3 film should cost £8 to £15 and A3 bromide £7 to £12. Bear in mind, however, that most bureaux set a minimum charge of around £25. If you want a faster service then you can arrange it at a premium. Similarly if you are prepared to wait until the imagesetter isn't busy then many bureaux will give a discount. Discounts are also sometimes made for files that can be sent directly to the imagesetter rather than PagePlus .PPP files - and you now know how easy that is. If you send any particularly complicated layouts to an imagesetter then the bureau may charge for the extra time. But don't worry - even if it takes 10 minutes on a PostScript laser printer it should still print fast enough not to incur a surcharge.

Most bureaux also offer services such as producing Cromalin proofs, typically £30 per A4 print, and scanning originals. This is relatively expensive, expect to pay up to £20 for an A6 colour photo.

The price that varies most widely is the cost of printing the finished product. Look out for specialists in the specific type of output you require. For example, using a specialist A5 booklet printer can work out at less than half the cost charged by a general jobbing printer. The same is true of process colour printing.

» Find a specialist and always get more than one quote.

Finally when you are getting quotes don't worry the printer with any talk of DTP - just say that you will supply film or CRC to their specification!

Key points

» Simple spot colour designs can often be printed using nothing but a laser printer. In this case don't try to position colours too close to one another.

» Process colour always needs to be printed to film and you may need cromalin proofs to check the colour balance and quality.

» Spot colour can be used almost as effectively as full process colour as long as you keep your design simple and use tints and gradient fills.

» Always remember that in a spot colour design you get white for free!

» A bureau can be used to produce film or bromide from files delivered in person, sent through the post or delivered electronically using a modem.

» You will need one film or bromide per colour. So, black and one spot colour requires two films and full process colour requires four - one each for cyan, magenta, yellow and black.

» It is well worth shopping around as bureau charges vary widely.

Chapter 10

Tools and Tips

PagePlus is a sophisticated package with many separate tools that are designed to do particular jobs. The initial task when you first start to use it is to discover what facilities are on offer and the most convenient way of using them all. As with any software, however, once you get beyond the basics there is a new level of challenge and the opportunity to experiment. Part of the skill in using a DTP package is in seeing how its tools can be made to work together to provide unexpected, and for that very reason, effective results.

In this chapter you will find the final tour which concentrates on using all of PagePlus's facilities and a collection of good ideas, hints, tips and problem solvers. Some of the features have already been described briefly within earlier chapters or used within tours but they now deserve a little more attention.

» Tour Nine: an advertising brochure

Tour Nine is a design for the front and back cover of Tour Three's holiday brochure. You do not need to have completed Tour Three, however, to do this one as it is an entirely separate publication. The tutorial assumes you are working at PagePlus 3's Professional level.

The design is concerned with the use of PagePlus together with its mini applications or *applets*. So you will need to have DrawPlus, TypePlus and TablePlus to be able to complete the tour. All of these are included in the PagePlus Professional Suite but are also available individually as add-ons.

Most of the clipart comes from the Travel category of the ArtPack1, which is also included in the Professional Suite, with one picture coming from the Transport category. If you do not have access to these graphics you can, of course, substitute suitable alternatives.

» Page setup

By now you will be aware of how to set up your page. So briefly, just double-click on a free area of your page to open the Page Setup dialog and set your page to A4 Tall (portrait) and set all the margins to 0.5 inches. As these pages are the cover sheets you don't have to worry about having separate margins for facing pages because the centre binding won't be a problem. You also needn't define a master page as there are no headers, footers, or page numbers involved.

» Front cover background and headline

The background for the front cover is simply a box which has a graduated fill effect. This effect is a gradual changing of colour or tint occurring in a particular direction along an object. In this case it is a faded cyan colour which fades into blue and then begins to get darker (increased tint).

The heading is produced by making a hole in the fill background, which acts as a mask, allowing a 'stars and stripes' flag to be seen behind. These effects are all created within DrawPlus.

● To create the main object on your front cover, select the Import Picture tool from the ToolBox and then select the DrawPlus icon from the flyout. Then, with snapping on,  drag the cross-hair cursor from the top left corner of your margined page down to the bottom right corner. This defines the size of the OLE object that you are going to create.

DrawPlus then opens automatically, with a page area equivalent to the size of the drag you just made. This saves you having to define the page/object size manually using the DrawPlus Page Setup dialog.

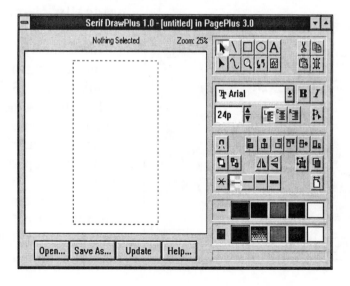

Many of the DrawPlus icons and tools will already be familiar to you as they have PagePlus equivalents. DrawPlus, like PagePlus, also has a HintLine which informs you of the use of various icons and tools as you pass the cursor over them. If the HintLine comment includes the > sign it informs you that double-clicking on that icon will open a dialog box.

● Select the Box tool, in DrawPlus, and then drag from the top left of your margined DrawPlus page to the bottom right corner.

This creates a box that will eventually form the background to your PagePlus publication.

DrawPlus has five predefined graduated fills. Single-clicking on one of these would select it. Alternatively you can create your own fill effect by double-clicking on any one of the Object Fill buttons.

● When you double-click the Edit Fill dialog opens. Select the Linear Fill Type which allows you to create a fill of

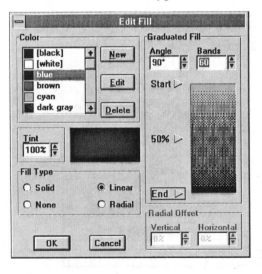

gradually changing colours. You can define exactly what colours and tints make up this effect. Select the Start box on the fill window and then select the cyan colour from the Color drop down list and set the Tint to 100%. This means that your fill starts off with cyan colour at 100% density.

- Next select the 50% box on the fill window, select blue as the colour and set a tint of 60%.

- Finally, select the End box and set the colour to blue and the tint to 90%.

These settings ensure that the starting colour of 100% cyan gradually changes to 60% blue by the time it is half way down the box. The blue then increases in intensity in the lower part of the box reaching 90% at the bottom line. You can adjust the position of the intermediate point on the fill so as to define the colour and tint of the 75% point, or the 25% point, etc..

- Increase the value in the Bands box to 60 so that the change in the fill colour and tint is more gradual, i.e. smoother, and then select OK to apply the fill to the object.

- When you return to the DrawPlus window make sure that the border thickness of the fill (the box object) is set to no border.

Next, you need to create a hole in the fill, in the shape of the words 'USA TOURS'.

- Click on the Text tool and then click on the DrawPlus page, on top of your fill. The Edit Window then opens so that you can type in:

USA

TOURS

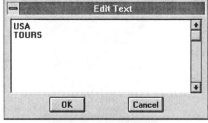

- Click on OK to apply the text.

- Set the text to an attractive sans serif font (such as BahamasHeavy used here) of size 72.0p, apply bold to it and centre align it. It doesn't matter what colour or style the text has for this effect.

- Use the Pointer tool to position the text object, by dragging, so that the baseline is about a quarter of the way down your page, and horizontally centre it using the Align center horizontal icon.

- Send the text behind the fill using the Send object to back icon. If the text remains on top, the effect will not be created in the way that you want.

- Next select the Select All icon followed by the Combine Selection icon to combine the fill and the text which has the effect of creating the mask with hollow text.

- To complete this object you need to place the 'stars and stripes' flag behind the text so that it shows through giving the text a colourful effect. Select the Import Metafile icon and import the picture flag.wmf which we used in Tour Three.

- Drag the flag, and stretch it if necessary, so that it covers the text completely. Then, with the flag still selected, click on the Send object to back icon. The flag should then show through the text heading. That completes the effect.

You can save the DrawPlus object as a separate file (.dpp) for use in other documents but it is not necessary here as the OLE object will be saved as part of your PagePlus publication anyway.

● Once you are happy with your design, select the Update push button to apply the object to your PagePlus page and then close DrawPlus so that you can return to your PagePlus window beneath.

You can select, move, resize, stretch, copy or delete this OLE object just like any other object. If you decide you need to modify the design at all, just double-click on the object to return to DrawPlus with the object open for manipulation.

» **Front cover pictures**

The picture design on the front cover - a set of snapshots scattered over a 'stars and stripes' background - is fairly simple to create and uses the Crop tool which we met in Chapter 7.

● Select the Import Picture tool from the ToolBox and select the Art & Borders icon from the flyout. Then select the flag picture (flag.wmf) before clicking on your page to place it. This acts as the backdrop to your snapshots but first it needs squaring off with the Crop tool.

● So that you can see what you are doing, use the Pointer tool to make the flag object bigger, by dragging on a corner handle with the Shift key held down.

● Next, select the Crop tool and drag inwards on one of the corner handles until both of the adjacent edges of the flag become squared off. Then do the same with the opposite corner until you end up with a rectangular area which is filled with the 'stars and stripes' colouring.

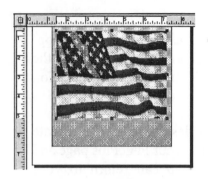

● Now select the Pointer tool and drag on one of the object's corner handles, to stretch it until it is approximately 5.75 inches wide and 4.5 inches high. Then place it centrally in the width of the page, with the bottom of the picture about 10.25 inches from the top of the page. You may need to turn snapping off to position it exactly.

To finish this graphic design you need to import the other pictures and just place them on your pasteboard for now. We used clipart of Mount Rushmore (rushmore.wmf), the Pentagon (pentagon.wmf), the White House (whithous.wmf) and a Caribbean bay (carib.wmf) but you might choose different ones. The rest of this stage is left up to you - resize the pictures, rotate some of them with the rotate tool, flip them if you want, and then drag on them to scatter them over the cropped flag backdrop.

» Front cover text

● The text for the top of the cover page is the single line:
  KEELY TRAVEL LTD

● Using WritePlus apply the text to the page and set its font to Arial of size 24.0p and make it bold. Also increase its letter spacing property to 20% to spread the letters out a little more and centre align the text. To centralise the text object, make sure snapping is on, and with the Pointer tool drag the text's left and right handles across to the left and right margins respectively.

● There are two lines of text for the bottom of the cover:
  SUMMER BREAKS BROCHURE
  1994

● Give the text an appropriate font (such as BahamasHeavy used here) of size 28.0p. Increase the letter spacing a little - to about 10% - and centralise it.

That's the front cover completed!

» **Back cover table**

● Now click on the page forwards button on the Status Bar and then click on OK on the Add Pages dialog to add a second page (the back page) to your design.

● Select the Import Picture tool and then the TablePlus icon. The cursor then becomes a cross-hair so that you can drag to define the size and dimensions of the OLE object. Drag from margin to margin, with snapping on, at a point 2.5 inches from the top of your page down to 5.5 inches.

TablePlus then opens, initially with a dialog allowing you to select a predefined table style. Click on OK to proceed. The TablePlus window then pops up containing a preview of your current table, which in this instance has the size and dimensions defined by the drag you just made on your PagePlus page with the cross-hair.

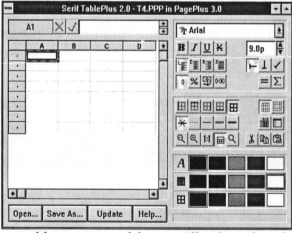

In common with most spreadsheet applications the table has rows labelled 1,2,3,... and columns headed A,B,C,.... These headings are for design purposes only and will not form part of your object.

● The default table is not quite right for your purposes, so select the Resize Table icon from the panel of icons on the right of the TablePlus window.

● Set the number of columns to 7 and the number of rows to 6 using the Edit table size dialog. You can change the values incrementally using the arrow buttons or you can type into the data-entry boxes. Click on OK when you've made the appropriate changes.

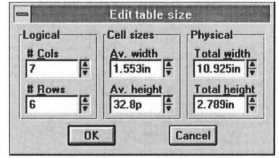

Click on the A1 cell to select it and then type in:

TOUR

The text appears in the text window as you type it, and clicking on the tick icon applies the text.

Do the same to put the appropriate text in the following cells:

```
B1:   JULY
C1:   AUG
D1:   SEPT
E1:   OCT
F1:   BUSINESS CLASS
G1:   EXTRA NIGHTS
A2:   NEW YORK STATE
A3:   THE GREAT LAKES
A4:   THE WEST COAST
A5:   THE BLUES STATES
A6:   THE FLORIDA EXPERIENCE
```

Some of your text will be too big for the cell that it occupies and will consequently appear as '*****', so you need to resize your cells so that the text becomes readable.

● To set the column widths required just drag on the lines between the cell headings. For example drag right on the dividing line between the F and G cell headings to increase the size of the cells in column F.

You will need to increase columns A, F and G. As the Fit table in window option is set by default, as you increase the size of cells, the table will appear smaller in the preview window - but not in reality. The table will always be sized to fit the original area you defined on your PagePlus page.

● Now to start applying some properties to the table. First, drag from cell A1 to cell G6, to select all the cells in the table, indicated by the subsequent highlighting of these cells. Then set the text font to Arial and the size to 12.0p. You may need to make some adjustments to the cell size again to accommodate this increase in text size.

● Click on the Select All Lines icon and then select the hairline icon followed by the black colour in the Lines selection box, if it is not already selected. This creates thin black grid lines throughout your table. Set the text to black for this area if it is not already set.

If a colour that you want to use is not available in the five quick selections, just double-click on one of them to open the Edit Color dialog where you can customise a colour and tint for your own use.

You now need to apply properties to individual rows, columns and cells in your table as opposed to the whole table itself.

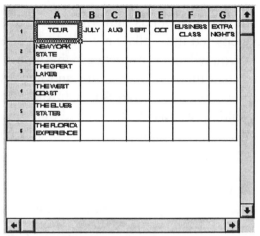

- Click on the row 1 heading to select all the cells in 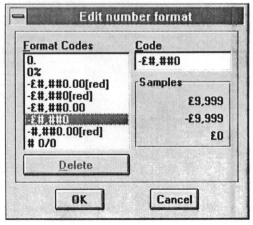 row 1, then select the Center text icon to centre the text in these cells. Drag to select the cells B2 to G6 and then again select the Center text icon. Although there is no data in these cells at the moment, when some is entered it will immediately become centre aligned.

- With the data area still selected, double click on the Currency Format icon, which is one of several format icons allowing you to specify the number of decimal places, leading zeros, how to show negative numbers, and so on.

- This opens the Edit number format dialog which enables you to select a predefined format or create your own. Select the format -£#,##0.

This code provides a picture of how a number will be displayed. This choice means that the pounds sign will be used as a prefix to the numbers entered into cells, only whole numbers will be displayed, so you will not show pence in this case, the comma will be used as a thousands separator and negative figures will have a preceding minus sign. So, to illustrate, the number -2035.95 would appear as -£2,035. Note that you can enter your own custom formatting code if you want to use a style that is not listed.

● When you've selected the appropriate value, click on OK to apply the formatting to the selected cells.

● Now you need to distinguish the heading cells from the data cells by reversing the colours. So click on the A column heading to select all of column A and then set the text colour to white, the lines to white and the background to black. Do the same with row 1.

● All that remains to be done is to enter some figures in the data cells. Just click on cell B2 and type in 550, click on OK and move on to the next cell. Continue entering numbers until all the cells are filled.

	A	B	C	D	E	F	G
1	TOUR	JULY	AUG	SEPT	OCT	BUSINESS CLASS	EXTRA NIGHTS
2	NEW YORK STATE	£960	£900	£576	£476	£260	£40
3	THE GREAT LAKES	£960	£910	£580	£485	£260	£40
4	THE WEST COAST	£960	£920	£576	£720	£425	£45
5	THE BLUES STATES	£920	£700	£840	£510	£335	£30
6	THE FLORIDA EXPERIENCE	£900	£990	£920	£485	£260	£30

So that's your table complete.

It's worth noting that if you want to use a pre-defined table style you can select the Quick Format icon and then preview the available styles in the Format entire table dialog, before choosing one to apply to the data you've entered.

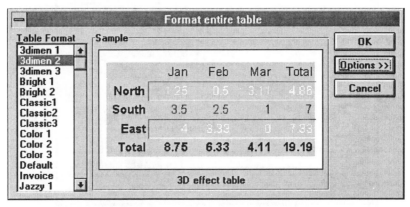

- With your table complete click on the Update button to apply the object to the PagePlus page and close TablePlus so you can return to your PagePlus publication.

- Make any necessary positional and sizing adjustments to your table. Remember, if you need to edit the object, just double-click on it to return to TablePlus with the object open for use.

» Fancy writing for the back cover

The telephone number and the Airline logo in the bottom right corner of the page are both to be created using TypePlus.

- Select the TypePlus icon from the Import Picture flyout. Then, with snapping on, drag the cross-hair cursor from just beneath your table from margin to margin, to a depth of about 1.5 inches.

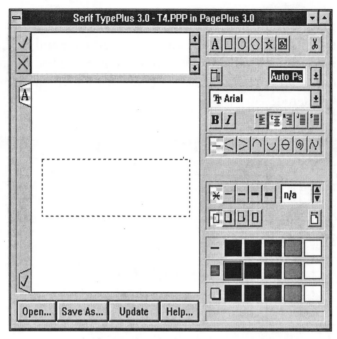

TypePlus then opens for use, with a page area equivalent to the area you just dragged. The window has the usual Serif applet style, with the panel of tools and icons on the right and the preview window on the left.

- In the text window at the top of the display type in:
  081-911-9191
- Having clicked on the tick icon to apply it, use the property icons on the right-hand side of the window to set the text to Arial font of size 70.0p and make it bold.

- Use the Position icon and its pop-up dialog to centre the text on the page area. The arrow keys move the object in the direction indicated.

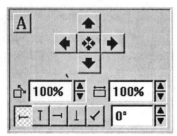

- Set the text to red and the outline of the text to blue, and leave the shadow colour at grey.

- This text is going to be shadow text so double-click on the Shadow icon to customise the shadow - a single click would apply the predefined shadow properties.

- The Edit Shadow dialog has properties for the vertical and horizontal offset of the shadow, which effectively govern how far the text appears to be raised off the page. Increase these values to 10% to exaggerate the shadow effect. Click on OK to apply the property changes to your object.

This object is now complete, so you can apply it to your page by selecting the Update push button and return to PagePlus by minimising the TypePlus window.

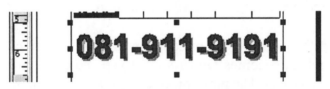

- There is a second TypePlus object to design so select the TypePlus icon again and drag an area about 1.5 inches by 1.5 inches in the bottom right-hand corner of your page using the Shift key to constrain the area to be square.

- TypePlus then opens and in its Text Window type in:
  All Flights . Air Atlantic .

- Press Ctrl-Alt-. (or Ctrl-Alt-8) for the two bullet characters. Then select the tick icon to apply the text to your page. Set the text to Arial, make it blue with a red shadow. Leave the text at its automatic size so that it will fill the available area.

- As with the previous TypePlus object, give the text a shadow and use the Edit shadow dialog to increase the shadow offset to 10% in both directions.

- Then set the text to the circular effect you want using the Button Text icon.

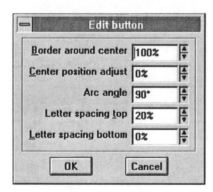

- Double-click on the Button text icon to change the point at which the text starts, using the Edit button dialog. Set the Arc angle value to 90° so that the text starts at the 9 o'clock position (0° starts it at the 6 o'clock position).

- You now need to import the picture of a jumbo jet (jumbojet.wmf). Click on the Metafile icon and use the Windows dialog to specify its location.

When the picture is imported it appears over the top of your text, which becomes fainter so that you can concentrate on the new object. The new object also has a new tab at the side of the preview window. These tabs are provided so that you can select the object you want to use. You don't need to make any adjustments to this object, except to send it behind the text. This is done by dragging the object's tab up the page until it goes behind the other tab.

- This object is now finished, so use the Update button and then switch back to PagePlus where you may need to make some final sizing and positional adjustments to the object.

- Now you need to set the object to wrap around. But, because the circular border is made up of text, the automatic avoid-me perimeter is rather ragged. Rather than spend a lot of time adjusting the perimeter, it's easier to create an invisible circle on top of the OLE object, and set it to wrap to act as a wrap mask around which the text can flow.

- Select the Oval tool and, with snapping on and the Shift key held down, drag outwards from the bottom right-hand corner of the page where the margins meet until the circle covers the OLE TypePlus object.

- Use the ChangeBar and Properties Palette to give the circle no border and give it a clear colour. Finally set the object to wrap around.

» Additional back cover text

- All that remains to be done to this design is to add two items of text. So open WritePlus and type in:
  ### HOW TO BOOK
- Apply the object to your page. Choose a sans serif font and increase the text size to about 40.0p, set its colour to blue and centre align it. Then with the 45° Line tool drag beneath the text to create a red line with a thickness of 4.0p.

- Open WritePlus again and type in something like:
BOOK DIRECT ON THE ABOVE NUMBER OR AT ANY OF THE FOLLOWING AUTHORISED TRAVEL SHOPS: Pitt and Goddard Tourism.... (list of names)
.... BreakBusters.
- Include a bullet point before every travel agent's name.

- Click on OK when you've finished typing in your text and increase the size of the text to 14.0p.

- Drag the object's right handles to the right margin and the left handles across to the left margin, to enable the text to flow up to the TypePlus logo and wrap around it.

You may find that you need to alter the right side of the circle's perimeter that you are using to wrap around, so that no text is able to fit in the gap between the circle and the right margin. Just drag the avoid-me perimeter on the right of the circle right up to the margin.

The design is complete and you can save it in the usual way except that the OLE objects will be saved as part of the design. If you ever re-open the design you can amend the OLE objects by double-clicking on them to open the appropriate application with the object automatically loaded for use.

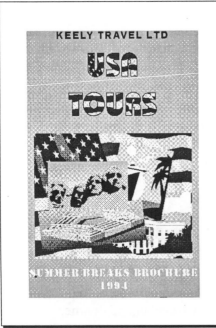

HOW TO BOOK

TOUR	JULY	AUG	SEPT	OCT	BUSINESS CLASS	EXTRA NIGHTS
NEW YORK STATE	£550	£600	£575	£475	£250	£40
THE GREAT LAKES	£550	£610	£580	£485	£250	£40
THE WEST COAST	£850	£920	£875	£720	£425	£45
THE BLUES STATES	£820	£700	£840	£510	£305	£30
THE FLORIDA EXPERIENCE	£500	£560	£520	£485	£250	£30

081-911-9191

BOOK DIRECT ON THE ABOVE NUMBER OR AT ANY OF THE FOLLOWING AUTHORISED TRAVEL SHOPS:
•Pitt and Goddard Tourism, •Hassan, Syed and Geraghan Ltd, •Dixon, Marmaduk and Bereguio Holidays, •Colin Hay International, •Durow, Hackey & Jefferies International World Associates, •EXTRA, •Bucket Bookers, BreakBusters.
Note: Please quote Keely Travel Ltd when making all bookings.

» Hints, tips and good ideas

Tour Nine has made good use of the extended capabilities of PagePlus Professional Suite and has demonstrated various special effects. It should have given you a lot of ideas for your own designs. In the rest of this chapter we explore some new features and expand on some introduced earlier in this book.

» Special characters

You can enter the most common special characters by using the Text,Insert Symbol command and then selecting from the list that appears.

Insert Symbol		Bullet	Ctrl+Alt+8
Insert Hyphen	Ctrl+ -	Dagger	Ctrl+/
Insert Page Number		Copyright	Ctrl+Alt+C
		Register	Ctrl+Alt+R
Text Style		Em Rule	Ctrl+Alt+=
		Em Space	Ctrl+Alt+M

Other special characters can be created from the character map by using the Edit,Character Map menu command, see Chapter 5. However, the fastest way of entering these and other special characters is to use the Ctrl and Alt key combinations. This method is also the only way that you can enter special characters into WritePlus.

The Ctrl and Alt keys are often used as if they were additional Shift keys. The list that follows shows how to produce various special characters. In each case the key in the table is entered while holding down both the Alt and the Ctrl key. Notice that you release the third key before you release the Ctrl and Alt keys - just as you would when using the Shift key to type a capital letter.

Character	See	Key	Character	See	Key
Bullet	•	.	Single open quote	'	(
Bullet (alternative)	•	8	Single close quote	'	)
Dagger	†	\	Double open quote	"	[
Double Dagger	‡	/	Double close quote	"	]
Copyright	©	c	Comma space		'
Registered	®	r	Digit space		1
Trademark	™	t	En-space		n
Em-rule	—	-	Em space		m

» Know your spaces

If you examine the list of special characters given above you might be puzzled by the number of different spaces included in the list - Comma, Digit, En and Em spaces are all different widths of space. Why should you need different types of space? In most cases the answer is to make columns line up. For example, if you are trying to make columns of numbers line up you need to know that in every font all digits take the same amount of space - a digit or figure space. If you want to pad a value that has fewer digits to occupy the same space as a value with more digits then you should use *digit spaces*. In the same way a *comma space* is the space take by a comma and can be used to leave small, punctuation-sized, gaps.

You can also use the different sized spaces to adjust the space between two words in a way that will not be changed by any justification you may select. The *em-space* is the width of a capital M and the *en-space* is the width of a capital N in the current font. You can also use a comma space as a *thin space* when you want to keep characters close together while still having a space between them. This is useful for example when you want to keep a unit of measure close to a number.

As well as being different widths all of these special spaces are no-break spaces. When you type a normal space, using the space bar, PagePlus treats it as being both breakable and paddable. It is *breakable* in the sense that it marks the division between words and it is *paddable* in the sense that additional space can be added to justify the line. By contrast a *non-breakable* space is not treated as a split between words and it is not padded with extra space when a line is justified. You can think of a non-breakable space as if it was any other character in the font set as far as justification and padding go.

» Keep together

The most common application of a non-breakable space is to keep two words together. For example, if you need to write Windows 3.1 then is very annoying to discover that PagePlus breaks the line just after the word Windows and so puts the 3.1 on the next line. To keep words together separate them by a suitable non-breakable space - an en, em, digit or comma space. So in this case you would enter

Windows en-space (Ctrl-Alt-n) 3.1

Notice that you should leave no space between Windows, the en-space and 3.1. If you do then PagePlus will simply break the line at the space - which is what you are trying to avoid.

» Left and right justification

A less obvious use of non-breaking spaces is in conjunction with the force justify alignment option. If you enter words separated by non-breaking spaces then they are treated by PagePlus as a single word as far as justification is concerned. This can be used with force justify to align one part of a line at the left margin and the other at the right margin.

If you enter the two groups of words with each word separated by non-breaking spaces, but separate the two groups by an ordinary space, then force justifying the line will send the first group to the left and the second to the right. The reason is simply that each group of words is treated as a single word and the only way that the line can be justified is if one word is aligned at each margin.

For example, try entering the text

Dear en-space Sir space 1 en-space April

There must be no normal spaces between the words apart from the one between Sir and 1. Notice how the en-spaces show as square blocks in WritePlus. If you use the ChangeBar to select force justify you will see the 'Dear Sir' and '1 April' spring apart to the opposite sides of the bounding box.

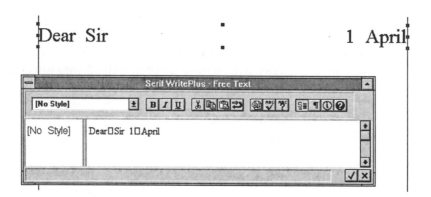

» Tint panels

As was first demonstrated in Tour Two, tint panels can be used to distinguish between different text elements in a design. In particular, they can be used to make an attractive backing for a main headline or for a message of special importance.

Broadly speaking, there are two types of tint panel. You can simply use a coloured background, which can be any hue and any tint or pattern, to black (or coloured) text. Or you can create a 'reversal' in which the text is the same colour as the page (normally white) on a coloured tint panel.

Tint panels are simple to produce by creating a box using PagePlus's own Box tool, then changing the properties of the box to give it the appropriate colour, tint and pattern. You may also need to change the size and colour of the surrounding border. When you have done this, create the text and place it on the box.

If you perform the procedure in reverse order, by creating the text and then the tint panel, you must remember to bring the text to the front, using the icon in the Wrap flyout, to prevent the text being obscured.

» Creative rules

PagePlus has two line drawing tools. One is used for drawing any line between two points while the other, known as the 45° Line tool is for drawing horizontal, vertical or diagonal (i.e. 45°) lines and is the more widely used. One of its most common tasks is to create rules - used to break up a design, to differentiate between text objects, and as a border at the top and bottom of a page. We have used rules in this way in many of the tours in this book.

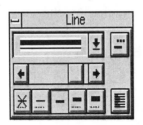

You can create double rules quite easily by selecting from the available line styles which include dashed and a number of pairs in different thicknesses. If the double line pattern of your choice doesn't appear you need to increase the line thickness.

Rules can also be used to underline text. Although you can underline any text object using the ChangeBar, there is no option as to how thick or how close to the text this underline is. Consequently, you will often find that the underlining passes through the descenders of text rather than going beneath them. Using rules, normally at the hairline thickness, you can create your own underlines and position them precisely. To align such rules it is often easier to use a vertical ruler marked in points and use the snap grid that it generates.

A combination of rules known as *thick and thin* is often used in publications to highlight and emphasise a phrase or quote. They consist of an inner 1-point line separated by a few points from an outer 2-point line. These thick and thin lines are then placed either side of the quote or phrase.

"I'm forever blowing bubbles..... and die."

Dan Dare

» Rotated text

It is easy to rotate text objects in PagePlus. You can do it either by eye using the Rotate tool or by specifying a precise rotation factor using the Status Editor dialog.

Rotated text can be a useful aid to design if used properly. Titles or slogans in adverts etc. often look good if the text is rotated, provided that the text is relatively large. Be careful to make sure that you do not rotate text to unreadable angles. You are advised to keep rotated text within 30° of the horizontal.

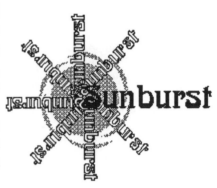

» Cropping text

We have frequently used the Crop tool to edit pictures. It can also be applied to text objects. This can be used to produce interesting design effects.

» Text to a path

As well as rotating an entire line of text, you can use a slant angle to rotate the individual letters. It you rotate a line of text by a given angle and then slant the letters by minus that angle the result is that the letters appear to sit on a sloping baseline.

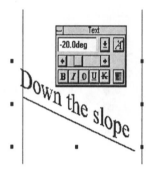

For example, if you enter some text and rotate it by -20° and then slant it by +20° the result will sit happily on a line with a -20° slope. Notice that when you enter a negative angle PagePlus automatically converts them to a positive one by subtracting from 360°, so -20° is converted to 340°.

There is a way to fit text to a general path but it is time consuming. The basic idea is to create a free text object for each letter and then rotate each letter by the desired amount. For example, if you want to fit the text 'Round' to a semicircle the 'R' is rotated by 90°, the 'o' by 45°, the 'u' by 0°, the 'n'

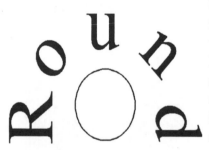

by -45° and the 'd' by -90°. The final task is to assemble the word by positioning the letters. If you are going to be using this sort of design feature often then it is a good idea to invest in TypePlus which makes it easy.

» Patterned text

PagePlus allows you to apply a fill pattern to the interior of text. However, unless the text is very large you will not be able to see the pattern. You may find it useful on occasion to apply such patterning, but generally it should be avoided as it often looks unattractive, ruining the message the text is trying to communicate. It is worth experimenting with contrasting pattern fills in text and tint panels. It is also useful when used with dropped or raised capitals.

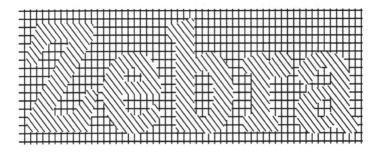

» Dropped and raised capitals

Dropped and raised capitals are commonly used in publications to mark the start of stories. They are very easy to create and are often very productive in brightening up a design, particularly if there are no other graphics.

A raised capital is a large first letter of a paragraph that stands above the other letters. A dropped capital is also a larger letter but it drops below its normal baseline. These effects are often used just for the first letter of an article, but they can be applied to every paragraph if necessary.

Tour Three illustrated how to create a dropped capital. Simply create a separate text object consisting of the letter to be dropped or raised and then increase its size and alter its properties, including setting its wrap status to on. You may also need to alter the object's avoid-me perimeter so that the remaining body text flows very close to the letter.

The letter can be in a different font from the remaining text and can be bold, italic or a different colour. Sometimes dropped or raised capitals are surrounded by attractive borders; placed on tint panels; made to look 3D; patterned; or given a shadow. The choice is yours.

uis lorem dolor ipsum sit am Yub sulpegap won! Sti os hcus taerg eulav. Ro, yub ı ypoc. Tahw tuoba eht net resu k senoj? Dna llet lla ruoy sdneirf, dı hcir seno eciwt.

The main problem with dropped caps is that they are separate text objects and so do not reflow with any frame text they might belong to. This doesn't matter too much if you are only adding dropped caps to the start of the story but if they are added to each paragraph then it can be a difficult task to keep them all aligned.

A raised cap can be created in the same way as a dropped cap but there is, however, a way of doing it that keeps the text as a single object. If you select the single capital letter that you want to raise using the Text tool, you can then use the ChangeBar to set the point size to something larger than the rest of the text. This creates the enlarged capital letter and, as it sits on the same baseline as the rest of the text, it extends above the top of the paragraph - hence it becomes a raised cap. To make sure that the raised cap doesn't run into the top of the previous paragraph you need to remember to set the paragraph's Space above to a suitable value. You may also find that you need to adjust the kerning to produce an attractive effect.

Puis lorem dolor ipsum sit a
sulpegap won! Sti os doog,
eulav. Ro, yub ruoy tac a yp
eht net resu kcap nywg sen

You cannot use the same method to create a dropped cap by adjusting the baseline because the text in the lines below will not automatically wrap around the larger capital letter.

» Shadow text

It is easy to add a shadow to almost any object by making a copy of it, setting the copy to black and sending it to the back. All you have to do is to position the copy relative to the original so that it gives the impression of a shadow cast by light from a particular direction. You can even use this method to create shadowed text.

Make the copy of the text using Ctrl and drag. Set its properties to a black fill and send it to the back. Next align both copies of the text so that only the top one shows. With a suitable snap grid on select the top object and move it one increment up and one increment to the left. If you are using shadows more than once on a page make sure that you use the same relative shift between objects and their shadow copies. Otherwise it looks as if the light is coming from more than one place.

» Shadow boxes

A shadow box is the term given to the effect where a particular area of the page is placed upon a different coloured background. This gives the impression that the page is slightly uplifted from the page in a 3D way, with the coloured background looking like the resultant shadow created on the page.

This trick should not be overused but can be attractive if there is a natural box of text which is separate from everything else on the page, such as the summary box created in Tour Three.

This effect is quite easily created by placing your text on a coloured box with a thin perimeter. Then draw a second box on top so that it is approximately the same size but displaced by a few points laterally and vertically. Give this box a coloured interior and tint and pattern if you wish, using the ChangeBar and Properties Palette, and then send it to the back so that your text is once again visible.

» Irregular shadows

If you want to add a drop shadow to a picture that has a clear outline simply import a second copy and use the Color Mapper to set all its foreground colours to black. Send the resulting shape to the back and position it behind the original.

» Irregular wrapping

If a picture is placed overlapping text and set to wrap, the text will wrap around it in a uniform manner defined by a rectangular outline around the object. You can opt for an irregular wrap outline and manually change this to produce any wrap shape.

This is a useful and relatively common effect, but should only be used if there is enough room beside the graphic to accommodate the text. If the graphic takes up a large proportion of the text area so that only one word, or less, is placed on each line, then the effect will look ungainly. So, if you want your design to be rigid and symmetrical do not use this effect.

» Text filled shapes

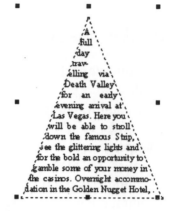

Using a method similar to irregular wrap around, you can pour text inside a shape simply by selecting Wrap inside. In most cases pictures are too complex to produce a pleasing result. However, you can create interesting effects by drawing a box and using its irregular wrap boundary to form a container for the text. As the wrap boundary can be edited you are not restricted to the square shape. In this case you should set the box to clear fill and 0 point line width so that it vanishes.

The biggest problem with irregular wrapping of this sort is ensuring that there are no loose lines. If there are then you can attempt to get rid of them by altering the wrap outlines slightly or by using selective tracking.

» PagePlus borders

Borders consist of a graphic image around the edge of the picture with a clear centre so that you can see other objects through it. These are not very useful if your publication consists of many columns of text etc.. But if you design a flyer or advert then a border can be an effective finishing touch.

PagePlus comes with a sample set of graphics including some borders. If you purchase the ArtPack you will have access to more borders. You can use a border simply by importing the border graphic and then placing it on your page. The border can then be resized and stretched or compressed to fit your design.

» White space

It may seem a little peculiar to recommend that you leave white space as an effect in a design. However, one of the most common problems with novice designers is their desire to fill the page up with too many pieces of rotated text, too many pictures, too many tint panels, etc.. White space is an important aid to design. It makes designs more open, more readable and less confusing.

White space is particularly important if your readership is not a willing one (for example your publication is a booklet entitled Give up Smoking! or a flyer entitled Vote for Bell!). You need to make proselytising as easy as possible to read. Give the document pictures if possible and make the text large, serif in style and give the page lots of white space by putting main points in numbered or bulleted lists, having large headlines, gaps between paragraphs, and large margins. Just generally keep the work well spread out.

» Indented bullet points

Indented bullet point lists are easy to create as long as you follow a simple recipe. The first thing to remember is that every bullet point has to start with the same set of characters, usually a bullet (Ctrl+Alt+.) followed by an em space (Ctrl+Alt+m) and then the start of the paragraph text. There must be no ordinary spaces between the bullet, the em space and the paragraph text. If there is, justification will alter the spacing and make lining up the start of the first line impossible. Next, select the paragraph and use the command Text,Tabs & Indents to set a negative first line indent and an identical but positive left indent. It is easier to work in points so change the horizontal ruler to points and enter the indents in points.

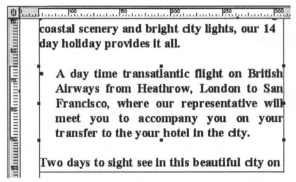

coastal scenery and bright city lights, our 14 day holiday provides it all.

• A day time transatlantic flight on British Airways from Heathrow, London to San Francisco, where our representative will meet you to accompany you on your transfer to the your hotel in the city.

Two days to sight see in this beautiful city on

The negative first line indent pulls the first line to the left while pushing the rest of the text to the right. You need to adjust the indents to line up the first letter of the first line with the first letter of the second line. The easiest way to do this is to use a high magnification and measure the outdent needed using the ruler line. For example, using 12 point New Times Roman you need a 16 point first line outdent.

The size of the indent that you need depends on the point size and the font you have selected. It is, of course, a good idea to define a paragraph style for the bullet point.

» Superscripts and subscripts

Although there is no superscript or subscript property in Page Plus it is easy to create both using a combination of font size and baseline shift. To create a superscript it is usually necessary to roughly halve the point size and shift up by the same amount. For example, working with a 12 point font a reasonable looking superscript can be formed by changing it to 6 point with a baseline offset of -6 points. You can create a subscript in the same way but in general the drop in point size and baseline shift is less - roughly two thirds and one third respectively. So for a 12 point font, change to 8 points with a baseline shift of 4 points.

$$y = x^2$$

The 1st of May

sum over a_{ij}

Unfortunately you cannot create sub- and superscript styles for two reasons. Firstly, a style applies to a whole object not just part of it; secondly, baseline shift isn't recorded as part of a style.

» Short cut to property dialog boxes

You can set an object's properties in a number of different ways - using the Properties Palette and ChangeBar, the menu command and the property dialog boxes. As a short cut way of getting to any of the property dialog boxes simply double click on the properties icon in the Properties Palette - not the ChangeBar!

» Function key tips

There are a number of function key presses that are worth knowing about.

Two keys, F2 and F4, are concerned with moving text in frames. The F2 key will move the insertion position of a text block in a frame to before or after the highlighted block. The F4 key changes free text to frame text and vice versa.

The F3 and F5 keys can speed things up. If you press the F3 key then no updating will be done until you release the key. Try holding this key down if you find that adjustments that you are making are being slowed down by PagePlus reflowing text or redrawing the screen.

The F5 key swaps between the currently and previously selected tool. And don't forget that you can select and keep a tool by holding down the Shift key.

» Using the rulers

PagePlus's rulers are a valuable aid to layout and it is worth
making sure that you know how to use
them. You can set the scale that they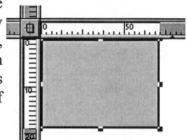
use via the Tools,Preferences,
General command. The scale chosen
determines the snap grid that is
available. Hiding the rulers turns off
the snap grid, even if snapping is on.

You can drag the rulers to any position on the screen that you
want them by dragging the box at the intersection of the
horizontal and vertical rulers. If you drag the rulers while
holding down the Shift key then the current position of the
zero stays put. You can use this to measure displacements on
the page. To move the zero point to the current intersection
of the rulers simply click once on the ruler box.

If you double click on the ruler box then they both jump back
to the screen edge with the zero aligned to the edge of the
page. If you double click on the ruler box when an object is
selected the rulers jump to surround the object - enabling you
to measure it accurately. A second double click moves the
rulers back to their default positions. If you want to keep the
rulers fixed then use the command Page,Layout Tools and
select Lock rulers.

Another, and sometimes more direct, way of setting the size
and position of an object is to use the Status Editor.

» Customising PagePlus help

There is a great deal you can do to make PagePlus work the way you want it to. By selecting the particular help facilities that you find useful you can create levels that are intermediate between Intro, Publisher and Professional. Simply use the command Tools,Preferences,Ease of Use and fill in the dialog box that appears to customise the program as you want!

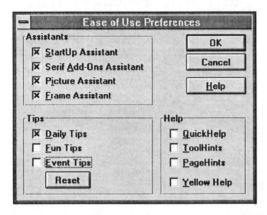

So, if you do not find the colourful Assistant dialog boxes helpful then unchecking their boxes disables them. Conversely, if they have been disabled by checking their own Don't show again boxes this is where you can reinstate them.

Whatever level you are working at you can check the QuickHelp or ToolHints to be confident that you have selected the correct tool. You also have a choice as to whether QuickHelp and ToolHints are displayed in grey or more prominently in yellow.

You can control which types of tip you are shown in the Tips section of this dialog but there is no option that disables them entirely. Notice, however, that you can slowly get rid of any tips that you have do not find helpful by checking the Do not show this tip again box after you have read the tip.

» Using PageHints

One of the standard and embarrassing errors is to leave a note to yourself in the margin of a layout only to discover that it has made it all the way to the finished document! The safest thing is to adopt the rule - never put anything into a design that you do not want to see in the final product. This is safe but it makes it impossible to leave yourself or a co-worker notes about the layout, its problems, what has to be done etc.. The solution is to use PageHints. A PageHint shows on the page as an icon but when you double click on it you can read it - of course a PageHint doesn't print so there is no danger of it appearing in the final product.

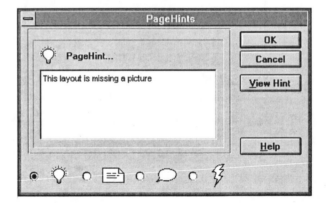

To insert a PageHint use the command Help,Insert PageHint. The PageHints dialog box then appears. You can type in your note and select the icon that you want it to display. Double clicking on the icon reveals the message.

Index